John Middleton Murry

John Middleton Murry:

THE CRITIC AS MORALIST

SHARRON GREER CASSAVANT

THE UNIVERSITY OF ALABAMA PRESS

Library of Congress Cataloging in Publication Data

Cassavant, Sharron Greer, 1939–
  John Middleton Murry, the critic as moralist.

  Bibliography: p.
  Includes index.
  1. Murry, John Middleton, 1889–1957—Knowledge—Literature. 2. Critics—Great Brit-
ain—Biography.
I. Title.
PR6025.U8Z54   820'.9   [B]   81-19717
ISBN 0-8173-0107-0   AACR2

To Martin Green

Contents

ACKNOWLEDGMENTS ix

CHRONOLOGY xi

INTRODUCTION: A BRIEF HISTORY OF A CRITIC 1

1. BETWEEN TWO WORLDS 6

2. CRITICAL PERSPECTIVES 33

3. SPIRITUAL HEROES 55

4. KATHERINE MANSFIELD AND THE ANTIPODES:
D. H. LAWRENCE AND T. S. ELIOT 82

5. VICES AND VIRTUES OF AN AUTOBIOGRAPHICAL CRITIC 112

NOTES 138

BIBLIOGRAPHY 153

INDEX 160

Acknowledgments

I am indebted to The Society of Authors as the literary representative of the Estate of John Middleton Murry, for permission to quote from Murry's journal and manuscripts.

Portions of *The Letters of D. H. Lawrence*, edited by by Harry T. Moore, copyright 1932 by the Estate of D. H. Lawrence, and 1934 by Frieda Lawrence, copyright 1933, 1953, 1954, and each year 1956–62 by Angelo Ravagli and C. M. Weekley, Executors of the Estate of Frieda Lawrence Ravagli, are reprinted by permission of Viking Penguin Inc., and Laurence Pollinger Ltd.

Extracts from unpublished letters of T. S. Eliot are reprinted by permission of Mrs. Valerie Eliot and Faber and Faber, Ltd., copyright© 1981.

Extracts from *The Letters of John Keats*, edited by Maurice Buxton Forman, are reprinted by permission of Oxford University Press.

Extracts from *The Letters of Aldous Huxley,* edited by Grover Smith, are reprinted by permission of Mrs. Laura Huxley, Chatto & Windus and Harper & Row, Publishers, Inc.

Though I am solely responsible for any errors and omissions in this work, I am grateful to Martin Green, who patiently read and responded to the manuscript, to Priscilla Khachadoorian, who cheerfully typed it, bending her schedule to mine, to Roland, who assisted me in incalculable ways, and to Stephen and Sara, who suffered a sometimes impatient mother.

SHARRON GREER CASSAVANT
Northeastern University
August 1981

Chronology

1889   John Middleton Murry is born, August 6, Peckham, London.

1901   Wins scholarship to Christ's Hospital.

1908   Begins classics studies at Brasenose College, Oxford.

1911   Edits *Rhythm* and meets Katherine Mansfield.

1912   Leaves Oxford to begin career as journalist, living with Katherine Mansfield. Age 22.

1913   Meets D. H. Lawrence.

1916   Publishes first critical study, *Dostoevsky*, and first novel, *Still Life*. Age 27.

1918   Marries Katherine Mansfield following her divorce from Bowden.

1919   Becomes editor of the *Athenaeum*.

1923   Katherine Mansfield dies. Murry has a mystical experience which marks a turning point in his life. He establishes the *Adelphi*.

1924   Marries Violet le Maistre.

1931   Marries Betty Cockbayne shortly after Violet's death; announces conversion to Marxism.

1935   Founds the Adelphi Center to promote a socialist society.

1936   Joins Peace Pledge Union, a pacifist society.

1938   Meets Mary Gamble.

1941   Leaves Betty Cockbayne to begin new life with Mary Gamble.

1942   Establishes communal farm in Norfolk. Age 52.

1954   Marries Mary Gamble, following Betty Cockbayne's death.

1957   Dies from heart attack on March 12. Age 68. Buried in churchyard, Thelnatham, Norfolk.

John Middleton Murry

Introduction

A BRIEF HISTORY OF A CRITIC

John Middleton Murry published his first book, *Dostoevsky*, in 1916, his last, *Love, Freedom and Society*, in 1957. Known primarily as a literary critic and editor (and even more widely as the husband of Katherine Mansfield and the friend of D. H. Lawrence), Murry also thought and wrote about broader cultural issues. He was a failed creative writer, a spokesman for causes, and a founder of many enterprises, including a communal farm which provided a haven for pacifists during the Second World War. An astonishingly prolific writer, he produced almost fifty books and innumerable pamphlets, essays, and reviews in the course of a complicated, energetic life.

Murry's reputation as a man of letters rose and fell dramatically. In the years surrounding the First World War he was the young man on the rise, the "bright, particular star"[1] of English criticism. Before the war he founded the little magazine *Rhythm* (later the *Blue Review*), which attracted the attention of the avant-garde and introduced him to the literary establishment. With D. H. Lawrence, Murry contributed to *Signature*, the short-lived journal published during the war to vent Lawrence's spleen about war and power politics.

Murry's great opportunity came in 1919 when at age thirty he became editor of the *Athenaeum*. Under his leadership the moribund journal gained an ephemeral international brilliance. The talents he drew upon were the writers who created the literary history of the twenties, many of whom gained their first forum in the *Athenaeum*. His approach was intensely serious—too serious, some said, for his high intellectualism lacked broad appeal—and the journal suffered financially, merging with the

Nation in February 1921. Soon after, Murry was invited to give the Raleigh Lectures at Oxford. Published as *The Problem of Style*, these essays solidified Murry's position as a serious, original critic who could attack old problems freshly. He was subsequently offered a post at Oxford but declined, as he did throughout his life, the invitation to an academic career. His energies were too diffuse and variable to be channeled principally into scholarship, and unlike F. R. Leavis he didn't see how to make a challenge of it. For Murry, academia represented too easy a choice.

The two years with the *Athenaeum* were the peak of his reputation. He moved in the circles of success, admired by Bloomsburyites and Sitwells, a guest at famous houses. Urged toward greater ambition by his wife, Katherine Mansfield, Murry treated his sudden influence with naive arrogance, telling a bemused Ottoline Morrell, the most celebrated literary hostess of the day, that he and Katherine were beginning to be recognized as the most important literary authorities in England, adding, "If *we* believe in you, it shows that you are of value."[2]

In 1923, a few weeks after Katherine Mansfield's death, Murry underwent a mystical experience which led him to make a holocaust of his former life and deliberately renounce his specialized role as literary journalist and critic. He emerged as a cultural critic with a mission. His new magazine, the *Adelphi*, offended most of the intelligentsia and D. H. Lawrence, for whom it was purportedly founded, but the journal acquired a broad public following, and Murry gained disciples. The broadly ambiguous credo, "faith in life," gave him latitude for conversion to a variety of social, religious, and political doctrines, by which he made zig-zag progress through the 1930s and 1940s. In 1936 Rayner Heppenstall called Murry "the best-hated man of letters in England,"[3] and no one contradicted him.

Bloomsbury dismissed Murry as soon as the earnest moral questing of the *Adelphi* revealed his reach for a wide, unliterary audience. ("Can you imagine a man of education could sink so low?" Dora Carrington sneered after reading the first issue.)[4] Murry created controversy in other quarters by filling the early issues of the *Adelphi* with Katherine's unpublished letters and journal, disregarding her written wish to destroy her papers. Her friends thought him disloyal and accused him of ghoulishly profiteering from his wife's death. Retrospectively, it is clear that Murry was almost solely responsible for the posthumous growth of her reputation, and no one now doubts that he served her and the world well by publishing the material. Indeed, since Katherine's account of events was often critical of Murry, he served himself ill by releasing the papers. But he had cast Katherine in the role of Keats, the young genius cut off before the peak of achievement, regarded the unpublished work as a revelation of her promise, and felt driven to give it to the world.

The accusation that Murry was an opportunist rose again after D. H. Lawrence died. Murry's relations with Lawrence had been tempestuous and occasionally rivalrous since 1916. There had been misunderstandings on both sides, and in his last letter to Murry, Lawrence told him to give up hope of finding a meeting ground. But Murry found Lawrence so potent a force that he meditated on Lawrence's significance all his life, continuing that exploration even in his last book, *Love, Freedom and Society*. However, *Son of Woman*, published the year after Lawrence died, aroused instant controversy by portraying Lawrence as a driven, Oedipal figure, obsessed by a sexual doctrine he could not express in his own being. Lawrence's friends regarded the book as a betrayal, and Murry became involved in endless justification. He sued Catherine Carswell for libeling him in her memoirs of Lawrence and forced the first edition of *The Savage Pilgrimage* to be withdrawn, events which enhanced his notoriety and Lawrence's fame. Such controversies produced a one-dimensional public image of Murry, seen at its worst in Aldous Huxley's caricature of him as the hypocritical, childish, self-deceiving Burlap of *Point Counter Point*.

Meantime, Murry's approach to literary criticism had taken an unfashionable turn. Early in his career he had led revolt against the genial laxness of Edwardian literary journalism, and *The Problem of Style* can easily be described as a precursor of the New Criticism. By the mid-twenties he was standing against the tides of technical criticism. He defended the worth of the romantic tradition and of critical intuition against T. S. Eliot's neoclassicism, insisting that too much intellectual formalization robs literature of its primary function, arousing a subjective response in the reader which leads to creative restructuring of life and values. More and more discontent with the literature of his own day, he turned to Shakespeare and the nineteenth-century romantics for art that could be taken seriously as a guide to conduct. To him, the great artist was a spiritual hero, a bearer of transcendent truth. Keats became, and remained, his touchstone.

In the early thirties Murry made the first of his political conversions. He gathered followers readily but lost them with each turnabout, from socialism to Marxism, from Marxism to pacifism, so that former disciples became enemies or scoffers. Because he maintained a pacifist stance during World War II, Murry's general unpopularity grew. His books were scantily reviewed, and he was not offered the regular reviewing assignments which had been his principal livelihood.

After World War II Murry became for the first time a proponent of conservative political and economic values. The repudiation of extra-literary preoccupations, along with some of his iconoclastic values, freed him to explore the possibilities of professional literary criticism, which he had abjured since the twenties. His biography of Swift was widely and favorably reviewed; so, too, were the miscellaneous essays he produced in the last few years of his life. When he died in 1957 the old rancors had abated, he no longer threatened any important set of ideas, and the last reviewers added judicious praise to largely patronizing accounts of Murry's feuds and ideological oscillations. Within a few years some critics began to lament the abuse he had suffered and issued more generous assessments of his achievements.

However, the extent of Murry's contribution to twentieth-century letters has never been widely acknowledged. Many commentators have praised the early work and the late work, in which he deliberately strove for objectivity, but dismiss the subjectivity and confessionalism of the long middle period. Since Murry viewed criticism as a creative act in itself, he quite consciously breached ordinary decorum and taste. He often claimed a special access to intuitive truth, interlaced literary commentary with autobiographical revelation, and insisted that the critic must surrender himself to the artist, must become an enthusiast, if he is to gain true insight. Understandably, many readers have set Murry aside before recognizing the astuteness of his judgments.

Our access to Murry's thought is also impeded by the noticeable unevenness of his work. He wrote rapidly, easily, and with a remarkable absence of self-criticism. He made his living by writing and once remarked that he couldn't afford the time to consider an idea unless he wrote about it. His most loyal admirers were frustrated by his resistance to rewriting. Richard Rees, his closest associate on the *Adelphi*, says that Murry refused to consider deleting weak passages on the grounds that "the book's faults are part of the book. It may as well be seen as it is, warts and all."[5] This vague justification is typically Murryian in its implication that a book acquires an ontological status which renders its parts sacrosanct. To rewrite, he implies, would violate the purity and integrity of his thought, as though he had produced the words by automatic writing and believed that metaphysical truths would be violated by clarification. That attitude is fittingly punctured by Collis, fundamentally an admiring critic, who points out that "no one wants our second-best on paper. Style, like clarity, is often a kind of sincerity. It is certainly a mark of respect for the reader. . . . Mr. Murry . . . frequently prefers, in a frenzy of insincere sincerity, to spray a pot of ink in the public's face."[6] These traits, as well as the often unfair and partial accounts of his relations with more famous and gifted contemporaries, have made Murry too often ridiculed and too little understood. All limitations considered, he produced a considerable body of illuminating criticism, and he made literature accessible to unsophisticated readers. He repeatedly placed himself in costing positions because he believed what he said and, to an astonishing degree, allowed ideas to act upon him. The principles that underlay his judgments—that the great literary work must demonstrate a comprehensive moral vision which universalizes experience, that such works must be placed in a hierarchy according to the profundity of that vision, that art and life must not be held separate—are principles most great critics have held by.

More than with most figures, the biographical facts shed light on the evolution of Murry's thought. He was the most personal of critics and insisted that his life and his work must be seen as being of a piece. His personal life was unusually troubled. His first two wives died of tuberculosis, and his third marriage was bitterly unhappy. He knew very little private peace until age fifty, when he formed a fulfilling and pacific relationship with the woman who became his fourth wife.

In a review of F. A. Lea's biography of Murry, Tims humorously pointed to the links between the shifts in Murry's career and his marriages. "With Katherine Mansfield he was literary; with Violet le Maistre (also doomed to an early death from T.B.) metaphysical; with Betty Cockbayne (a good cook but a poor scholar) socialist and, under the stress of reconciling the irreconcilable, pacifist; with Mary Gamble, who provided him for the first time with the married bliss he craved, he was to become—bucolic."[7] This description, though amusingly apt, fails to acknowledge the countertruth—that Murry's marriages, like other important life decisions, were shaped by his reactions to ideas. His disastrous marriage to Betty Cockbayne was prompted by his conversion to Lawrence's doctrine of sexual fulfillment, in contrast to the "idealistic," "spiritual" love ideal which underlay his relations with Katherine Mansfield and Violet le Maistre. He lived his beliefs, though often without fully understanding where they would take him.

This study of the development of Murry's literary criticism attempts to trace the interaction of experience and idea which led Murry to take the paths he did. F. A. Lea's account of Murry's life, to which I am indebted for much biographical detail, deliberately emphasizes his role as a social thinker and largely neglects his literary criticism, while Griffin's study of the criticism, though often illuminating about particular works, excludes biographical data. My aim is to place Murry's critical work in its full context by describing how his personality, private values, and life experiences shaped his approaches to literature and how his response to literature shaped his actions. "Criticism," he said near the close of his career, "as I wanted to practice it . . . depended on values—a determination of what is good for man."[8] Certainly, the task of evaluating Murry's literary criticism is complicated by the entanglement of idea and personality, but that entanglement is the source of his vitality, the enlivening enthusiasm which more disinterested criticism too seldom attains.

Chapter One

BETWEEN TWO WORLDS

Between Two Worlds, John Middleton Murry's autobiography, written in mid-career, takes its title from Matthew Arnold's poem of the same title. His appropriation of the phrase points to the two most important elements of his life work. It calls attention, first, to Murry's allegiance to Arnold's mode of criticism, his effort to achieve the same sort of comprehensive vision and to write about literature in a way that sustains life, "to see life steadily and to see it whole." Even more tellingly, the phrase "between two worlds" defines Murry's sense of himself as a displaced person, uncomfortable in his own time and uncertain of his own identity. He said that since undergraduate days his life had been "largely spent in an effort to make sense of myself" and quoted approvingly Katherine Mansfield's description of him as a "monk without a monastery."[1] The important movements in Murry's thought are unvaringly related to stages in his search for meaning and personal being.

The Early Years

John Middleton Murry, born in 1889, was the eldest son of a civil servant, John Murry, who had by enormous struggle just raised himself from the laboring class. The father was self-taught and even more ambitious for his son than for himself. Young John Middleton Murry's obvious precociousness must have seemed to his father full justification for the forced education which began, literally, in the cradle. The family legend is that the boy was reading newspapers aloud at age two.

When John began day school at age two and a half, his father initiated the pattern of constant, unsatisfiable criticism which was to haunt his early years. John Murry senior was then working torturously long hours in his desperate effort to establish a foothold in the middle class. He left home at dawn while his son slept and returned long after the boy was in bed. No matter how late his return, John Murry nightly examined the sums and letters his son had produced. A stream of admonitions and suggestions issued from this remote, inaccessible figure, whom John encountered briefly on weekends. The combination of physical and psychological distance meant that the boy did not know his father and had no means of evaluating the impossible demands in relation to a fallible human being. The pressure was enormous and soon made of him, his aunt said, "a little old man."[2]

The counterbalancing softness in John's early world issued from his sensitive, affectionate mother and his grandmother and aunt, who shared the home for several years. Domestic warmth, laughter, emotional security came solely from the maternal and the female. Given the classic psychic imbalance of this family structure, it is not surprising that Murry describes himself as suffering from a split between his emotions and his intellect and as having a pervading sense of alienation and emotional, if not physical, impotence. His constant need for approval was the source of many of the contradictions in his personality and of what others frequently perceived as inconsistency and inconstancy.

Although Murry habitually wrote a kind of introspective autobiography, it is interesting that he defensively ignored the emotional implications of this rigid opposition of male/female traits and denied the relevance of Freudian doctrine to his own psychic situation. He professed puzzlement at D. H. Lawrence's pronouncement that "you, in particular, ought to be very concerned about the Freudian theory" and was surprised by the "passionate indignation" that Lawrence summoned against his father. Murry described himself as "quite incurious about my complexes and my repressions. . . . I could see no good reason why I should get bothered about them, supposing that they existed. The dogs were asleep, as far as I knew, so why not let them lie."[3] Murry was to live through three complicated and tragic marriages before finding, at age fifty, a comfortable, fulfilling relationship with a woman who offered him unconditional warmth and approval, yet he never looked more closely at the sleeping dogs.

Rather, Murry attributed the major conflicts of his early life to the rigors of the early intellectual demands and the stress attendant on the change of social class which accompanied his educational progress. He was among six scholarship boys admitted to the noted school Christ's Hospital in 1901, the first year the institution opened its doors to board-school boys. By winning the scholarship, Murry became socially dispossessed, caught up in the first wave of change in class barriers which was to transform England in the twentieth century. He was without precedents and guideposts, the more adrift since his mother and father were imperfectly removed from the laboring class. In essence, he was to skip the middle class altogether, and he could not do so without disowning his parents. At Christ's Hospital Murry was terrified not so much of the exams or his relations with boys of more advantaged backgrounds as of being embarrassed by his parents. His mother's cakes were inedible, his aunt chattered familiarly with the porter, his father asked altogether the wrong questions of the headmaster. Murry was increasingly ashamed of his parents, aware of the want of taste in his home, and guilt-ridden by the deceptions he was forced to practice, at home and at school, in order to survive in the incompatible worlds.

The price of assimilating so much change was that Murry tried to be several people at once and so retarded the process of self-knowledge. Throughout his life friends charged him with obliviousness to his effect on others. That trait was probably both a consequence of his early identity confusion and a habit of mind that became convenient. The commitments Murry evaded by appearing not to understand what was wanted of him were legion, yet the evasions hardly conscious, since he was no less confused about himself than others were about him. Perhaps the search for a fixed truth assumed such a major place in Murry's criticism because he found the truths of his own nature so difficult to fix.

Predictably, Christ's Hospital was followed by Oxford. Murry won one of the few available scholarships and went up in 1908. There he was one of an even more select minority. There were hardly a dozen board-school boys at Oxford and Cambridge in 1908. Murry himself knew only two.[4] His classmates knew nothing of his background, and Murry did not betray himself, though he continued secretly to consider himself a fraud and an imposter, as he had in public school.

However, at Oxford Murry discovered an intellectual life which could excite him beyond self-consciousness. His forced education had not allowed time for the play of mind and idea. Through the Milton Society he met a group of able undergraduates which included Joyce Cary and Arnold Toynbee. Murry said: "There was nothing precious about them, yet their intellectual interests were various and widespread; and they judged for themselves. To me they were vastly stimulating; I can hardly have been that to them."[5] Murry's friends, in fact, found him an impressive personality, brilliant in argument.[6] He was exceptionally responsive to new ideas, having none that were preconceived, and the intellectual life became, for the first time, an end in itself rather than a means of satisfying his father.

Dreading vacations at home, Murry gratefully discovered a haven on a prosperous farm near Oxford. The family who let him a room were named, appropriately enough, Peachey, and Murry soon became a quasi-member of the family. The rural setting and spontaneous warmth of the Peacheys freed Murry from his self-estrangement. "I suppose that I was as near as I ever could be to my real self in the kitchen at Waterloo. There I had no need, and therefore no desire, to defend a precarious position."[7] That easeful tone did not recur for many years. Trapped in London by the exigencies of editing and journalism, he longed for a rural home. When he did, finally, become the proprietor of Lodge Farm, he also achieved contentment.

Life with the Peacheys offered a sustenance which filled the emotional vacancies of Murry's personality. He fantasized himself a real member of the family and became briefly engaged to the niece of the village vicar. In fact, he was not one of them and could not become a farmer without capital. He could only fulfill the destiny prescribed by the scholarships he'd been granted and put his able intellect to work in the professions.

Ironically, it was at the Peacheys' that Murry met the French novelist Maurice Larrouy, who convinced him that he could not understand contemporary culture and ideas without going to Paris. Murry's trip to Paris in December 1910, was to refocus his life. Not for the last time, Murry disowned his past associations and involvements. He never contacted the Peacheys again. He had tried on the role of gentleman farmer and found no practical way to wear it. The world of ideas Paris presented to him was another matter.

Murry and the Avant-Garde

Paris in 1910 was a center of avant-garde thought and experimentation. A resurgence of postimpressionism, the birth of symbolist poetry, and Bergson's recently proclaimed doctrine of creative evolution mingled to produce an intoxicating climate of discovery in the Bohemian circles Murry joined. Greedily absorbing all he saw, he found in Bergsonism the connecting thread, the notion that art was a quality of being—an achievement of, or an effort toward, integrity.[8] That interpretation of Bergsonism owed much to Murry's friendship with the Fauvist painter J. D. Fergusson, who described the essential integrity of the artist as deriving from his capacity to live in harmony with the rhythm of the self, a rhythm to be apprehended by the workings of the Bergsonian intuition.

If at Oxford Murry had discovered a life of the mind, in Paris he gained a raison d'être. There art was a life force in which he found his vocation. He wrote to a friend, "I have got clear on things that shifted vaguely before me and the whole vividness and directness has reacted back upon me and given me myself an end to live for—which will be a life of Art as far as I can make it so."[9] His elation and sense of wholeness owed something, also, to his first love affair. He was exceptionally naive in his relationship with Marguéritte, the young French girl he met amid the café crowd. Too idealistic to regard his attraction as wholly sexual, he soon found himself promising to marry her. In the meantime, he was bound to return to Oxford. He did so reluctantly, but by the time he returned to Paris over Easter vacation his ardor had cooled sufficiently for him to consider the practical impossibility of marrying before completing his degree. His promise to come again in the summer was more dutiful than passionate. He sent her money throughout the spring but instead of returning to Paris accepted a tutorship in Devon and then spent a month in Heidelberg learning German. He stayed twenty-four hours in Paris on his way home, trying to make up his mind and then left without seeing her. Marguéritte's letters went unopened and unanswered. For years he was haunted by his cowardice and betrayal of her. In *Still Life,* Murry's first novel, the hero, Maurice Temple, journeys to a French village looking for the girl he deserted years before, but Murry could not summon a fictional resolution of his abandonment. Like Murry, Temple cannot face the encounter and flees before meeting his former mistress.

The permanent influence of Murry's Paris experiences developed from his artistic, rather than his sexual, initiation. He immediately began giving form to his determination to bring the literary, artistic, and philosophic innovations of Paris to England. Upon his return to Oxford early in 1911 he enlisted the support of a fellow undergraduate, Michael Sadlier, in publishing a journal dedicated to his Bergsonian aesthetic, Sadlier's father agreeing to subsidize its beginnings. During the Easter vacation he and Sadlier gained promises of contributions from a number of French artists and literary figures, including Fergusson, Picasso, and the leaders of the fantaisiste movement, Francis Carco, Edouard Gazinin, and Tristan Derème.[10] The first issue of *Rhythm* appeared in June, 1911, six months after Murry's first trip to Paris.

The opening essay, "Art and Philosophy," which Murry had composed immediately on return to Oxford, is marred by a strained effort to link Bergson and Plato and by excited elliptical terminology. Nonetheless, it is significant as an early effort to explain the implications of Bergsonian philosophy for aesthetic theory.

> We attain to the truth not by that reason which must deny the fact of continuity and of creative evolution, but by pure intuition, by the immediate vision of the artist in form. But the pure intuition is no mystical surrender of reason and personality to a vague something, which, because it is nothing, is called God. It is the triumph of personality, the culmination and not the negation of the reason. The intuition is that point, as it were, at which the reason becomes most wholly itself, and by its own heightened working conquers the crude opposition of subject and object, from which at a lower

level it cannot become free. . . . so when the workings of the reason become most concentrated and intense it reaches that utter consciousness of its own all-embracing power, which the blind call mysticism but which is the very essential rationality of reason. This is the truth which Plato declared so many years ago. Interpreted into the crude hallucinations of Neo-Platonism, it is the most blind and feeble of all doctrines. Taken in its real truth and meaning, it is the final word in aesthetic—a truth which Bergson, as I interpret him, is declaring once more today.[11]

In this essay Murry articulated some of the fundamental principles of modernism long before others did so. Pondrom points out that Hulme did not begin to discuss Bergson and art until 1913, and his interpretation of the aesthetic implications of the theory of intuition is very like Murry's. The Imagism movement was founded on the same principles.[12] Hulme, the Imagists, and Murry use Bergson's higher empiricism, the notion that the intuition combines with the form-making faculty of the intellect to produce a total construct of reality, to define art as "the true and only expression of reality," which interprets life with the "eye of the heightened reason."[13] That reality is immediately, pragmatically accessible. The artist presents his intuition of the real nature of things through image and analogy, providing an occasion for a succeeding intuition by the reader or viewer.

The notion that art can provide a completed version of reality (in contrast to the partial, distorted knowledge of the intellect) led Murry to propound a doctrine of form which is an interesting antecedent to the aesthetic doctrines Pound began to articulate three years later.

The artist attains to the pure form, refining and intensifying his vision till all that is inessential dissolves away. . . . He must return to the moment of pure perception to see the essential forms, the essential harmonies of line and colour, the essential music of the world. Modernism is not the capricious outburst of intellectual dipsomania. It penetrates beneath the outward surface of the world and disengages the rhythms that lie at the heart of things, rhythms strange to the eye, unaccustomed to the ear, primitive harmonies of the world that is and lives.[14]

Murry's stress on the concentrated perception in a moment of time derives from Bergson's definition of intuition's power to contact the full continuity of consciousness in an "immediate vision," but the emphasis on presentness is also allied to his corollary theme, that art must be revolutionary, continually fighting submission to the past. It was that theme of rebellion against the nineteenth-century sensibility which dominated the avant-garde world of Paris and which Murry proposed to carry to England.

When he returned to Oxford in the fall of 1911, he substantially withdrew from academic activities. Life for him lay in London, where Dan Rider's bookshop served as the small center for experimental English artists and Murry found "some counterpart to the wonderful republic of art in Paris."[15] Engrossed in producing *Rhythm*, he found his Oxford studies irrelevant to his real concerns.

In December he was invited to a dinner party to meet Katherine Mansfield, the young writer from New Zealand whose short story "The Woman at the Store" he had published in *Rhythm*. Each was prepared to be impressed by the other, and both shared at this juncture a cultivated cynicism, what Murry melodramatically called a "revulsion from life."[16] He thought Mansfield's story by far the best that had been submitted to *Rhythm*. She was curious about this precocious undergraduate. The coincidence of literary interests and a rather neurotic psychological balance of personalities created a quick, powerful attraction. Murry's vacillations and dependencies were attractive to Katherine, whose life had consisted of a series of revolts against male domination. She enjoyed being in charge of the relationship; Murry enjoyed having choices made for him. He recognized and envied Katherine's creative spontaneity and emotional responsiveness. In his relations with her he achieved for the first time the kind of security his emotionally ambiguous personality required.

When Murry told Katherine of his restlessness at Oxford, his impatience to begin living real life, she advised him to give it all up, leave the university at once, and do what he felt he needed to. He did so, only three months before he would have gained a certain First in Greats. His renunciation of academic honors for an uncertain and ill-paid post as a part-time art critic for the *Westminster Gazette* is an interesting measure of Murry's extreme suggestibility and the abruptness with which he was capable of making major decisions about his life. The practical wisdom of waiting out the term which would have stayed another man did not stay Murry because he had been awakened to a new mode of being. He never stuck to the safer path when he was convinced of the worth of the new one. Ever after he distrusted and devalued the purely academic; his criticism was unorthodox by scholarly standards, and he frequently opposed the conventions of the academic world.

Murry and Katherine began living together as soon as he left Oxford. He was twenty-three; she was ten months older. There was no question of marriage, since Katherine had not divorced George Bowden, the husband she had lived with for only ten days in 1909. Together, Murry and Katherine produced *Rhythm*, which had become a monthly—and a severe drain on their combined incomes. They gladly seized a chance to turn it over to a publisher, staying on as editors, but the publisher shortly went bankrupt and left them with the printing bills. It became a point of honor to keep the journal going and to pay off the debts, so that 1912 and 1913 were filled with financial struggle, the bonding engendered by idealism in the service of a losing cause, and the constant strain of trying to satisfy personal, creative, and emotional needs without enough time and money.

The general philosophy and character of *Rhythm* changed in tune with their vicissitudes and Murry's shifting enthusiasms. His infatuation with modernism subsided long before *Rhythm* ended publication in 1913. Although the postimpressionists were celebrated in the first issues (provoking vehement attacks from the *New Age*), the *Egoist* was the forum for imagism and vorticism, and the literary side of *Rhythm* never equaled the pictorial. Murry did successfully recruit contributions from his French literary acquaintances, but they were unballasted by English talent of equal caliber. Katherine Mansfield remained the only memorable new writer. There were fine illustrations by Picasso, Derain, and other French artists, but the articles were generally weak, and from the beginning Murry was compelled to publish nonmodernists like Hugh Walpole alongside the French fantaisistes.

The "modernism" of the journal had always been a rather hazy ideal. Murry's first embrace of the new aesthetic was eclectically indiscriminate. In a letter from Paris written during his first visit, he had tried to explain what he understood the movement to mean. "Modernism means, when I use it, Bergsonism in Philosophy—that is a really *Creative* Evolution with only in the end an intuition to put the individual at its heart roots: an intuition which is the raising of Personality to the nth degree, a conscious concentration of vision. . . . "[17] But once away from the intoxications of Paris, Murry began to question Bergson's view of reason and by 1913 was openly disavowing his former faith. "There is no fundamental rightness in the victory of instinct over the intellect. . . . they cannot be reconciled— even by a Bergsonian 'intuition.' "[18] Although he was never to abandon the view that art is a product of the whole personality, he came, increasingly, to focus on the "religion of art," art as reflecting the spiritual integrity of the artist, a concern which led him to find models in Russian literature and the English romantics rather than in the technical experiments of the French symbolists.

Having rejected the aesthetic of Bergsonism and without yet any allegiance to an alternate set of ideas, Murry was left to a youthful, uncertain exploration of new British literature. He became one of the idolaters of Frank Harris and inadvisedly proclaimed him "the greatest writer of short stories England has ever possessed . . . , the greatest creative critic the world has known," just before discovering that Harris was a plagiarist. Murry ruefully acknowledged that "I was and am the kind of fool who always has to believe in somebody or something,"[19] and his exaggerated estimate of Harris was not the last effusion he was to regret.

The necessity of financial help to maintain the journal led, in the end, to an influx of Georgian poets who transformed *Rhythm* into the "centre of the Georgian literary scene."[20] The literary pages were dominated by contributions from De La Mare, W. H. Davies, Wilfred Gibson, James Flecker, and John Drinkwater. In his autobiography Murry defensively insists that he and Katherine controlled the tone of *Rhythm*, even after Eddie Marsh contributed financial and editorial assistance, but in fact they eventually allowed Marsh to take the lead and were relieved to do so. Katherine wished to concentrate on her writing, and Murry needed to produce quantities of journalism to earn a livelihood. In May 1913, *Rhythm* ended publication. Issued under a new title (to avoid the burden of debt) as the *Blue Review*, it lasted for three issues. The end of the magazine was less a defeat than a long overdue freeing from obligation. Neither Katherine nor Murry could develop creatively while burdened with the financial disaster of a journal which had lost its sense of direction.

Murray's creation of *Rythm* was an astonishing enterprise for an undergraduate, a suggestive beginning for a career checkered by ambitious literary and social projects. In its early issues, *Rhythm* opened new channels of communication between French and English artists and displayed a cosmopolitanism that no other British journal possessed in those years, enlarging the creative possibilities of British culture.

Katherine Mansfield and D. H. Lawrence

The nature of Murry's critical career was fundamentally determined by the two significant relationships of his twenties, with Katherine Mansfield and D. H. Lawrence. His liaison with Katherine cemented his vision of himself as a man of letters bent on effecting change in English culture. His intense friendship with Lawrence served to locate those significant ideas which he examined for the rest of his life. From the beginning the love relation and the friendship were in partial opposition. Katherine and Lawrence were both possessive in relationships, jealous of other influences, and they represented very different models of being, Katherine allied to a genteel, romantic love tradition which gained its seriousness through cultivation of a Keatsian melancholy and a Russian exaltation of the suffering soul, Lawrence passionately embracing the "life" values of eroticism, viewing himself as the prophet of a new mode of consciousness.

When Murry and Katherine met Lawrence and Frieda in 1913, the two couples were attracted by the similarity of their situations and concerns as well as by the considerable intelligence and personal charm all possessed. Both were unmarried couples in revolt against conventional society and fossilized literary values. Murry recognized Lawrence's novelistic genius, recalling years later the "impression of warm, rich darkness which the opening pages of that great novel [*Sons and Lovers*]" made upon him.[21] Murry's impressionability, his readiness for discipleship, fostered Lawrence's instinct for directing other people's lives. He evidently over-estimated Murry's place in the critical world and expected him to further Lawrence's reputation in high places. While Murry and Katherine were enchanted by the quick warmth and intimacy Lawrence brought to his friendships, they were appalled by the ferocity of Lawrence's and Frieda's marital battles and discussed the superiority of their own romantic rela-tionship. Lawrence, meantime, diagnosed Murry as suffering from fail-ure to confront the real issues of manhood, sensuality, and primordial feeling, in part because of the protective warmth of his relationship with Katherine. Since Murry thought that he and Katherine were "unusually happy as lovers" and was repelled by Lawrence's treatment of Frieda as "a sort of incarnation of the Female principle, a sort of Magna Mater in whom he deliberately engulfed and obliterated himself,"[22] he was not prepared to accept Lawrence's prescription. So as early as 1914 the issue between Murry and Lawrence was the nature of the man-woman relation-ship.

Lawrence's love doctrine, which he articulated during this period in *The Rainbow* and later in "The Study of Thomas Hardy," "The Crown," and *Women in Love*, rested on the mutual attraction and antagonism of love, an eternal dualism which insists upon the integrity of the single being, the recognition of the otherness of the beloved. This Lawrentian theory of love posits only momentary interludes of integration in the perennial struggle, but the "state of still tension, life-sustaining and life-creating, forbidding forever the merging of opposites, and maintaining both in a state of mutual, complementary balance" which is the ideal, can be at-tained only by the necessary opposition of polarities which flow before and after the balance.[23] As Lawrence admitted, his love journey was lacerating.

The element of hatred and antagonism in the Lawrences' marriage alarmed and bewildered the Murrys, the more so because their own love cocoon was unraveling. Murry was resisting both Katherine and Lawrence, withdrawing into a "curious intellectual mysticism" which reached its apogee in obesssive discussions of Dostoevsky with his friend Gordon Campbell. Theirs was a masculine, intellectual relationship which Murry posed against Lawrence's call to blood consciousness. Retrospec-tively, Murry discerned that he allied himself with Campbell's assertion of the male principle of "knowing and self-consciousness and mental 'love' " against Lawrence's "female principle of being" as part of his simultaneous attraction and repulsion from Lawrence and his need to compensate for the poverty of his own instinctive nature in the face of Lawrence's "rich spontaneity." "I took refuge in my tower of 'intellectual mysticism,' not merely to vindicate the essential apartness of the Male from the Female, but at least equally to confirm myself in the sense of some superiority to Lawrence—to save myself from the peril of being annihilated by him in my own estimation."[24] Katherine, finding herself eclipsed by Lawrence on the one hand and Campbell on the other, retaliated by bedding with the painter Mark Gertler after a Christmas party during which she and Gertler had played a charade enacting her leaving Murry. Murry wholly exasperated Lawrence and Frieda by passively and miserably acquiescing to Katherine's behavior.

Lawrence had reason to claim that Jack's and Katherine's love relationship lacked the full commitment of his and Frieda's. They had been married in July 1914, following Frieda's divorce. The worm in the apple for Frieda was that she had never foreseen losing her children when she ran away with Lawrence, and the terms of the divorce annulled her custody rights. Although her grief at that loss enraged Lawrence, Frieda had, in effect, chosen between Lawrence and her children, and the degree of her commitment was measured by what she had given up for him. Jack's and Katherine's situation was quite different. They were unmarried still, and although he evidently believed that she could not obtain a divorce, her husband, George Bowden, has stated that he offered her one but she took no initiative.[25] Even more damaging evidence of Katherine's duplicity in intimate matters is the fact that over the years that she and Jack desired a child and did not have one, she allowed him to assume responsibility for the failure. Murry learned that Katherine was sterile in consequence of peritonitis, contracted after an abortion, only from reading Anthony Alper's biography of her, years after her death.[26]

If Katherine was insufficiently committed to Jack to promote actively the possibility of marrying him, he was too passive to set a direction himself and characteristically found intellectual grounds for their modus vivendi by asserting that he and Katherine allowed one another growth and freedom by maintaining their distinct beings. To some degree they found gratification in the melancholy sense of impending separation and catastrophe which punctuated their lives together, lending a mock-heroic and self-dramatizing quality to their use of the term "lovers." After Katherine announced that she was leaving for Paris to join Francis Carco, the French novelist she'd met through Murry, she recorded in her journal feeling "deeply, strangely in love" with Jack after he had accepted her forthcoming departure. "We gave each other our freedom in a strange way."[27]

Lawrence, who believed Murry was substituting romantic martyrdom for commitment of the whole, instinctive self, viewed Katherine's desertion as the crucial opportunity for Murry to "come to himself at last."[28]

After nursing him through a severe bout of flu, an incident Lawrence drew upon in the scenes of Lilly's nursing of Aaron in *Aaron's Rod*, Lawrence strove to enlist him as a follower and enunciator of his doctrine of a new revolutionary society, where all personality would be surrendered to "some great and all-inclusive religious purpose."[29] This was to be the occasion of Murry's rebirth into a "correspondence of being" with Lawrence; he was to be "one of the men of the future . . . , my partner—the only man who quite simply is with me—One day he'll be ahead of me. Because he'll build up the temple if I carve out the way."[30]

This interlude of intimacy between Murry and Lawrence in February 1915 significantly influenced all that was to happen later between them. Murry was shaken by Katherine's departure and by his illness, eager for all the comfort Lawrence offered and momentarily caught up in the great scheme. Lawrence urgently needed a disciple. The outbreak of World War I was a horror to him, terrible evidence of the destructiveness of mechanized society and of the absolute necessity of his revolution of the human consciousness. Frieda's Germanness, her family's association with German military tradition, made Lawrence's agony over the war deeply personal as well as ideological. Like many writers living amid great public events, he felt compelled to action but was at a loss about what to do. In Murry he recognized a capacity for public action. Despite the element of personal insubstantiality, Jack had a talent for making things happen. It is not surprising, then, that Lawrence seized upon his potential discipleship.

Murry had never come to terms with the war, personally or impersonally. His reaction was wholly introverted and self-conscious, a "woe is me" engulfment in the horrors of life. While Lawrence was constructing a schema for the new order that was to arise from the ashes of the old, Murry was discussing Dostoevsky's suffering soul with Campbell. While Lawrence was calling him to join in striving for a great impersonal bond with all mankind, Murry was struggling to survive Katherine's rejection, and his intimacy with Lawrence grew out of the "warm atmosphere of love" in which he proposed their comradeship. At bottom, Murry never accepted Lawrence's assertion that the source of new being lay in the acknowledgment of the "animal of oneself," for he was unwilling to repudiate the validity of his own love experience.[31]

Clearly, the founding terms of the comradeship were incompatible. Murry later described his failure to reject Lawrence's plans decisively as a betrayal of friendship. At the time he kept his reservations to himself. His sense of self was too vulnerable to permit an open assertion of differences; he evaded demands which threatened his psychological defenses by a passive, ambiguous noncompliance, a trait which was the source of numerous charges of betrayal in the course of his life. The full disparity between Lawrence's expectations and Murry's willingness to fulfill them was not clarified then because Katherine returned from Paris and Murry turned his attention to her.

The tangible product of Lawrence's search for a vehicle to express his outrage with the war was the *Signature* venture. He and Murry produced three badly undersubscribed pamphlets in the summer of 1915 which are chiefly noteworthy because they contain Lawrence's essay "The Crown," a philosophical explication of his theory of polarities. Murry's contribution, "There Was a Little Man," is unremarkable save for the verbosity with which he expressed his confusion amidst a world at war. When Murry summoned the courage to tell Lawrence that he believed in Lawrence himself but not necessarily in his ideas, Lawrence vehemently denounced Murry and his other false supporters. "They say to me, 'You are wonderful, you are dynamic,' then they filch my life for a sensation unto themselves, all my effort, which is my life, they betray, they are like Judas."[32] The suppression of *The Rainbow* shortly after its publication heightened Lawrence's frustration and sense of betrayal.

Murry shared Lawrence's indignation over the censorship, although he found the "warm promiscuity of flesh"[33] in this novel symbolic of all that differentiated him from Lawrence. In any case, his attention was centered on Katherine, who was grief-stricken by the death of her beloved younger brother on the front. Murry initially reacted away from the responsibility of supporting her grief, but by the new year, 1916, he had joined her at Bandol, in the south of France, and genuinely comforted her. This new balance, in which Murry was the source, rather than the recipient, of emotional security, fostered a creative harmony which Jack and Katherine were to look back on as the idyll of their lives. During the three months at the Villa Pauline, Katherine wrote "Prelude," the first of her fine stories about her New Zealand childhood, and Murry produced his first full-length critical work, *Dostoevsky*. The interlude of peaceful concentration was broken by Lawrence's urgent calls to join him in Cornwall, where, he wrote, he had discovered their "Rananim." "No more quarrels and quibbles," he promised. "I am a *Blutbruder:* a *Blutbrüderschaft* between us all. Tell K. not to be so queasy."[34]

Despite Katherine's misgivings, Murry found Lawrence's warm personal appeals to his loyalty irresistible. The Murrys' move to Cornwall in April represented another swing in Jack's alternation between Katherine and Lawrence. She felt displaced from the start, wanting, as Frieda discerned, Murry all to herself,[35] while the Murrys' coming did not cure Lawrence's black depressions. The two couples wrestled with the conflicted relationships for two months. Murry's coming had not altered his resistance to Lawrence on the love doctrine issue nor lessened Lawrence's need for a male comrade who would be at one with him in his purposes, a reassuring alterego, who would not, like Frieda, challenge him by opposition. The crisis came when Lawrence proposed a Blutbrüderschaft ritual with Murry, a "mingling of the blood so that neither of us could go back on it."[36] Murry, envisioning "some sort of ceremony of black magic to be performed amid the great stones of the eerie Cornish moors,"[37] refused and proffered simply "love" in place of a male sacrament. Lawrence turned on him: "I hate your love. *I hate it.* You're an obscene bug, sucking my life away."[38] Murry yielded to his consistent impulse to escape moments of confrontation. He and Katherine moved to the south coast of Cornwall, the possibility of a real alliance between him and Lawrence ended. Lawrence's ironic description of their departure connotes the sexual struggle which divided them. "The Murrys do not like this country—it is too rocky and bleak for them. They should have a soft valley, with leaves and the ring doves cooing. And this is a hillside of rocks and magpies and foxes."[39]

Katherine's jealousy of Lawrence had contributed to the break. She resented his propagandizing of his love doctrine and interference in her relations with Murry, and she was piqued by his low estimate of her work. Lawrence did not take Katherine's "little" stories seriously; portraying her as Gudrun in *Women in Love,* Lawrence emphasized her "miniature" art, and he took Murry to task for overrating her. But like most people, Katherine was attracted to Lawrence, and when the specific rivalry over Jack was not at the center, she and Lawrence spontaneously enjoyed one another.

If Murry had "chosen" Katherine rather than Lawrence, leaving did not restore the contented intimacy they had felt at Bandol. Katherine was again restless and disillusioned, and Murry was shortly called up for war service, which he performed as a translator in the Intelligence Office. Katherine left again for Bandol and was stranded for months in war-torn France. When she finally made her way back to England, she was ill, with the first symptoms of the tuberculosis of which she later died. Katherine and Jack were married in May 1918, but the ceremony was scarcely emblematic of a new beginning. He sent her off to the country to recuperate while he carried on at the War Office. The immediate parting was a harbinger of the constant separations and reunions which marked their lives until her death in 1923. As Katherine's disease waxed and waned, she journeyed between England and the south of France (where the beneficent climate offered some hope of recovery), while Jack remained bound to his work in London.

Athenaeum

After the armistice and the relief from war preoccupations, Murry was appointed editor of the new *Athenaeum.* This post was the first substantial opportunity of his career; through it he became generally regarded as an important man, what Lawrence had earlier fancied him to be, a person who could influence the literary ethos of a generation. The journal he built was brilliant by any standard. Successful in assessing the significance of new talent, as well as in coaxing the famous to contribute, Murry took his role seriously. He was committed to building a new, vital literary culture in the aftermath of destruction, on being a "light to lighten the intelligentsia."[40] The list of his eminent contributors is formidable, including Eliot, Bertrand Russell, Santayana, Valéry, Lytton Strachey, Aldous Huxley, Herbert Read, Virginia Woolf, and Clive Bell. Many younger writers gained their first hearings in the *Athenaeum*, while Murry's own essays in the *Athenaeum* and the *Times Literary Supplement* cemented his reputation as one of the finest critics of the age. His repudiation of the Georgians and ensuing quarrel with the *London Mercury* and J. C. Squire was the first of his many public controversies. Describing the 1920 issue of *Georgian Poetry* as the product of "startingly uneducated minds" which have "jettisoned the past," Murry accused the Georgian poets of "impatience of structure and technique, contempt for technical method, the exaltation of sensational immediacy," and concluded that "there is something rotten in the state of English literature."[41] The vigor of the attack did much to enhance Murry's reputation. Certainly the feud with Squire increased his standing with the Bloomsbury set, who were similarly appalled by the facile sentimentalities of popular poetry. But, as Gross points out, Murry's positive essays were a greater achievement. "He chose major subjects and ranged widely. His illustrations were freshly chosen, his comments were acute. And there was a quality of unyielding seriousness which commanded respect. . . . Traditionalists as well as moderns were impressed."[42]

In 1921, having lost almost ten thousand pounds in two years, the *Athenaeum* merged with the *Nation*. Its demise was generally regretted. H. G. Wells remarked that it had been "the one hope of literary decency in England,"[43] but Murry's intellectual seriousness was not appreciated by a sufficiently wide audience. As Gross suggests, it was "too good to last,"[44] although a harsher critic claims that "the aim was . . . so superior as to be right off target."[45] Murry himself was undiminished by the closure; he was promptly invited to deliver the Raleigh Lectures at Oxford, the fruits of which, *The Problem of Style*, became a classic of critical theory.

The only dissonant note came from Lawrence, who had been freshly embittered with Murry when he refused to publish Lawrence's short essay "Adolph." In the years since the Blutbrüderschaft quarrel, Lawrence had alternately vilified and wooed Murry. Soon after the break Lawrence wrote wistfully: "I think that one day—before so very long—we shall come together again, this time on a living earth, not in the world of destructive going apart. I believe we shall do things together, and be happy. But we can't dictate the terms, nor the times. It has to come to pass in us. Yet one has the hope, that is the reality."[46] Murry made no reciprocal gesture at restoring the friendship, and a few months later Lawrence attacked him as a "small stinker . . . How is it that these foul-loving people ooze with such loving words. 'Love thy neighbor as thyself'. . . . I can't do with this creed based on self-love. . . . Murry, *not being an artist*, but only a little ego, is a little muck-spout, and there is an end of it. I never said he was honest. I said we *had* liked him and therefore we still liked him. But one can mend one's ways. I have liked him, and I don't like him any more."[47]

The extent of Lawrence's need of Murry, his belief that Jack was uniquely fitted to act as his particular comrade, is evident in the overtures he made two years later, through Katherine. He expressed to her his notion that Jack was a victim of the "mother-incest idea" and reiterated his own need for male comradeship. "I do believe in friendship. I believe tremendously in friendship between man and man, a pledging of men to each other inviolably. But I have not met or formed such friendship. . . . Please give the letter to Jack. I say it to him particularly." This letter closes with a warm plea for Jack and Katherine to spend Christmas with the Lawrences.[48] There was no Christmas reunion, but in January 1919 Murry was putting together the first issue of the *Athenaeum*, and he wrote Lawrence asking for contributions. To Lawrence, this response must have seemed a fulfillment of his earlier belief that Jack would be the person who would build up the temple, although his reply was diffidently couched: "You must tell me exactly what you would like me to do, and I will try to be pleasant and a bit old-fashioned. I don't mind if I am anonymous—or a *nom de plume*."[49]

Murry was delighted with Lawrence's first contribution, "The Whistling of the Birds" (published under the pseudonym "Grantorto"), but the next piece, Murry and Katherine agreed, was too angry and embittered to suit the purposes of the *Athenaeum*. No doubt Murry was treading cautiously in his first months as a major editor and did not care to risk alienating his readers. Nonetheless, Lawrence's memoir of a pet rabbit who escaped to wildness was of the mildest order—from the author of *The Rainbow*, such a tale was a concession to the most conservative taste. Clearly, Lawrence could produce nothing that would satisfy Murry if "Adolph" was defined as revolutionary, and Murry's refusal is difficult to fathom. Not surprisingly, Lawrence found this rejection the last straw, coming from the man to whom he had offered deepest friendship. For the next several years Lawrence was venomous about the Murrys, calling them "two mud-worms . . . playing into each other's long mud-bellies," rejoicing in the downfall of the *Athenaeum* and the "Murry-worms,"[50] finally writing Katherine: "I loathe you. You revolt me, stewing in your consumption."[51] The insult to Katherine enraged Murry, who angrily wrote Lawrence of his intention to hit Lawrence if they ever met again, a threat which provided a fittingly melodramatic closure to the early phase of this ambivalent friendship.

Death and Rebirth

Katherine Mansfield died at the Gurdjieff Institute in Fontainebleau on January 9, 1923. She had fought tuberculosis for five years, moving restlessly between England and various "healthy" spots in France, Italy, and Switzerland, never consenting to the prolonged rest in a sanatorium which doctors agreed offered the only possible hope of recovery. She and Jack were separate more often than together from the time of their marriage, since she could not endure English winters and he could not make a living outside of London. She blamed him for his absences and his unwillingness to live frugally with her on her allowance, although she also constantly complained of financial problems and pressed him for supplemental money to help meet the extra expenses of her illness. As a general practice, Mansfield lived on an allowance provided by her father, Murry on his income as writer and editor. They shared common household expenses. After Katherine became ill, Murry regularly contributed to her support, but his assistance ensured only basic comfort, and Katherine was fond of luxuries.

Circumstances dictated the length of their separations during these years, and Murry seems to have made real sacrifices in order to join her at intervals, but his visits were never long enough or frequent enough to quench her need for him. Murry needed her presence less than she needed his, leading her to complain that he was happiest with a remote, consecrated image of her rather than with her real self. Obviously, Murry was busily productive in London, while Katherine, a semiinvalid, had ample brooding time. The charges of neglect which permeate her letters to him ring false when one realizes that Murry consistently wrote to her once, often twice, a day. Any relationship conducted habitually at long distance is susceptible to misunderstandings, however. As Benet points out, the "mutual flattery of love letters" creates a world of small relation to the actual.[52]

Moreover, Katherine's new state of dependency altered their prior equilibrium. Katherine, who had fought for independence, for egalitarian status as an artist, for free Bohemianism, now exclaimed, "I am become—Mother!" Implicit in her discovery is her need of a man like her father, "a man . . . all action, all resolution."[53] Murry was not that, nor would she have chosen him had he been, for it was Murry's particular literary sensibility, combined with his need for association with a stronger personality, which allowed him to appreciate and nurture her talent unjealously. Such wholehearted support of female literary achievement is rare; one thinks of Murry and Katherine Mansfield, of Leonard and Virginia Woolf, of Lewes and George Eliot, and then pauses in search of another example.

Murry had always met Katherine's requirement for artistic comradeship. They admired the same writers, cultivated the same critical standards, and shared a romantic vision of themselves as solitary warriors in the service of "real" literature (in other words, that which repudiates cynicism and aestheticism in the search for a moral vision that can act on life). This embattled sense that their credo was not shared by their contemporaries allowed Katherine to tell Murry, "You and I are the only people who can write and think and whose opinion is worthwhile,"[54] and led Murry to reflect, just before his death, that the kind of "seriousness" he had shared with Katherine and Lawrence was not that of Eliot or of Bloomsbury. "To us, there was a sense in which they were all 'phoneys'. . . . Love meant more to us."[55] (Murry is precise, of course, in defining the difference in terms of love, for the struggle with Lawrence occurred precisely because each construed the aim of the artist to be the reformation of the human personality, particularly in the essential relationship of male and female. Their disagreement was about the nature of the reformation.) Because Murry and Katherine agreed about the nature of the central artistic task, he conferred on her a sense of herself as a symbolic writer, a modern Keats, questing toward a final integrity, a whole vision of moral beauty, while she applauded the same values in his critical work, his exploration of literature as something that really matters in the life of man. Their attitude of isolated superiority enhanced their mutual ability to wrest the best from one another, positing a symbolic standard which helped them guard against their weaknesses. It also biased their judgments. Katherine made Keats and Shakespeare her guides. Chekhov was the only modern who influenced her writing. All writers must select from the past that which fosters their own creative imaginations, but it is interesting to note how completely Murry adopted her literary heroes. His early interest in modernism was abandoned under Katherine's influence. He saw the importance of works like *The Waste Land* and *Ulysses* quite clearly, but he was uneasy with their cynicism and disillusionment and impatient of technical experimentation, and he turned to literature which posited an ideal to strive for.

This intellectual camaraderie flourished during the *Athenaeum* period, particularly, but it was accompanied by Katherine's resentment of Murry's passivity and self-absorption, her demand that he become another kind of man who would know how to care for a sick woman, and her letters became increasingly trivial and petulant. Her bitter portrait of him in "The Man without a Temperament" records the petty faults with which she charged him. In the last year of her life even their intellectual sympathies split, for Katherine had relinquished hope of a physical cure and was seeking spiritual salvations—with Ouspensky and Gurdjieff—and Murry, a skeptic about all that verged on the occult, was violently opposed to this program. Katherine's refusal to obey the doctors and accept the need for prolonged rest, her restless quest of a special cure, unquestionably hastened her death, and Murry felt all his life that he had failed her by yielding to her refusal of institutional care.

Shortly after Katherine's death, Murry had an experience of illumination which profoundly altered his future life and led him, he declares, to make a holocaust of his former self. The visionary moment, which he describes in the autobiographical section of *God*, followed the classic pattern of mystical enlightenment—a state of solitude and terror, descent into an abyss of unknowing, the dark night of the soul, and ascent to an ineffable recognition of unity, coherence, of "belonging" to the universe. Murry had always been temperamentally susceptible to discovering emotional portents in mental moments; his studies of Dostoevsky had been conducted as metaphysical explorations, and he was addicted to mysteriously oracular pronouncements such as "the inhuman is the highest form of the human."[56] Katherine once irritably remarked that "Jack can't fry a sausage without thinking about God."[57] However, his previous transcendental moments, such as the nightmare vision of the "ship of death" which he shared with Katherine during their first year together, or his discovery in Keats's phrase "the beauty of necessity" of a means of reconciling existing with suffering,[58] had embodied his own existential anxiety. When Murry blamed the war for his morbidity and overwhelming angst, Katherine reminded him that his state of mind preceded the war, that the war was "a supreme justification of all you had trembled towards (like a compass) all your life."[59]

His mystical experience of March 1923 was distinguished instead by affirmation and reintegration. Murry emerged with a holistic zeal which dominated his thinking for the rest of his life. The dividing line between the old and the new was 1923. *Between Two Worlds*, his autobiography, ends with Katherine's death, when he was thirty-four, and its candid confessions were made possible by his dissociation from his former self. His subsequent truth-seeking was conducted with evangelistic fervor, although what he was converted to was vaguely defined, a doctrine simplistically labeled "faith in life." The new perspective required a broader range of inquiry and exploration of social issues he had ignored as a professional literary critic. One might speculate that Katherine was largely responsible for Murry's straightforward devotion to literature, that without her influence his interests would have become diffuse at an earlier date. And it is significant that at this moment in his life, Murry veered straight back to Lawrence.

Lawrence had written a deeply sympathetic note on hearing of Katherine's death. A few days after Murry's mystical experience, he received a copy of Lawrence's *Fantasia of the Unconscious* and found it the inspired receptacle of his new life conception. "This book contains all my deep beliefs—all,"[60] he cried. He reviewed *Fantasia* effusively and decided suddenly that his great purpose would be the founding of a new journal, to be an organ for Lawrence as much as for himself. The first issue of the *Adelphi* appeared in May 1923, four months after Katherine's death, two months after Murry's mystical conversion.

In the *Fantasia* Murry found, along with Lawrence's familiar doctrine of the falsity of spiritual love and the alternating battle and reconciliation of the sexes, a definition of the source of "self-consciousness" in the stultified possessiveness of the mother toward her child and a call for man to find his salvation through possession of his own soul, gained by "retreat to the very centre . . . , there to be filled with a new strange stability, polarized in unfathomable richness by the very centre of centres."[61] Murry, long frustrated by his hypertrophy of the intellect, convinced now that Lawrence was correct about the deathliness of spiritual love (such an intensity of love, he now believed, had killed Katherine), had just discovered such a center in himself, a core yielding inner harmony and immediate, spontaneous contact with life. *Fantasia* promised that his ephemeral vision could regenerate his life, that he could be liberated from his own temperament.

From New Mexico Lawrence gave neutral assent to the *Adelphi* project, whose first issues serialized *Fantasia,* and he tried to let Murry down gently, but inevitably Murry's conventionalized, self-dramatizing version of the regenerated life did not impress him. He wrote, though not to Murry: "I was badly disappointed. It seemed to me so weak apologetic, knock-kneed, with really nothing to justify its existence. A sort of beggar's whine through it all . . . No really! Is this the best possible in England? One's got to *hit* nowadays, not apologize."[62]

Nonetheless, the *Adelphi* was an astonishing success. Murry had directed the *Athenaeum* to an intellectual elite; the *Adelphi* was deliberately middle-brow, aiming at "being comprehensible and interesting to as many people as possible."[63] It opposed the cult of art, favored earnest exploration of moral, social, and intellectual issues, and was imbued with Murry's ineffable religious exhaltation. Although Leonard Woolf compared Murry with Mr. Pecksniff, the working-class intellectual found him a prophet, a serious accessible writer propounding ideas of "significance for life."[64]

The *Adelphi* continued publication until 1948, although Murry handed the management of the journal over to his colleagues Plowman and Rees in the thirties. Although it was never embraced by the cultural establishment, the magazine significantly influenced British thought for twenty-five years. From the time he established the journal, Murry made himself an outsider, excluded from central intellectual circles and the stylish social fringes of the arts to which he had had prior access. His unfashionableness cost him the stimulus of association with first-class minds during the same period that he lost Katherine's exacting scrutiny of his emotional excesses. The mass audience he now wrote for encouraged his propensity for self-projection and inflated rhetorical gesture. Murry rather welcomed his suspect status—it freed him of the pretense that he had been wholly translated from his class of origin—and if the intellectuals shuddered at his emotional exhibitionism, he in turn found them too narrow to assimilate the genuinely relevant.

The *Adelphi*'s enthusiastic reception beguiled Murry into thinking that great numbers of people shared his passionate convictions, that a mass change of consciousness, a new brotherhood of man, was imminent. The misconception reinforced his decision to publicize his intuitions, to preach the integration of body and soul. Like others before him, Murry found it impossible to convey his revelation, and his efforts at explanation were decidedly murky. Attempting a definition of his "confidence," Murry resorted to writing passages like this one: "confident because he has acknowledged a destiny of which the end and process are unknown; confident because they are unknown: because everything matters and nothing matters, because he does not care and cares infinitely, because he loves men dearly and loves them not at all, because he is bound and free, waiting and not anxious, himself and not himself."[65] Meantime, he was proclaiming himself a forerunner of Lawrence (announcing that he was acting in locum tenens for a better man), and *Adelphi*, meaning "brothers," is an interesting title for a magazine founded on such terms. He was effectively signaling acceptance of the Blutbrüderschaft Lawrence had offered nine years before. But, as Martin Green suggests, there was a "flawed ambiguity" about Murry's dealings with Lawrence, even when his admiration was most fulsome.[66] The *Adelphi* was Murry's magazine, launched at a time when Lawrence was utterly renouncing European civilization. Moreover, by presenting himself as an ideologue, Murry became a rival. He must have been aware that Lawrence would never take over, as he was inviting him to do. Lawrence's eventual counteroffer was an invitation to Murry to come to New Mexico, to join him in building the community of brotherhood, and that offer Murry resisted, as he always resisted Lawrence at the decisive moment.

The jealousy between Murry and Lawrence during Lawrence's brief visit to England in 1923-24 culminated in the famous scene in the Café

Royal when Lawrence drunkenly pleaded with Murry not to betray him, and Murry responded, "I love you, Lorenzo, but I won't promise not to betray you."[67] The statement has become famous precisely because it encapsulates so many of the tensions between the men. Lawrence, who had fought for recognition, was jealous and contemptuous of Murry's ready success in presenting his ideas, piously diluted for popular appeal. Nor was he pleased by Frieda's too-fervent admiration. "After all," she was reported to say, "Murry is Somebody! And the Adelphi is Something!"[68] There were, additionally, sexual tensions, since in the interval before Lawrence joined her in England, Frieda apparently proposed an affair to Murry. He painfully declined, out of loyalty to Lawrence, but their "chumminess" was evident.

The "betrayal" scene also delineates the terms of discipleship with which Murry and Lawrence struggled. Seeking a master, Murry tried to make a Jesus of Lawrence, to assimilate him to a civilized, Christian ideal, for Murry rebelled only within conventional limits. He was committed to the rebuilding of English life and regarded Lawrence's retreat to New Mexico as escapist. He was ready to be John the Baptist to a civilized prophet, while Lawrence insistently played the centaur, celebrating the preconscious and the erotic. By rejecting Lawrence's central identity, Murry became Judas. The label was applied by Lawrence, accepted by Murry, and embodied in the Café Royal dialogue. Lawrence fought being "loved" or turned into a savior, for he believed that adoration falsified and invited betrayal, a Dostoevskian martyrdom. To him the "Judas trick" was false deference, pseudoloyalty born out of mental love—behavior he attributed to Murry. Murry acquiesced to the label by associating himself with a Russian version of Judas as the loving disciple who tried to reveal the true, hidden nature of Jesus. This Russian view of Judas is best exemplified by Leondin Andreev's play *Judas* (1907). Murry probably knew the work, since Katherine Mansfield assisted Koteliansky in the translation of Gorky's *Reminiscences of Leondin Andreev*. In *Reminiscences of D. H. Lawrence*, Murry describes a conversation with Lawrence in which Murry defines Judas as the only disciple who understood Jesus—by divining his true nature and trying to reveal him.[69] Murry eventually enacted both versions of the Judas figure, by having his long-deferred affair with Frieda immediately after Lawrence's death and by writing *Son of Woman*, in which he claimed: "In this book I have betrayed you. . . . This 'betrayal' was the one thing you lacked, the one thing I had to give, that you might shine forth among men as the thing of wonder that you were."[70]

The "revelation" of this book is Murry's interpretation of Lawrence as sexually inadequate and conflicted, an Oedipal figure who built an erotic theory in compensation for his own sexual dilemma. In it Murry again insists that Lawrence never expressed his full genius because he denied his spirituality. Although Lawrence renounced Murry's last effort to find a meeting ground and wrote, just before he died, "Even when we are immortal spirits we shall dwell in different Hades,"[71] neither man was ever really indifferent to the other. As we shall see, Murry pondered the enigma of Lawrence until his own death, twenty-five years later.

Aftermath

In 1924, shortly after refusing to accompany Lawrence to New Mexico, Murry married Violet le Maistre, a young short story writer whose resemblance to Katherine Mansfield eerily impressed his friends. This marriage underscored Murry's rejection of Lawrence and his effort to return to the past, for he acquiesced in Violet's efforts to make herself over into Katherine. Violet had modeled her own short stories after Katherine's, and before meeting Murry she saw a newspaper photograph of him and told a friend, "That's the man I'm going to marry."[72] She submitted her stories to the *Adelphi*, captured his attention, and told him her feelings, and Murry quaintly discovered that he, too, was in love. He gave her the pearl ring he had given Katherine, and they set up housekeeping with Katherine's possessions, so that visitors were startled to find the table napkins monogrammed KM.

Happiness lasted for two years. They lived reclusively most of the year on the Dorset coast, where Murry puttered in the garden and wrote *Keats and Shakespeare*, bringing to fruition his long years of reflection on Keats. But the idyll was broken after Violet became pregnant. Because Katherine had longed for a child, Murry had assumed that Violet would, and he was shaken by her sudden refusal of the role for which she had been cast. When the baby (a girl inevitably christened Katherine) was born, Violet refused all contact for several months, and Murry had to take over. Violet was soon pregnant again and, after the birth of their son, Colin Middleton Murry, was persistently weak. The medical diagnosis gave tragic meaning to Violet's imitation of Katherine. She had tuberculosis, and her first words to Jack after hearing the verdict were grotesquely significant: "O I'm so *glad*. . . . I wanted this to happen. . . . I wanted you to love me as much as you loved Katherine—and how could you, without this?"[73] As soon as Violet's illness was established, Murry announced the end of the *Adelphi*. Dismayed subscribers sent money to ensure its continuance, but Murry turned the journal into a quarterly, reducing the demands on his time so he could devote himself to caring for Violet. The little writing he did in the next three years was centered on religious, rather than literary, exploration; his chief continuing project was editing and publishing all Katherine's remaining manuscripts.

Violet grew steadily worse. Then Murry learned that Lawrence, too, was dying of tuberculosis. He sped off to the south of France to see him but arrived too late. During his two-week stay he and Frieda had their long-deferred affair, and he learned, he said later, "what fulfillment in love really meant,"[74] but he could not abandon a sick wife and two children, even for Frieda, so he dutifully returned to England, and Frieda turned to Angelo Ravagli. But Lawrence's death spurred Murry to write again. Within six months he had written *Reminiscences of D. H. Lawrence* (published in installments in the *Adelphi*) and had begun work on *Son of Woman*. The reimmersion in Lawrence bore more peculiar fruit. When Violet died, a year after Lawrence, Murry immediately turned to his housekeeper, Betty Cockbayne, for solace. They were married within two months, and Murry's journal entries show that he was quite consciously acting out his idea of the Lawrentian love ethic, that he defined Betty as the incarnate female. A few months earlier he had written: "Probably I couldn't love anyone but a girl. Katherine was a girl. I don't know what a Woman is; and never shall. Not that I have avoided Woman. It is simply that I can't see, can't make contact with, Woman. She doesn't exist for me: a sort of Bogey of whom I hear report. Not in my destiny. In my destiny only Love, and the inevitable disaster of love."[75]

Having altered his fate by marrying Betty, a decidedly physical, unintellectual being, he declared: "This looks like being my baptism into direct knowledge of the Female—the thing that I have always eluded."[76] This event, coinciding with publication of *Son of Woman*, had the distinct appearance of marriage to a surrogate Frieda.

The result of the experiment was, according to all observers, totally disastrous. Murry's two children by Violet suffered the legendary abuse of a jealous stepmother, and Betty and Jack's own two children were not exempt from the consequences of Betty's horrendous temper. Colin Murry recalls an occasion when his infant stepbrother, David (named after Lawrence), was flung across the breakfast table into Murry's arms in the midst of one of Betty's rages.[77] Betty was spurred, evidently, by her sense of social and intellectual inferiority to Murry's friends. The "primeval intensity" of her tantrums was designed to elicit response from a husband whose primary instinct was to withdraw from conflict. According to Colin, "Once things were down on all fours she no longer felt herself to be at an intellectual disadvantage. If she finally managed to goad my father into hitting her then her triumph was complete."[78]

Betty was not Frieda, as Violet was not Katherine, but Murry tried to endure the catastrophic marriage with Christ-like submission—an attitude which infuriated rather than appeased. The impossible marriage ran its course for ten years, punctuated by separations and renewals. Murry coped chiefly by burying himself in writing and committee work, leaving his children to bear the brunt of Betty's frustration, which was especially great during his six-month lecture tour in America.

Those years, his forties, marked the height of his activities as a social critic; eight of the fourteen books he produced between 1931 and 1941 deal with sociopolitical theory. Most of these works are unmemorable, not only because they were topical. Murry's thought is least valuable when it is removed from the particular. His abstractions lack clarity and integration with disciplined theory, and he is too content to generalize without fact. Equally, none of the books is without germinal ideas, and reading them one is struck by the reach of Murry's mind as well as by the unity of his central belief in the values of the individual and his distrust of pure intellection. (Murry's model of the reformed state was of a socialist democracy with strong agrarian roots. He opposed nationalism and capitalism and totalitarianism and believed the good society would cultivate social responsibility by providing all its members with a moral education founded in Christian values.) And he brought to social theory the same criterion he applied in his own life, that when ideas cease to be "costing," they cease to be valuable.

Incredibly, since Murry's life with Betty was described as unrelieved hell by every witness (Murry's own feelings were obliterated; he destroyed the portion of his journal covering those years), he wrote his two best books during this period. *Shakespeare* is the most illuminating of all his treatments of major figures and *Heaven—and Earth*, an account of the cultural growth of the democratic idea through profiles of pivotal thinkers, combines acute historical consciousness and literary sensibility in a perennially interesting book which could have been produced by no other mind.

In 1941 Murry broke with Betty and began a new life with Mary Gamble. He paid the price of leaving his two youngest children, whom he was permitted to see only once before Betty died in 1954. She characteristically refused him a divorce, so he and Mary weren't able to marry until they had lived happily together for thirteen years. The final relationship was pacific and fulfilling, offering a fifty-two-year-old Murry his first taste of settled domestic comfort. The happiness of his fourth marriage tempered the hectic political activity and the desperate search for a social utopia. He did not wholly withdraw from such concerns (the community farm experiment during World War II he directed with Mary) so much as he ceased looking for personal salvation. That, as he made clear in *Adam and Eve* (1944), lay in the felicities of achieved marriage. Mary's effect on his literary attitudes was to revive his central faith in the doctrine of love, reinterpreted in the light of tardy sensual knowledge, making him, therefore, more Lawrentian. The revivified society, he now preached with greater ardor, depended on individual self-transcendence. That, in turn, depended on the birth of consummating spiritual/physical love between men and women. His search for an adequate creed ended in simple affirmation of the potentiality of human marriage, of the "true man-woman relationship." It was what he had always believed in, but Mary Gamble proved to him that this sort of fulfillment was really possible.

Murry spent his last ten years as a gentleman farmer, attended by a devoted wife, on happy terms with his four children and a growing company of grandchildren. Perhaps not coincidentally, he adopted more centralist political positions and turned, at the close of his career, to writing orthodox literary criticism of a sort he had not done for years. In addition to the widely praised biography of *Swift*, he wrote several volumes of essays which cast light on the English romantic tradition and scrutinized again the two presiding genuises of his life, Katherine Mansfield and D. H. Lawrence. The turbulent career ended bucolically, and his gravestone was capped with the seemly Shakespearean epitaph "Ripeness is all." He died at age sixty-eight of a heart attack.

Glancing over Murry's bibliography against the background of personal turmoil, one is struck by the sheer force of will which drove him. As leader of a small, earnest subculture, he performed largely outside the cultural establishment, and his reputation was marred by the character of his nonliterary interests, the unevenness of his work, and the publicity of his conversions. Thus, when he briefly flirted with the notion of taking orders in the Church of England, he gave a newspaper interview proclaiming his intent; the idea was quickly discarded, but Murry had enhanced his reputation for eccentricity and instability. One friend summed up the general exasperation: "John will think aloud."[79] Retrospectively, it is clear that Murry's political postures in the thirties were no more various than those of most contemporaries. Indeed, his forthright proclamation of new truths seems uncommonly honest in comparison with the concealed Marxist conversions and defections of others. But Murry was peculiarly vulnerable to slander because he was never fundamentally certain who he was. His quest for identity led him sometimes to enact roles chosen in relationship to individuals and ideas, and the roles shifted as allegiances changed. His inconsistencies and vacillations coincide with his quest for the definitive hero, the master idea. It was a search for an absolute ground for personality and was, like most quests for absolutes, bound to fail. Murry's inconstancies were linked to his hunger for a constant, and he was often self-deluding in his brief and too-hasty enthusiasms. His early successes arose from his unusual efficiency at practical, outer-directed activity, but as his autobiography reveals, that achievement was all on the surface. Personally Murry was disintegrated and inchoate.

This linkage of traits had much to do with the continued outcropping of charges of betrayal from his associates. His accomplishments led people to expect from him what he couldn't fulfill.

But Murry's unusual lability, what Lawrence called his "valuable inertia," equipped him to be an unusual critic. Because he was so ready to respond and to merge his own personality with the work he was studying, he was able to recreate his experience for the reader and express insights no one else had articulated; if he sometimes read his own conflicts into the writers he was treating, he also dealt with matters that a more circumspect criticism avoids.

The general view of Murry has been that he can be admired often before 1923 but not often after. The alternative view I am offering is that Murry's later achievements equaled and sometimes surpassed his early ones. If he had always written with dispassionate orthodoxy he would be remembered mainly as a minor imitator of Eliot; it was his particular combination of fervent, often ill-advised enthusiasm and acute sensitivity which made him a genuine force in British letters.

Chapter Two

CRITICAL PERSPECTIVES

The Failed Artist

In 1916 Murry published his first two full-length books. The first, *Dostoevsky: A Critical Study*, was a provocative introduction of Russian "spiritual biography" to English criticism; the second, *Still Life*, a novel, exposed the paucity of his creative gift. Murry lacked, and knew he lacked, the transforming artistic imagination he recognized in Lawrence, in Katherine, and in the sculptor Gaudier-Brzeska, but despite Lawrence's advice that Murry stick to criticism and Katherine's frequently devastating honesty, he produced three novels, two collections of lyric poems, a long dramatic poem, and a verse drama before he relinquished the effort to join the fraternity of artists and restricted himself to "creative" criticism. The frustrated longing for a talent he didn't possess underlay Murry's vicarious criticism and his pattern of self-identification with literary heroes.

Still Life is an unhappily appropriate title for Murry's first novel, for despite an elopement, a shifting love triangle, and settings in London, a country cottage, and Paris, nothing seems to happen in this book. Maurice Temple is a transparent self-portrait, and insofar as the novel has a definite point it is the portrait of his confused and confusing search for identity amidst a band of similarly lost souls. Murry later accurately described the writing of *Still Life* as "analyzing my own inward life to immobility."[1] It is a very dull novel whose dreariness is aggravated by Murry's insistence that we take the plight of his characters as seriously as he does. Their long, quasi-philosophical dialogues are never lightened by a hint of recognizing absurdity. Collis remarks that Murry would have profited by remembering Chekhov's observation that "if a writer wishes the reader to weep over his characters, he himself must be rather hard on them: for if he weeps, readers won't."[2] Instead of criticizing the human folly which leads his characters to find life pointless, Murry endows them with an irritating pride in their dissatisfactions, as if unhappiness proved sensitivity. Without capacity for self-objectification, Murry recorded his own nebulous emotions—and revealed how little he understood their source. Joyce Cary, his old friend from Oxford days, made a telling, if spiteful, judgment. "The novel sounds just the sort of thing I would have expected from him—confused sex relations, neurotic love affairs—and a great anxiety for originality at all costs."[3]

Still Life bears some superficial resemblance to *Women in Love* in its theme of a few men and women working out sexual relationships in the arty circles of London and the continent, and it is easy to see how Lawrence would have made Murry's plot and characters electric. Murry lacked the sure sense of comedy which underpins all Lawrence's best work, his gift of rendering social setting and, most importantly, the faculty for giving action symbolic content. The deliberately indefinite plot of *Women in Love* is given form by Lawrence's skill in centering significance in a fragment of action, such as the familiar episode in which Gerald Crich's character is defined by his forcing his horse against the railway crossing as the train is going by. The only discoverable parallel in *Still Life* is that Maurice carries an unopened letter from his mother about for several weeks. Whenever Murry suspects that the reader has forgotten that Maurice can't make decisions, Maurice is made to haul out the unopened letter. The sadly overworked gimmick typifies Murry's failure of invention and the strained, unsatisfactory quality of his fiction.

Conscious of the thinness of his novel, Murry turned to poetry as a better medium for his special sensibility. It was a move Katherine Mansfield supported, but her enthusiasm was always curbed by the warning that he had not yet achieved the goal. "Every new thing that you send me seems to be surer, to be more absolutely *poetry*. Ah, God! Why can't you simply give yourself up to your power *now*? why must your bird be still chained to your wrist when it is so ready for flight? But, my soul, it won't be for long, and nothing can stop you. I feel, with quite a new, 'special' feeling you are a poet."[4] The poems appeared in two editions, the first published in 1918, the second, including both early and late poems, in 1921. The 1916–18 poems are uniformly marred by archaic rhetoric and arch sentimentalities. Murry's children are always "little children," whispers are always "soft." Lacking a natural ear and without aptitude for compressing meaning, Murry veers between prosiness and melodramatic exaggeration. After 1918 he occasionally ventures into a more modern idiom which bears the palpable imprint of his reading of T. S. Eliot. One poem, "Sublunary," reads like an unfortunate parody of "The Love Song of J. Alfred Prufrock."

> What is the sense of this late afternoon
> Nudging my elbow: d'you dare to see the moon
> Just like a dirty post-card seller in the Rivoli?
> We have had tea,
> And we shall dine together very soon.
> I'll cut a cardboard thought or two, and spoon
> Some transcendental soup to show that I am he
> Who was at tea.[5]

Murry quickly abandoned this mode of imitation, but he never found a natural poetic voice. Even in 1921, after his brilliant editorship of the *Athenaeum*, he wrote and published poems he would never have praised in another poet. Unusually discerning as a critic of poetry, a champion of young talents, Murry was bizarrely unselfaware.

The Critic in Judgement, a discursive dramatic poem, was one of the first publications of the Woolfs' Hogarth Press, although not one on which they rested much hope. Both form and subject were better attuned to Murry's talent than the lyrics, and though *The Critic* is a negligible work, it is not embarrassing. The poem takes its inspiration from the Platonic theory of the ultimate spiritual unity of all things. The critic engages in a series of dialogues with personified ideas and ends with his affirmation of a vision which comprehends "all philosophies . . . , all beauties, all desires."[6] Hardly a helpful manual for critics, *The Critic in Judgement* was Murry's self-justification of the eclectic breadth of his literary enthusiasms and a tentative statement of what later became a fundamental tenet of his critical creed—the belief that the critic's task is to judge literature hierarchically, according to the wholeness of a life vision. Murry's intellectual ecstasy in *The Critic* pivots around his doctrine of the unity of body and sense, matter and spirit. Plato is the penultimate figure in the dialogue series because he represents the critic's most potent temptation, to judge by reason without reference to the sensual world.

Cinammon and Angelica (1921), an antiwar verse drama in the commedia dell'arte tradition, suffers, like the poems of the same period, from Murry's propensity for archness, whimsy, and artificial imagery. The tone of the piece is defined by Murry's decision to give the characters the name of spices, in a vain effort to lend the play an air of faerie. Even if Murry's blank verse were less execrable, it would be difficult to find pathos in the fatal love of King Cinammon of Peppercorn for Princess Angelica of Cloves. The antiwar theme is overridden by Murry's sentimentality about despairing romantic love, and the piece is a catalog of clichés about separated lovers. Katherine Mansfield, eager to bolster Murry's confidence in his work, suggested minor alterations in letter after letter, but her fundamental disbelief in its quality reveals itself. "I am a perfect fiend about this play, aren't I . . . ? Your play suggests so much—that's the trouble—and I can't be quite sure that what you have imaginatively apprehended yourself has *got into it enough*. You know how, beyond a certain point, if one is deeply in love with a piece of work, it's almost impossible to say what is there and what's not there."[7] Murry was, in fact, pinning many hopes on the success of this work, but his poetry still turned to hackneyed personifications of the moonlight:

> She is a queenly mistress
> Whom we do clasp in anguish to be held
> Close in her arms for ever; yet she turns
> Thrusting us from her: so we fall and weep.
> And then she is a gentle child who leans
> Over our sobbing and demented heads.
> And through our tears she shows us rainbow beauties
> Til we are comforted, and happy grown.
> Would be children no more but very lovers;
> We clasp her and she turns away again.[8]

With such a passage it is hard to know whether to blame most the exploitation of the pathetic fallacy or the insensitivity to cadence and precise diction. A phase like "sobbing and demented heads" surely establishes that Murry lacked fundamental poetic taste.

The critical silence met by *Cinammon and Angelica* finally discouraged Murry, and he turned back to the novel, the long break in his intimacy with Lawrence having loosened his inhibitions about trying that genre again. *The Things We Are* appeared in 1922. Murry's second novel is undoubtedly the best creative piece he did, and it earned a variety of mildly flattering reviews. The novel has the virtue of being nonautobiographical, hence created at a greater emotional remove than *Still Life* or the poems. Murry's most embarrassing lapses were connected with sentimental self-disclosure; his taste was always surer from a distance. The hero of *The Things We Are*, Boston, does embody many Murrian traits, including the habit of using New Testament tags such as "one must lose one's life to save it" with annoying repetition, but this tale of a mild London clerk who makes an upheaval of his life by suddenly quitting his job and retreating to a country inn has moments of realistic vigor. The transformation of the central character, and the triadic complications created by his emotional recrudescence are persuasive. So, too, are the scenes of talk and card playing at the country inn. The innkeeper and his wife approach Dickensian caricatures of the hearty, robust, *good* people of rural England, but that ideal Murry always held very sincerely (in later life he was always on excellent terms with the villagers of Lapham and Thelnetham) and he managed the portraits of these minor characters with observation, feeling, and humor which he never achieved when dealing with "sophisticated" characters. His downfall in this novel, as elsewhere, lies in his effort to analyze feeling intellectually. As a contemporary critic pointed out, "the characters talk too much and act too little." They are "dreadfully concerned with their motives"; they give everything an "appalling significance."[9] The endless soul-searchings of Boston and his friends turn to murky gropings toward defining the meaning of life, and the novel cannot bear too much ill-defined philosophizing, particularly when the issues are purportedly resolved by New Testament quotations which are brought into no explicable relation to the actions of the characters. Despite the occasional vivid passage, *The Things We Are* eludes success.

Murry's last novel, *The Voyage* (1924), was a dismal finale to his novelistic career. A depressing, gray-mooded book, it suffers, like its predecessors, from a cargo of emotional significance heaped upon lifeless characters. Wickham, a Murryish figure, fails to carry out his scheme of opening an arty bookstore because he becomes embroiled with an Italian femme fatale who is married to his wealthy patron. The presence of this improbable siren suggests that Murry was trying to strike a popular note by sensationalizing his plot with sexual intrigue, but if *The Voyage* was an attempt at a potboiler, it didn't succeed. Murry's inveterate preachiness invades the melodrama as Wickham pontificates about making love a religion, an occasion for self-surrender, as men once surrendered to God. In the muzzy atmosphere of this novel, such a declaration seems simply silly, as it doesn't when Murry explores that doctrine in relation to Keats. In 1924 Murry's critical reputation was in decline, and no one felt obligated to pay much attention to *The Voyage*. It was hardly reviewed.

Murry's success as critic and failure as artist demonstrates his gift for appreciation linked with an absence of inventive power. As Griffin suggests, Murry could not aesthetically resolve the theme of dissatisfaction; his novels offer "perplexity without solution," a "turmoil of feelings which subside without developing a sense of tragedy or comedy."[10] Rebecca West explored the disparity between Murry as critic and as artist in a 1922 review:

> Mr. Middleton Murry is one of the most distinguished of our younger critics, and he will be always remembered as having been an inspired editor. . . . he was also a most lucid critic. He would condense a deal of hard thinking and hard reading into something clear and globed like a raindrop. Now this is not true of *The Things We Are*. About Mr. Middleton Murry one could come to very definite conclusions. It is very hard to bring anything definite at all from a reading of *The Things We Are*, except perhaps a desire to

congratulate Mr. Murry for having found a title for his book that would suit
almost every novel that ever was written.

West ponders the separation between artist and critic in other writers and
concludes that no one save perhaps Henry James has combined the two
successfully. "It would almost seem as if there were something pythonic
about that state of true inspiration; that there must come first the trance,
during which the knowledge garnered by one's consciousness passes into
nothingness." Interestingly, her example of the "truly created story" is
one of Lawrence's: "No amount of thinking gave Mr. Lawrence the power
to write *Wintry Peacock.* . . . But the vision was attained. . . . It is impossible
to detect how these queer, unattractive fragments of events are arranged
so that they reveal the significance of these people's passion for one
another. . . . This is the great, the undeniably inspired Mr. Lawrence:
wandering like King Lear on the blasted heath of his own temperament."[11] One supposes that West's pungent comparison with Lawrence
must have been particularly damning to Murry.

Indeed, one explanation of this string of failures, on which Murry
labored so vainly, without talent, is that Murry was driven to place himself
in relation to Lawrence and Katherine. She promoted a vision of Murry as
artist, although her attitude was always double-edged. She kept telling
him he was *almost* a poet, then defining the nature of his artistic faults, so
that one suspects she needed to contemplate her own achievement in
relation to his failure. In any case, Murry wrote only one novel after
Katherine's death, and *The Voyage* was executed halfheartedly.

West's theory of pythonic inspiration aside, the weakness of Murry's
literary work is related to his personal insecurities and blindnesses. As a
literary critic, he was constrained to establish some distance from his
subject. His worst criticism lacks that distance, his best blends the subjective and objective in a mode of subtle discernment which casts new light.
His literary works are subjective, grossly self-revealing, without the significant transformation which makes art out of life. Lawrence and Mansfield
did not display their personal flaws in their work as he did. His poetry and
novels seem written out of that uncomfortably childish world glimpsed in
the letters between Murry and Katherine in which they term themselves
"Tig" and "Wig" and speak of the "little, little child" they may have
someday. Reading Murry's literary efforts, one is tempted to echo Katherine Mansfield: "Cover yourself—cover yourself quickly. Don't let them
see!"[12]

Russian Fever

Murry's first full-length critical book, *Dostoevsky: A Critical Study* (1916),
is an interesting prelude to his later work because it reveals Murry's

characteristic precepts and biases in their most naive form. English interest in Russian literature had been kindled by Constance Garnett; her 1912 translation of *The Brothers Karamazov* created a cult of Dostoevskyites, Murry among them. Dorothy Brewster declares that "while the fever lasted, Mr. Murry ran perhaps the highest temperature."[13] Murry's emotional mysticism made him a natural disciple of that school of criticism founded by Rozanov which represented Dostoevsky as a religious figure and found mystical significances in his work. Murry's *Dostoevsky* not only approaches the writer as prophet rather than novelist but denies that he *is* a novelist, a judgment precariously founded on the statement that Dostoevsky "could not represent life" because "he was obsessed by the *vision* of eternity."[14] This approach to Dostoevsky was the first manifestation of Murry's allegorical approach to writers he admired. He frequently described his soul heroes as prophets, insisting that they not be judged by ordinary aesthetic standards.

The study traces Dostoevsky's evolving spiritual biography through his novels, a method founded on Murry's description of Dostoevsky as an unbeliever "seeking perpetually to believe." Discovering a pattern of exploration beginning with *Letters from the Underground*, Murry calls Svidrigailov the true hero of *Crime and Punishment* because he is an incarnation of the single will asserted to the extreme in an effort to discover a God who will punish him and brought to metaphysical despair by the absence of retribution. Myshkin of *The Idiot* is a prototype of perfect goodness, but his goodness is impotent. "To do evil and to suffer it—each is vanity." Stavrogin of *The Possessed* tests the limits of human consciousness, becoming "pure spirit" by killing both his virtues and his instincts. But he, too, is vanquished. The human will can "will to annihilate itself." Only Alyosha of *The Brothers Karamazov* attains a consummation, representing a new dispensation, a post-Christian era "wherein even the physical being of man is changed."[15]

The argument he unfolds in the novels reflects Murry's own horror in the face of the "metaphysical terror and obscenity which is the appointed end of the striving of the human consciousness"[16] and his finding of hope only in the dream of a reformation of personality which would permit him to become, like Alyosha, a being "conscious only of his unity, and feeling within himself that which binds him to all humanity, the knowledge that he is the appointed end of all their striving."[17]

Murry inherently claims that he is revealing the true but previously undiscovered pattern of Dostoevsky's thought. Indeed, in *Between Two Worlds* Murry writes that he felt himself "the amanuensis of a book that wrote itself . . . the objective 'pattern' of Dostoevsky had declared itself, through me as instrument."[18] The argument that his "experience" of Dostoevsky revealed the essential nature of the novels did not convince many reviewers, who found Murry's conclusions "whimsical" or "heretical" and suggested that he had read more into Dostoevsky than the author intended. "One may say that this volume resembles rational criticism much as Dostoevsky's heroes resemble average humanity,"[19] one reviewer complained, although another acknowledged that "his study is in many ways the most profound which the great Russian has inspired."[20] This spate of approving and disapproving reviews shows that Murry had a knack for arousing controversy by pursuing a tantalizing thesis to an extreme. Almost always the result was that he induced his readers to return to the text and rediscover it more intimately.

The danger of Murry's approach is that the facts are always in danger of being wrenched into conformity with the thesis, and in *Dostoevsky* the supporting textual references are slighter than in a work like *Keats and Shakespeare*. The lurid, dramatic style of Murry's revelations is off-putting, even when the logic holds, and when the exclamatory prose becomes confessional, ideas have the appearance of originating with the critic rather than the author. "There have been moments when I have been taken unawares by a sudden *vision* of that which is beyond time, and the timeless world has terribly put on a physical shape. These moments I cannot forget, and they return to me sometimes when I read and meditate upon Dostoevsky. Because I am convinced that this terror is a part of Dostoevsky's creation, and that he himself was haunted by it even to obsession."[21]

Murry's *Dostoevsky* is not among those of his works which hold interest today for their own sake, although it certainly aided the growth of Dostoevsky's reputation in England. Its exclusive focus on Dostoevsky's spiritualness engenders judgments that are neither very useful nor necessarily true—for example, that Dostoevsky was not a novelist, not a Christian, believed in a miracle, had a secret to reveal. The list more accurately reflects Middleton Murry's preoccupations than his subject's. His fascination with Dostoevsky arose from his own God-seeking, that intellectual self-consciousness which Lawrence condemned in Murry and Dostoevsky alike. But Murry had discovered in the Russians, Dostoevsky in particular, a "passionate synthesis of thought and life" which was missing in contemporary English literature, and he passed on to his readers the conviction that literature could be the catalyst of a personal resurrection.

Soon after writing *Dostoevsky* Murry published an essay, "The Honesty of Russia," which amplified his view of the potency of Russian literature to a war-maimed English generation. Tolstoy, Dostoevsky, and Chekhov, Murry argued, are writers who still have a sense of connection between "all the great activities of the human soul," who don't compartmentalize but attack all philosophical questions and try to find a place for all human potentialities.[22] But it is in a later essay, "The Significance of Russian

Literature" (1922), which contrasts the Russian concern with the "problem of conduct" with the French formalist conception of art, that Murry offers a cogent and illuminating definition of the special character of Russian literature. "The Russian writer holds it instinctively as an axiom that a way of life to be truly satisfying must be based on a harmony of the human faculties. Heart and mind must be at one. There must be no piecemeal realizations. If the claims of the moral nature of man are in conflict with the claims of his intellectual nature, then the house is divided against itself and must fall. What is good, says the Russian, must be true."[23] The unity of the practical and contemplative in Russian literature, Murry suggests, has to do with Russia's political history; the democratic political institutions of the West have furthered a sense of compromise, an acceptance of life's imperfections, and a divorce between man's religion and his temporal condition which does not exist in Russia. "We fix the rules of conduct according to our practical knowledge of what men do if they get the opportunity, and feel that we can safely leave the motives of their conduct to themselves." For the Russian, the act is only a manifestation of thought. "The moment you take the emphasis off the act and put it on the mind expressed in the act, the inclination to definite moral judgment diminishes; and not only the inclination, but the possibility also."[24] This "instinctive suspension of moral judgment" leads both to difficulty in ascribing guilt to individuals and to a hunger for moral absolutism, typified by the "god-seeker" types who people Russian novels. The result is that Russian literature has a greater range than English literature; it sounds both higher and lower notes. Only Shakespeare, perhaps, of English writers, has expressed "an apprehension of human life as something which in all its manifestations exists in its own right," as Tolstoy, Dostoevsky, and Chekhov did. As Griffin astutely points out, the answers the Russians provided to the question "Is life worth living?" were peculiarly apposite in the middle of World War I, and the Russian belief in art as the "supreme human activity" gave Murry and many others a source of hope.[25]

The generalizations proffered in *Dostoevsky* and "The Significance of Russian Literature" are very different. In the former Murry was essentially defending an arcane reading which was subjectively linked to his private conflict with Lawrence, endorsing, through his treatment of Dostoevsky as a striving, suffering soul, a spiritual ideal in direct opposition to Lawrence's life-affirming creed. Lawrence had explosively condemned Dostoevsky's humility and search for an absolute. "Humility is Death. To believe in an Absolute is Death. There are no Absolutes."[26] Murry's explanation of Dostoevsky was more privately than publicly useful, a vindication of his own salvational quest. "The Significance of Russian Literature" offers instead original generalizations which point beyond themselves to new dimensions in comparative criticism. The essay demonstrates how economically lucid Murry could be when he set to work on a very specific idea and how good the spatial limitations of the periodical essay were for him, acting to restrain his verbosity and effusion.

The only other Russian writer to whom Murry gave detailed attention was Chekhov, Katherine Mansfield's chief literary mentor. Biased by Katherine's aesthetic preferences, Murry proclaimed Chekhov an indispensable master ("Tchehov is a standard by which modern literary effort must be measured, and the writer of prose or poetry who is not sufficiently singleminded to apply the standard to himself is of no particular account"),[27] but he could also be illuminating about Chekhov's technique, as when he defined the source of his genius in his capacity to find "unity in multiplicity." Chekhov's method, Murry explained, eschews both the classical prescription that aesthetic unity is attained by rigorous exclusion of all that is not germane to an arbitrary argument and the modern assumption that "all that is . . . present to consciousness is *ipso facto* unified aesthetically." Chekhov sorted detail from the "saturated solution of consciousness" by determining the aesthetic impression he wished to produce. "Everything that heightened and completed this quality accumulated about it, quite independently of whether it would have been repelled by the old criterion of plot and argument." The quality of Chekhov's aesthetic Murry relates to the contemplative unity of life he had achieved; for him "the act of comprehension is accompanied by an instantaneous act of acceptance"; he doesn't "seek to judge the unity he perceives, as others have felt compelled to." Murry's analysis of the operation of this comprehensive intellect in the stories is explicit and convincing: "It is a sense of incalculability that haunts us. The emphases have all been slightly shifted, but shifted according to a valid scheme."[28]

Murry's earliest effort as a critic had been to deepen the contact between British culture and the new French aesthetic of symbolist poetry and postimpressionism; in the second half of the 1910–20 decade he gave impetus to the new Russian influence. The cross-fertilization enhanced the postwar culture, although the French influence proved more potent than the Russian. It was in Murry's own career that the Dostoevsky influence was most explicit, and in his effort to convert Lawrence to that model.

Critical Theory

Until 1919, when he became editor of the *Athenaeum*, Murry's time was consumed by endless book reviewing, succeeded by two exhausting years in the War Office. Once he had his own organ and time to write for it, he produced impressive journalistic criticism at an amazing rate. We must remind ourselves of the originality of Murry's achievement in 1919-23. The four important literary journals in England after the war were the *London Mercury*, edited by J. C. Squire, the *New Statesman*, where Desmond McCarthy acted as literary editor after 1920, the *Egoist*, an experimental imagist paper which recruited T. S. Eliot as assistant editor in 1917, and Murry's *Athenaeum*. Squire's anti-intellectualism earned him and his circle the nickname "Squirearchy," and he remained the sworn enemy of all the new literature; McCarthy, an affiliate of the Bloomsbury group, acted as the traditional man of letters, fostering enlightenment, urbane civility, and genial breadth. During that period the essays of T. S. Eliot, later collected in *The Sacred Wood*, and Murry's in *Aspects of Literature*, *Countries of the Mind*, and *The Problem of Style* were alike and unique in the seriousness with which they regarded the critic's task and in the ground they broke for what is generally called the New Criticism. The authority of Eliot's criticism, both because of its finely honed, deliberative argument and because of its congruence with his poetry, has been incalculably greater. Murry's role as a shaper of critical principles has been largely neglected. Frank Kermode stressed the significance of Murry's revolt against the genteel journalistic tradition of his day when he wrote:

> . . . he began, at a time when criticism was a "novel preoccupation" for men of letters, with a theory that criticism was important for its own sake, and that it was the "consciousness" of art; and he was obviously anxious to develop it as an "autonomous" activity. In so doing he touched upon many ideas that have subsequently been of great importance; and that at a time when Mr. Eliot was sharpening his tools (and testing their edge on Murry.) They have more in common than either allowed himself to think, and Murry can easily be presented as another pioneer of the modern criticism.[29]

Two essays, "The Function of Criticism" (1920) and "A Critical Credo" (1921), and *The Problem of Style* (1922), are the core works of critical theory, although other essays of the period contain supplementary statements. He wrote little formalist theory after 1922. Once the first principles of his style of criticism were articulated, he was more interested in literature itself. The *Athenaeum* period was Murry's classical phase, one in which he was influenced by Eliot and Eliot by Murry. Murry wrote Katherine Mansfield that Eliot was "the only critic of literature that I think anything of,"[30] while Eliot states that the essays of *The Sacred Wood* were mostly "written during the brief and brilliant life of *The Athenaeum* under Mr. Middleton Murry: some of them directly at Mr. Murry's suggestion."[31] Interestingly, Murry's Eliotic period coincided with the interval of his greatest alienation from Lawrence.

The fertile interplay with Eliot's theories is explicit in Murry's "The Function of Criticism," since the essay begins by taking issue with Eliot's ranking of Coleridge, Aristotle, and Dryden in "The Perfect Critic." Murry uses Aristotle as the exemplary critic, one who has developed "a system of moral values derived from his contemplation of life," and omits Dryden because he lacks the "organic interpenetration," the "mutually fertilising relation between . . . moral and . . . aesthetic values" possessed by Coleridge and Aristotle. Eliot had endorsed Aristotle for his detached contemplation of literature. Murry links Aristotle with Plato, and his sense of what the Greek critics represent is quite different. "Their approach to life and their approach to art are the same; to them, and to them alone, life and art are one. . . . in the Greek view art is the consciousness of life."³²

In emphasizing the integration of Greek culture, Murry is using the Greeks much as Matthew Arnold did, to uphold the conception of art as a humanistic activity, a "revelation of the ideal in human life" (p. 4), and like Arnold he insists that art must be measured by its breadth of comprehension. "The active ideal of art is indeed to see life steadily and to see it whole. . . . only he has a claim to the title of a great artist whose work manifests an incessant growth from a merely personal immediacy to a coherent and all-comprehending attitude to life" (p. 14).

As the argument proceeds, Murry defines the critic's role as intrinsically creative. Criticism is an "organic part of the activity of art." "As art is the consciousness of life, criticism is the consciousness of art." The critic's function is to appraise literature in relation to its apprehension of the ideal, and since "only by virtue of the artist in him can man appreciate or imagine the ideal at all," and "to discern it is essentially the work of divination or intuition," the critic is himself an order of artist. However, the literary critic must employ a conscious aesthetic system, while the artist's aesthetic philosophy may well be unconscious; the artist's difficulty in making his philosophy conscious makes Eliot's expectation that the good critic and the creative writer are likely to be the same person "confused" (p. 11). The hint of acerbity in Murry's tone was a reaction to Eliot's pointed comment that the artist is "oftenest to be depended upon as a critic; his criticism will be criticism, and not the satisfaction of a suppressed creative wish—which in most other persons, is apt to interfere fatally."³³ The lines drawn between Eliot's artist-as-critic and Murry's creative critic mark the fundamental distance between them, even in this early period of mutual appreciation and encouragement. Murry concludes "The Function of Criticism" by emphasizing the need to distinguish between significant intuitions and "to establish a definite hierarchy among the great artists of the past, as well as to test the productions of the present," in order to assert the "organic unity of all art" (p. 14).

Murry's belief that literature must be judged hierarchically is in tune with the Arnoldian precepts on which both he and Eliot based their idea of a critic's responsibilities, but he offers no criteria for the task. "Poetry and Criticism," also published in 1920, tackles the issue again, but reaches only the general formulation that "one must establish a hierarchy and decide which act of comprehension is the more truly comprehensive, which poem has the completer universality."[34] In "The Poetry of Mr. Hardy" (1919) Murry had praised Hardy's poetry and attempted to describe the order of comprehension which characterizes great poetry. "The creative act of power which we seek to elucidate is an act of plenary apprehension by which one manifestation, one form of life, one experience is seen in its rigorous relation to all other and to all possible manifestations, forms and experiences. . . . " Aesthetic vision is not a perception of beauty but "the apprehension of truth, the recognition of a complete system of valid relations incapable of logical statement. . . . In a 'moment of vision' the poet recognizes in a single separate incident of life, life's essential quality. The uniqueness of the whole, the infinite multiplicity and variety of its elements, are manifested and apprehended in a part."[35] Neither "Poetry and Criticism" nor "The Poetry of Mr. Hardy" was written primarily to articulate critical first principles. Murry was concentrating on educating the public to require more of poetry at a time when the feeble sentimentalities of Georgian poetry were very popular. Nonetheless, his difficulty in translating a value conception like "plenary apprehension" into a serviceable critical idea is characteristic of his weakness in employing abstractions without an equivalent concrete context.

In "A Critical Credo" (1921) Murry did provide an outline of a methodology for criticism; significantly, the criterion of comprehensiveness is qualified, while the creativeness of the critic is expanded. The core of the essay lies in a succinct paragraph suggesting five rules for the art of critical appreciation. (1) The critic should convey the "peculiar uniqueness" of the work he is considering, then (2) define the "unique quality of the sensibility which necessitated this expression" and (3) establish the determining cause of this sensibility, before (4) conducting a technical examination of the style. The final step (5) should be a close examination of a "perfectly characteristic passage."[36] Not very impressive as they stand alone, these principles acquire resonance from the rest of the "Credo" and from the fuller amplification of these ideas in *The Problem of Style*. In "A Critical Credo" he is concerned with diagnosing the interplay between the personality of the critic and essential rules of the craft of criticism, but he is also anxious to foster serious, responsible criticism by making the critic "conscious of himself as an artist." Although Murry acknowledged that "the man who is content to record his own impressions, without making an effort to stabilize them in the form of laws . . . is not a critic," he contends that "the function of criticism is . . . primarily the function of literature itself, to provide a means of self-expression for the critic." In this view the critic, like other writers, "stands or falls by the stability of his truth and to a less degree by his technique in expressing the truth." He should guard himself against "accidental and temporary disturbances of his sensibility" by using a set of principles to "control momentary enthusiasms and passing disgusts," but the critic will have personal predispositions which influence his verdicts, and he is practicing an "independent literary art" (p. 240).

Murry believed that a conscientious critic would "try to correct his predisposition by training his appreciation of other kinds," but he must make his own system of laws or rules, "refined by his own effort out of his own experience." Otherwise he is a pedant and not a critic. Since Murry had defined criticism as an art, it must, like poetry, be measured by its effect, which is to say that it must give delight by enabling the reader to discover "beauties and significances which he had not seen, or to see those which he had himself glimpsed in a new and revealing light" (p. 241).

The generalizations of the 1919–20 essays are all preliminary to the particularized statements of *The Problem of Style*. Reprinted more frequently than anything else Murry wrote, *The Problem of Style* has become a standard work. It is the book people refer to when they praise the early Murry and lament the religiousness or the romanticism of the later Murry. *The Problem of Style* gives evidence of being much more carefully written than any other item of the bibliography, and the gentlemanly, Erasmian tone of the book invites comparison with Forster's *Aspects of the Novel* in its deceptively easy mastery of a familiar style, its wide-ranging allusiveness, its effort to talk simply about big literary ideas. With these lectures Murry established his ability to be a conventionally "good" critic, to write with intelligent good taste. But the kind of intellectual performance involved in being an Eliot sort of critic was unsatisfying to Murry because it excluded other options important to his temperament. As we shall see, he rejected "decorous" criticism and returned to the more personal and radical kind of engagement with literature toward which *Dostoevsky* had pointed him.

The Problem of Style treats the term "style" in an absolute sense as "the complete realization of a universal significance in a personal and particular expression"[37] and gives the idea meaning by building a context of examples, from which the subject grows clear by accretion. The sample passages are inevitably useful, and the concreteness of the discussion lends substance and particularity to Murry's generalizations. Murry argues that using "style" in any but an organic sense leads the reader to confuse it with "applied ornament" and to regard style as separable from

the work itself, a view similar to that of metaphor as superficial incrusta-
tion of language. The metaphor of true creative literature, Murry contends, is actually neither ornament nor an act of comparison but a mode of
apprehension, "the unique expression of a writer's individual vision," just
as "style" is that essential quality which makes a literary work a genuine
creative achievement, one which recognizably belongs to a specific author
but which transcends personality and particular modes of expression.[38]
The definition excludes the concerns of most twentieth-century stylists.
David Lodge even complains that Murry's approach "implies the whole of
modern poetics."[39] But as Murry points out, definitions of style by writers
have "infallibly" fallen upon the organic nature of style. The core definition Murry accepts and reiterates is Stendhal's. "Le style est ceci: Ajouter à
une pensée donnée toutes les circonstances propres à produire tout l'effet
que doit produir cette pensée." (Style consists in adding to a given thought
all the circumstances calculated to produce the whole effect that the
thought ought to produce.) Stendhal's definition leads Murry to his main
original critical term, "crystallization," by which he refers to the method a
writer uses to evoke his own emotion in his readers.

Crystallization may occur through the discovery of a symbol or analogy
or similitude, or it may occur in a large, structural way as plot; it operates
whenever an author compels others to feel the particularity of his emotion. Murry says that in a "perfect" work (and his examples of perfection
are inevitably Shakespearean) crystallization is "complete on every plane,
in the first and fundamental creation of the plot, in the realization of the
characters themselves, and in the language which they speak, or by which
they are described."[40] "Crystallization," then, is a term functionally similar
to Eliot's objective correlative. "The only way of expressing emotion in the
form of art is by finding an 'objective correlative'; in other words, a set of
objects, a situation, a chain of events which shall be the formula of that
particular emotion; such that when the external facts, which must termi-
nate in sensory experience, are given, the emotion is immediately
evoked."[41]

Murry is clearly indebted to Eliot's concept and insofar as crystallization
is a rephrasing of the objective correlative, he becomes first among the
many twentieth-century critics who have occupied themselves with explicating Eliot's term. However, Murry makes "crystallization" a more holistic term than "objective correlative." Its definition is inseparable from his
treatment of style itself as the embodiment of a "core or nucleus of
emotional and intellectual experience"[42] which, we might say, crystallize
in a writer. Crystallization is illustrated by powerful cumulative reference
to familiar literature, through which Murry points to the constant interpenetration of the private and the universal which occurs in the course of

particularizing emotion. The technique is always associated with the necessity of concreteness, exemplified by Chekhov's reply to a friend who
had asked his opinion of a story: "Cut out all those pages about the
moonlight and give us instead what you feel about it—the reflection of the
moon in a piece of broken bottle."[43] Crystallization is also inexorably
bound up with metaphor, for metaphor is the result of a search for the
most specific equivalence. "Try to be precise, and you are bound to be
metaphorical; you simply cannot help establishing affinities between all
the provinces of the animate and inanimate world; for the volatile essence
you are trying to fix is quality, and in that effort you will inevitably find
yourself ransacking heaven and earth for a similitude."[44] A writer's struggle with the limits of language, his effort to communicate ineffables,
produces metaphors. Murry concludes that great writing is "not so much a
triumph of language as a victory over language."[45]

The principle argument of *The Problem of Style* revolves around Murry's
definition of "absolute style" manifested in crystallization and organic
metaphor, but Murry also introduced ideas which became increasingly
important to his practice of criticism. For Murry, the primary originating
emotion of the writer lies at the center. He is critical both of the displace-
ment of emotion by discursive reasoning and of writers in whom technique assumes a "life of its own," leading to stylistic idiosyncrasies that are
not necessary and inevitable. His argument that romanticism and realism
are both integral to great art anticipates the central tenet of "Towards a
Synthesis," the last major statement in his romanticism-realism controversy with Eliot, while the statement that the critic functions as a miniature
artist is the primary locus for his critical stance.

In chapter 2 Murry endorsed Eliot's view that the artist should be
impersonal. In "Tradition and the Individual Talent," Eliot said: "The
progress of an artist is a continual self-sacrifice, a continual extinction of
personality. . . . the more perfect the artist, the more completely separate
in him will be the man who suffers and the mind which creates.[46] The final
paragraph of *The Problem of Style* forcefully reiterates the idea. "Nothing
will teach a man to feel distinctly; but probably the best way for him to
discover whether he does is to leave himself out of the reckoning. To be
impersonal is the best way of achieving personality, and it gives him far
less chance of deceiving himself."[47]

In light of Murry's later fame as a "personal" critic given to confusing
himself with his subject, one might assume that Murry simply adopted the
idea from Eliot and subsequently discarded it. In fact, Murry made
considerable use of the idea of impersonality, but he expanded it to a
moral doctrine quite antithetical to Eliot's austere negation of personality.
The aesthetic principle of the artist's detachment of his personality from
his creation became associated for Murry with Keats's belief that great

artists possess "negative capability," that they lack a determined character and are therefore receptive to all experience because they are capable of obliterating their own limited personalities.

By extension, after his mystical experience, Murry came to believe that renunciation of personality is essential to spiritual growth. The New Testament phrase "whosoever shall lose his life shall save it" became one of his characteristic tags; it is quoted with irritating regularity by the hero of his 1922 novel, indicating that it became a cohering idea for Murry around this time. Despite Murry's contention that his autobiographical revelations were, in an absolute sense, impersonal, nothing more clearly marks his temperamental distance from Eliot than the contrast between his incessant self-disclosure and Eliot's total personal reticence.

The strengths of *The Problem of Style* amply validate its reputation as a minor classic of modern criticism; consideration of its weaknesses will suggest why it lacks major standing. The most pervasive problem arises from Murry's assertion that great style is marked by the writer's "apprehension of the quality of life as a whole, the power to discern the universal in the particular, and to make the particular a symbol of the universal."[48] The universal significance criterion leads back to the dilemma posed in "The Function of Criticism"—how to measure value concepts—and Murry comes no closer to providing a clarifying methodology. He always retreats to mystical language when pressed for a standard and, by definition, places these considerations outside the cognitive realm. Acts of imaginative apprehension are primary, he says, but incapable of definition. His consideration of style as "the complete realization of a universal significance in a personal and particular expression" results in valuable expatiation of the "personal and particular" term; universal significance, on the other hand, can only be intuited.

Two modern critics have considered this hiatus in Murry's argument and point to subsequent clarifications of similar value criteria. William R. Heath's appraisal in a 1955 *PMLA* article of Murry's work as a literary theorist concludes that Murry deserves to stand in the ranks of significant critics and that his effort to establish a hierarchy based on the comprehensiveness of the artist's vision is a useful concept in any age, even though Murry himself seldom used this criterion empirically. Heath cites Brower's *The Fields of Light* as a text in which terms such as "comprehensiveness of imaginative vision" and "integrity of imagination" have been divorced from "emotive vagueness and subjectivity,"[49] while James R. Bennett contrasts *The Problem of Style* with W. K. Wimsatt's essay "The Concrete Universal."[50] Both conclude that Murry's system is sound enough; his doctrine of significance is obscure because Murry never devised precise ways of describing it. "Better methods of understanding literary art have developed than Murry was able to imagine in 1921,"

Bennett notes in his defense, and, indeed, we should not tax Murry for not settling in *The Problem of Style* matters which have occupied two generations of subsequent critics.

A similar problem arises from the thesis advanced in chapter 2 that the critic can connect the creative result with a writer's originating emotion. Murry does not attempt to demonstrate such relationships in *The Problem of Style*, although what he had in mind was probably the kind of exploration of the genesis of poetry which he conducts in *Keats and Shakespeare*. The extreme subjectivity of such an approach is exactly what W. K. Wimsatt, Jr., and Monroe Beardsley repudiated in "The Intentional Fallacy" when they argued that "the design or intention of the author is neither available nor desirable as a standard for judging the success of a work of art."[51] Murry's persistent interest in the character of the original perception of the writer marks his distance from the objectivist critics who emerged in the latter part of the decade.

Since Murry, even in what I've termed his "classical" period, was essentially a romantic critic, the difficulties we have considered would probably not have concerned him. He was always illuminating when he looked closely at specific literary passages, but he was usually more interested in generalizing about the total effect of a piece than looking at its parts, and he was reluctant to apply rational techniques to the "mystery" of great literature. He was hostile to the scientism of the New Criticism as it developed, feeling that it missed the point of reading literature altogether. In some sense, then, the defects of his argument were willed defects.

Perhaps the most telling flaw of *The Problem of Style* is the relative slackness of Murry's vocabulary, his tendency to be content with vague, loosely defined terms. The interchangeable use of "precision" and "crystallization" in chapter 5, for instance, obscures a thought that wants refining. Unlike Eliot (or Arnold) he did not formulate tight, quotable definitions, even for his most resonant ideas. One may argue, with merit, that Murry's wide-ranging, allusive mind was uncomfortable with rigorous categories, that his charm as a critic resides in his colloquial, familiar tone and easy movement among ideas, but the price of his diffuseness is often inexactitude. These qualities make Murry a less substantial critic than Eliot. Set *The Problem of Style* against *The Sacred Wood* and the greater quality of the latter is evident both in originality and in the tautness of the concepts.

The Unprofessional Critic

Murry's "professional" criticism was written while he was editing the *Athenaeum*. The essays in *Aspects of Literature* and *Countries of the Mind*, along with those in *The Problem of Style*, contain his most widely respected writing, that which requires his most dedicated detractors to admit that Murry was a significant, original literary critic. When Eliot spoke of Murry's "solitary eminence in his generation"[52] he was referring principally to the impressive corpus written between 1919 and 1922. In addition to those essays on Russian literature and critical theory which we have already surveyed, these volumes contain a particularly astute series of essays on French writers, several treatments of the English romantics, trenchant reactions to contemporary English writing, and an interesting miscellany of essays on various subjects ranging from Burton's *Anatomy* to *Arabia Deserta*. In those years Murry's reputation outweighed Eliot's, both because of the volume of his excellent criticism and because of his wider influence on literary culture.

I have already discussed the events of the watershed year of 1923—Katherine's death, Murry's mystical experience, his renunciation of professional criticism and founding of the *Adelphi*, a journal which the literary establishment thought betrayed his intelligence and education—and good taste in general.

Murry has been consistently reproached for the volte-face of 1923. Heath's defense of Murry's literary criticism rests on the critical theory tendered between 1920 and 1922, and although he does praise a few pieces, such as the chapter on *Antony and Cleopatra* in *Shakespeare*, in which he sees some pragmatic application of the principles of "A Critical Credo," it is the theory he is defending, not the critic. Murry obscured his own critical principles, Heath explains, by being "driven away from literature into 'the fields of Eternity,' "[53] and he holds no brief for the romantic critic. Heath's concern was to point out that Murry was not always merely subjective, a statement worth making in 1955, when the early accomplishment was almost entirely disregarded.

In fact, Murry's focus on particularity and analysis of sample passages did anticipate central themes of the twentieth-century critical revolution, and Frank Kermode later joined Heath in seeing him as one of its pioneers.[54] However, both critics reject the bulk of Murry's work by assigning value only to his cognitively based judgments, and in trying to establish Murry's credentials, Heath obscures the essence of the Murry-Eliot controversy. Even in 1921 Murry was not using the term "impersonal" in the same way as Eliot, and far more than semantic differences were involved in the romanticism-classicism controversy, as we shall see.

Murry's critical terminology increasingly acquired metaphysical dimensions. The crystallization idea of *The Problem of Style* was centered in metaphor, and metaphor he was soon defining as essentially transcendent. "However much we struggle, we cannot avoid transcendentalism, for we are seeking to approximate to a universe of quality with analogy for its most essential language through a universe of quantity with a language of identities. Sooner or later . . . , a transcendentalism (which is only the name for a prodigious metaphor) is inevitable."

Murry's ultimate stand was that the poet's imaginative world is invulnerable to intellectual analysis. "This world of imagination is a universe wherein quality leaps to cohere with quality across the abysms of classification that divide and categorize the universe of intellectual apprehension."[55]

Had Murry remained a "professional" critic he would be more containable, his achievement easier to describe in conventional academic intellectual terms. But the excited rhetoric of *Dostoesky* had already suggested that he could not say decorously what he principally wanted to say, and his defection from professional criticism seems to have been a response to powerful psychic demands.

Katherine Mansfield had acted as a brace on his subjectivity and exhibitionism, encouraging intellectual sophistication. She frankly enjoyed sharing the public esteem he gained from the *Athenaeum*. With her death he lost that cool, restraining judgment of his work and the chief motive to be a "success." His mystical experience affirmed his emotionalism and reliance on intuition while showing him an alternative to the "intellectual hypertrophy" of which he had complained in the midst of his Dostoevsky studies.

In fact, there is much to suggest that Murry did not so much become a different man in 1923 as begin to follow his personal inclinations more freely. *Dostoevsky* is a more natural predecessor of *Keats and Shakespeare* than of *The Problem of Style*. The loss of his critical reputation had its gratifications, for he liked being regarded as an outsider and iconoclast, identifying literary and academic coteries with artificial aesthetic snobberies, the separation of literature from life. He had never been fundamentally at ease in those circles and may have felt it easier to be labeled a fraud than to feel an imposter. His response to Lawrence in 1923 and 1924 was not intrinsically different from the ambiguous deference he had shown before. Murry admired his own version of Lawrence (that is, Lawrence à la Russe and à la Keats) but did not abandon Civilization and spirituality to follow him to New Mexico. And, of course, Murry's 1924 marriage to Violet le Maistre bore the neurotic imprint of rewedding Katherine.

Moreover, Murry had returned to thoroughly impressionistic criticism before the cataclysms of 1923. Most of the romantic principles he had tentatively advanced before surface as dogma in the 1922 essay "The Nature of Poetry." In it he insists that genuine understanding of a work of literature occurs only when the critic enters a condition of vicarious participation in the creation of the work, when he "feels the presence" of the author and enters into a "secret communion" with him. From that peculiar intimacy the critic gains "secret" knowledge, itself ineffable but leading toward a "fuller reality, *i.e.*, God, or 'rhythm of life.' " He no longer admits the possibility of objectivity in the critic. "I believe that criticism is a personal affair, and that the less we try to disguise this from ourselves the better."[56]

Hero worship is a natural consequence of the belief that we understand literature by understanding a "master spirit." "The nature of Shakespeare's poetry is the nature of poetry," Murry declares, after extolling "The Phoenix and the Turtle" as the "most perfect short poem in any language. . . . It is pure poetry in the loftiest and most abstract meaning of the words. . . . it gives us the highest experience which it is possible for poetry to give. . . . [this] *is* the music of the spheres; this is indeed the hymn of that celestial love which 'moves the sun and other stars' " (pp. 25–26). The rhapsodizing is elicited by Murry's belief that in this poem Shakespeare most fully portrays his intuitions of ultimate reality, his apprehension of a mystery like that alluded to by Jesus: "Except ye be born again ye can in no wise enter into the kingdom of Heaven." Murry describes Shakespeare's poetry as sometimes "superhuman" because the "felt meaning so far exceeds the meaning understood, that in order to describe it at all we are driven even against our will into semi-mystical metaphor" (p. 28).

Murry employs so many mystical metaphors in "The Nature of Poetry" that it might serve as a catalog of his critical indiscretions. The exclamatory excesses of this essay show how exaggerated and insubstantial his judgments were when directed solely by private enthusiasms. His willingness to offer large generalizations, eschewing safety, often stimulates our interest, even when we disagree, but his contention here that the poetry of "The Phoenix and the Turtle" surpasses that of Shakespeare's great tragedies is not merely suspect but irresponsible, because it is radically distorted by the critic's private quest for transcendence. Murry argues that the highest, most absolute poetry shows "the white light of eternity," that such poetry is superior to "relative" poetry, which chooses symbols from the world of human experience (p. 43). The biased partiality of that standard, proclaimed rather than demonstrated, contradicts the crystallization maxim of *The Problem of Style* and entangles literary with metaphysical values.

The eccentric critical standard is attended by that loss of control of language from which Murry suffered when he plunged himself into the contemplation of mysteries, as the gush of the opening passage of "The Nature of Poetry" shows:

> There are moments when criticism of a particular kind, the only kind I care for, utterly absorbs me. I feel that I am touching a mystery. There is a wall,

as it were, of dense warm darkness before me. . . . This, I believe, is the reflection in myself of the darkness which broods over the poet's creative mind. . . . There is a moment when, as though unconsciously and out of my control, the deeper rhythm of a poet's work, the rise and fall of the great moods which determined what he was and what he wrote, enter into me also. I feel his presence; I am obedient to it, and it seems to me as though the breathing of my spirit is at one with his. [Pp. 13–14]

Despite its rhetorical and conceptual weaknesses, Murry included the essay in both the 1924 and 1930 editions of *Discoveries*. His later Shakespeare criticism was far more balanced and substantive, but he never recanted this early essay, as he did some others. It was really a romantic manifesto, the first uninhibited expression of literary attitudes that he defended for the rest of his life. It may not be coincidental that Murry made such a proclamation of faith in poetry as the key to metaphysical truths in 1922, the year in which *The Waste Land* and *Ulysses* were published. He had recognized the cultural force of these works as soon as he read them and acknowledged their genius, but he was dismayed by the moral nihilism of the former and the aesthetic ingenuity of the latter. Against these models of abstruse subtlety he posed the Keatsian standard of the unity of truth and beauty, a conception of literature as ideal and prophetic, the purveyor of spiritual and moral truths. He thought literature the principal surrogate for religion in a secular age and believed that an elitist literature which appealed to a severely restricted audience would rob the culture of the essential means of investigating values.

Thereafter Murry stood in opposition to the main currents of his age, celebrating the capacity of literature to enlarge the human spirit and proclaiming Keats, Shakespeare, and finally Blake spiritual heroes who point the way to individual regeneration. He continued to affirm that the deepest judgments of literature are moral and to demand that art be humane, finding little to stir his imagination in the literature of his own day. He candidly summarized his dissociation from his contemporaries in his journal shortly before his death:

I have the feeling that I have been completely outside the main stream of literature; that I don't "belong" and indeed never have belonged. My concern has been that of a moralist, and I have never been sufficient of an artist to be diverted from it. And yet the stubborn feeling persists that my "concern" was shared in the old days by Lawrence and by Katherine: that I was, in some sense, their critical counterpart, and that the kind of seriousness we had has been lost.[57]

Chapter Three

SPIRITUAL HEROES

Keats

Keats and Shakespeare, that brilliant, idiosyncratic, pivotal book which defined the depth of Murry's romanticism, appeared in 1925. In it Keats is portrayed as the greatest poetic successor to Shakespeare and as a prototypal spiritual model. The title reflects Murry's theory of Keats's poetic growth as a discipleship to Shakespeare, as man and as poet, and Murry's conviction of their "similar completeness of humanity."[1] Exploring Keats's soul history as he had Dostoevsky's, Murry treats the poetry as evidence of moral achievement, reflecting Keats's life experiences, and disowns the traditional role of literary critic: "It is no part of the purpose of this book to appreciate Keats' poems objectively as poetry; its concern is solely to elucidate the deep and natural movement of the poet's soul which underlies them."[2] Murry's Keats is a "hero of humanity" whose poetry's greatness reflects his great soul. "This achievement of his soul . . . is the inward and spiritual grace of which Keats' magnificent poetical achievement . . . is the outward and visible sign."[3]

Writing the book, Murry immersed himself in Keats and achieved that condition of vicarious identity he had spoken of in "The Nature of Poetry" as a prerequisite to genuine understanding of a writer. In Keats's case, Murry had been propelled toward ego identification for years. Both he and Katherine Mansfield promoted her linkage with Keats by virtue of youth and genius and disease; their affinity with him was so deep that after Murry unconsciously used Keats's phrase "I have made love my religion" in one of his own poems, Katherine quoted it back to him as her own words. Years before, Murry had experienced Keats as a cataclysm (although it is interesting that his sense of revelation was occasioned by reading Colvin's life of Keats rather than by rediscovery of the poems). He was struck then by the parallels with his own life—membership in the wrong social class, financial hardship, susceptibility to enervating depression, belief in the importance of passional love, and being short, even. Murry says, "Had Keats been six inches taller, the history of English literature in the nineteenth century might have been different."[4]

Such correspondences are emphasized disproportionately in *Keats and Shakespeare*. Collis's rather snide judgment, that the book owes its force "to the fact that the author is writing about himself. Indeed, no one has ever succeeded before in writing about himself with such full documentary evidence that it was about someone else,"[5] contains a partial truth, but like most easy generalizations about Murry, misses the whole. Murry far more obviously tried to make himself into John Keats than the reverse, although that attitude, too, is problematical; evaluation of *Keats and Shakespeare* requires a constant weighing of its insights against its excesses.

The vitality of the work is the direct consequence of Murry's steeping himself in Keats, becoming, as it were, an alter ego of the poet. That intimacy empowers his understanding and enables him to savor nuances others had missed, to depict Keats's poetic growth more comprehensively than any previous critic could. He conveys Keats's poetic mode of thought—imagination working upon sensation—with great immediacy and so teaches a great deal about the creative process itself. *Keats and Shakespeare* is a substantial achievement for that reason alone.

Murry approached Keats with deliberate intellectual naivete, claiming only to take him at his word, to believe he meant what he said: the study gains substantial emotional power from its consistency and total sincerity. Murry's exhortative moods inspire exasperation but not disbelief in the integrity of his commitment. His reverence for the "whole" Keats leads to discovery of patterns of thought neglected by previous critics. He knows the body of poems and letters so well that he can treat each line with a sense of its bearing on the whole, tracing delicate threads of association and experience with subtle perceptiveness, yielding a sense of the endless suggestibility of great poetry. His treatment of textual and chronological difficulties has almost always prevailed. His fundamental contention, that Keats made himself a poetic disciple of Shakespeare, turning briefly toward Milton before returning to the Shakespearean model, that the rededication liberated his imagination and led to the composition of the great odes, has been widely accepted. "The most intimate motion of Keats' inward life gradually revealed itself to me as a motion of loyalty to Shakespeare the man," Murry says,[6] his theory bolstered by citation of passages where Keats refers to meditation on Shakespeare, fancying him the "Presider," the "good Genius" of his life.[7]

The Shakespearean model lay at the root of Keats's formulation of the essential poetic character: "It is not itself—it has no self.—It is everything and nothing.—It has no character—it enjoys light and shade; it lives in gusto, be it fond or fair, high or low, rich or poor, mean or elevated. It has as much delight in conceiving an Iago as an Imogen. What shocks the virtuous philosopher delights the chameleon poet. . . . A poet is the most unpoetical of anything in existence, because he has no identity—he is continually in for and filling some other body."[8] In one letter Keats describes his personal formlessness as issuing in the sensation of being pressed upon by other identities, feeling annihilated by other people. To Murry this "state of extreme and agonizing receptiveness" which Keats describes is the essential condition of genius, the passive sensitivity of the ego, which amounts to a renunciation of the self, being the price of extraordinary responsiveness to experience.[9] This negative of self-anni-hilation, Murry posits, is the necessary counterpoint to self-achievement, part of the process Keats called "dying into life." The birth of a larger identity which can incorporate the changing material of experience and sensation requires giving up the old personality.

Although the poet lacks determined character, the "proper self" of "Men of Power,"[10] he is the most "genuine Being in the World,"[11] Keats asserts. The genuineness (or organic wholeness) of the poet, according to Murry, derives from his undivided consciousness, which transcends the partial realizations of the intellect through a synthesis of mind and heart. It results in "soul-knowledge," that is, a more complete comprehension of reality. Organicism erases egoism. Thus Keats identifies negation of ego with Shakespeare and the "egoistical sublime" with Wordsworth, who developed prideful intellectual self-consciousness and lost his earlier in-tuitive genius.

For Keats, the flexibility of the boundary between the self and experi-ence issues in "negative capability . . . when a man is capable of being in uncertainties, Mysteries, doubts, without any irritable reaching after fact & reason."[12] Negative capability, Murry explains, means that "the su-preme poet is he who can accept the fact that the mystery must be, and wait for the moment when he can comprehend it by the faculty of poetic intuition, instead of impatiently turning for aid to faculties less potent than his own."[13] Through negative capability man can assimilate and harmonize all experience, both good and evil, and attain the supreme condition of acceptance, an achieved wholeness, of the sort Murry distin-guishes in the poetry of Shakespeare and Keats—and in the life of Jesus. These three are unequaled masters of reality because they have proven adequate to great suffering. Keats's "Vale of Soul-Making" letter discloses the spiritual odyssey which culminated in his writing of the great odes. "Do you not see how necessary a world of Pains and trouble is to school an Intelligence and make it a soul?" Keats inquired.[14] In Murry's view, the

statement signals Keats's resolution of spiritual crisis—acceptance of
death and evil as part of life, a discovery of the "principle of beauty in all
things."

Soul making was so resonant a concept for Murry that he felt driven to
make his next book *Jesus: Man of Genius* in order to measure the profundity of Keats against the profundity of Christianity. Not surprisingly, he
concluded that both bore the same message, that Keats's discovery that
"beauty is truth," like Shakespeare's "ripeness is all," is a realization of the
integrated self completely analogous to the rebirth proclaimed by Jesus.
The parallel is absolute in Murry's essay "The Parables of Jesus":

> If it can be put into a word, this is the fundamental distinction between the
> teaching of Jesus and all other religious wisdom that I know: that he taught
> not goodness, but *wholeness*: and this both in the inward man, and the
> outward world. Wholeness in the man himself means that the soul is not a
> partial faculty of man; it is not something that can be opposed to and
> distinguished from mind and heart: it is a creation which includes both
> these within itself. The soul is simply the condition of the complete man.
> And to this completeness in the man, which is his soul, there corresponds a
> completeness and harmony of the world or his experience; it, also, without
> abstraction or denial of any of its elements, suffers a like transformation,
> and becomes organic, harmonious—it becomes God.[15]

This odd version of the teaching of Jesus reflects Murry's obsession with
uniting his heroes in a single truth, one fully synthesized vision. As Fogle
remarks, "he knows and is obsessed with one great truth—Oneness—and
without quite realizing it he is always striking inwards at it, though from
many angles and directions."[16] Reiterating his single principle, Murry
sounds too exclusively dogmatic and oppressively monistic: "The process
of poetic comprehension moves from the perception of harmony to the
perception of harmony, and these successive harmonies are its truths. . . .
Poetry is a knowledge of the unity and harmony of the universe which can
be reached only through the individual's knowledge of unity and harmony in himself."[17]

Murry interpreted "Beauty is Truth, Truth Beauty,—that is all / Ye
know on earth, and all ye need to know" quite literally. The lines hold all
Keats's realizations, his "vast idea of poesy" and "the mighty abstract idea
of Beauty in all things." In them Murry read his own belief in poetry as
revelation, a more direct route than religion to the discovery of essence.
Quoting Keats's letter to his brother ("I can never feel certain of any truth
but from a clear perception of its beauty"),[18] Murry insists that the poet
means just what he says. "His faculty of truth-perception . . . is of a
different kind from the ordinary."[19] Murry's Keats is a fully integrated

soul whose poetry expresses his deepest nature, without division between man and poet, a Keats who said, with equal literalness, "A Man's life of any worth is a continual allegory."[20] Murry's defensive posture toward other critics, who, he keeps telling us, derogate and misinterpret Keats because they do not take him seriously, is better comprehended when we contrast Murry's treatment of the beauty-truth problem with C. M. Bowra's argument that the lines have reference only to Keats's theory of art:

> The Ode is his last word on a special activity and a special experience. Within its limits it has its own view of life, and that is what Keats expresses. The belief that "Beauty is truth, truth beauty" is true for the artist while he is concerned with his art. It is no less true that, while he is at work, this is all that he needs to know for the proper pursuit of his special task. Unless he believes this, he is in danger of ruining his art. The "Ode on a Grecian Urn" tells what a great art means to those who create it, while they create it, and so long as this doctrine is not applied beyond its proper confines, it is not only clear but true.[21]

Bowra, in this passage, exemplifies the critic Murry has been chastising, one who anxiously rationalizes the poet's meaning in order to find grounds for agreement with him. Murry's errors were expansionist and systemizing rather than narrowing, and though his theories sometimes pass the boundaries of sobriety, he is never guilty of patronizing the poet.

In its basic terms Murry's treatment of the beauty-truth equation recapitulates his theory of art. His argument is: truth cannot be known by reason, only through the intuitive faculty, which recognizes truth by its beauty. Perceptions of beauty are premonitions of a final reality; the way to intuitive knowledge is a reverence for "the holiness of the Heart's affections, and the truth of Imagination."[22] In the final knowledge all contradictions and discords are reconciled. Poetry is actual religion, freed of dogmatic incrustations. The true poet is the *vates sacer*, potent with knowledge of the soul.

The moral criterion that informs these ideas is not narrow, of course, and for the most part it led Murry to discern great poetry. He refines Arnold's definition of poetry as a criticism of life, pointing out that it must be a *poetic* rather than a *philosophic* criticism of life, that poetic thought is perception, not cognition, a "comprehension by and through the concrete and particular."[23] To that we may add that Murry's ultimate criterion of greatness, a poem's adequacy to great suffering, is unarguable.

It is time to consider the limitations of Murry's application of soul biography as a means of penetrating literature. Inherent in his method is the reduction of the poems to incidents in the life of the poet. He warns us fairly of his design, but we are interested in Keats, after all, *because* of his poetry, and the inversion strikes us as wrongheaded. Moreover, we are required to accept Keats wholly on Murry's terms, as a being beyond judgment: "The proper attitude of criticism towards Keats is one of complete humility," he declares. "There is no man living, and no man has lived, who has the right to pass judgement upon Keats."[24] Performing more as lover than as explicator, Murry is jealous of conflicting interpretations and sententiously castigates his critical antagonists without feeling obliged to refute them. The attitude leads to distasteful rhetorical arrogance: "If we choose to believe that Keats was mistaken in everything and that out of this abysm of error he sent forth the great Odes,—then we will believe anything."[25] Reading the poems out of the life, he identifies Keats with his characters, including the Apollo of "Hyperion," an interpretation defended on the ground that it is "necessary and palpable."[26] The lack of rigor in such generalizations elicited F. R. Leavis's complaint that Murry's method is fundamentally wrong and Tillyard's criticism that "Keats is made the victim of a larger theory."[27]

Murry confesses himself that his famously harsh judgment, "Fanny Brawne killed [Keats]," arose from his private need to view Keats as always sane and truthful, unswayed by "sick passion." His 1949 recantation, which emphasizes Fanny's loyalty and integrity, was prompted by his discovery, while editing the letters, of the connection between Katherine Mansfield's bouts with disease and the emotional tone of her letters. Murry wrote in his journal: "Some strong unconscious motive was at work which forbade me to face the evidence of Katherine's emotional derangement—probably, since I was the one who suffered by it, a simple avoidance of pain. And mainly because of this I was impervious to the possibility of a similar emotional disturbance in Keats. I identified myself with him *too much*: as I identified myself with Katherine. It's an interesting example of how a bias may be produced."[28]

An idealizing web enshrouds much of *Keats and Shakespeare*. Keats must be too perfect—"one of the bravest and wisest and most beautiful spirits this England has been privileged to engender."[29] His thought must always build to a final coherence, all contradictions resolved, however wrenchingly. In fact, Keats's thought was elusive, contradictory and unsystematic, the more so because he died prematurely. The pattern Murry imposes is too tidy to be wholly true, as some of his own later essays acknowledge.

In his discussion of Murry as "Keatsian critic," Griffin shows that Murry's effort to build a philosophy based on poetry is muddled. Murry distinguishes between Keats's discursive language and his poetic language: "Keats means what he says always when he is being a pure poet. When he is using the language of discourse he cannot always mean what he says, for the simple reason that he cannot always say what he means. He has to use words that were not made for his purposes."[30] But, Griffin tellingly points out, "he then tries to make Keats' poetic thought yield arguable conclusions."[31]

Despite the overingeniousness of the pattern, many of Murry's theories about Keats's poetic development have been very suggestive. In some cases they have gained wide currency, while their source was forgotten. Among them is Murry's contention that Keats would have turned to the drama as the culminating genre for his talent. The idea is bolstered by passages from letters declaring Keats's intention of tackling the form, and it is a useful notion for Murry because it fits his paradigm that Keats was following in the steps of Shakespeare. Unfortunately, Murry then assumes that Keats would have met artistic success in a form that proved impenetrable to other nineteenth-century writers. His conclusion that Keats was greater than his actual achievement is not only impossible of proof but essentially irrelevant.

Murry's analysis of Keats's relationship to Milton is also a useful idea vitiated by Murry's bias against Milton, who represented for him the divorced mind and heart. He can explain Keats's turn from Shakespeare to Milton only as a tortured retreat from human emotion. "He was trying desperately to make the remoteness and abstraction of Milton his ideal; to find in the deliberate art of Milton and his proud neglect of human destinies for his majestic but inhuman theological drama a refuge from the torment of life."[32]

Murry's relief when Keats rejects Milton ("Life to him would be death to me")[33] is excessive. "I have failed in everything if I have not made it palpable that Keats' rejection of Milton was an integral part of a movement of Keats' whole being."[34] Tillyard is the certain victor in an exchange with Murry on the Milton influence. In *The Miltonic Setting* Tillyard calls *Keats and Shakespeare* "at once the best and the worst book on Keats" before quietly dissecting Murry's Milton argument. He points out interesting parallels between "Lycidas" and Keats's poetry and reasonably concludes that Murry "has not penetrated the facade of Milton's rhetoric."[35] Murry's defense in "Keats and Milton" rests on a generic distinction of "feeling-types," Milton belonging to the Protestant feeling-type, Keats and Shakespeare to the Catholic. "*Lycidas* is a poem of the intellectual imagination. . . . it is not the poem of one who has been oppressed by 'the burden of the mystery,' "[36] Murry argues. Griffin rightly says that Murry underestimates Milton because he refuses intimacy, and "a sense of intimacy with writers was both the strength and weakness of Murry's form of criticism."[37]

The most pervasive and influential thesis of *Keats and Shakespeare* is that Keats gained, toward the end of his life, a maturity of idea which established him as a major poet. It was not a status unquestionably accorded him in 1925; it has hardly been doubted since. Murry firmly established

Keats's poetic mastery by the authority of his concentration on the growth of thought which reached its highest embodiment in the resolution of fertility and death in "To Autumn." The corollary thesis, that Keats is thereby a significant spiritual figure has, of course, been ignored, and the religious ardor of *Keats and Shakespeare* has limited appreciation of its insights.

Keats remained the center from which Murry explored other ideas, the central figure in his pantheon of heroes. In 1947 Murry wrote: "How much I owe to Keats is indeed past all computation. He has been the voice of Life itself, speaking to me. . . . It is through him, and my slowly won understanding of him—an understanding continually deepened by love, and the love continually deepened by understanding—that I was carried on, irresistibly, to Jesus, to the same love and understanding of Him, and to that incessant grappling with the mystery of Christianity, which has become, in a sense, the main theme of my life."[38]

The essays collected in *Keats* (1955) were published at intervals over three decades, often in response to attacks on *Keats and Shakespeare* or to new criticism with which Murry disagreed. Among these, we have already considered his reply to Tillyard on Milton and his reassessment of Fanny Brawne. Perhaps the most famous is "Keats and Isabella Jones," the attack on Robert Gitting's theory, in *John Keats: The Living Year* (1954), that Keats had a love affair with Isabella Jones while he was engaged to Fanny Brawne. Murry was passionately indignant about the "slur" on Keats's character, and his lengthily reasoned rebuttal does refute Gitting's theory, which had gained a brief currency. The tone of the essay is competent restraint, but its publication was preceded by heated letters to the *Times Literary Supplement* venting Murry's animus against Gittings. It was an unattractive episode and unlike Murry.

Several substantive essays were written soon after the publication of *Keats and Shakespeare* in response to charges that the book paid insufficient attention to the poems. "The Realms of Gold" traces the unconscious thought process and train of associations preceding the composition of the sonnet on Chapman's *Homer*; "The Cave of Quietude" examines Keats's first elliptical expression of the beauty-truth equation in "Endymion," while "Beauty is Truth" explicates its development in "Ode on a Grecian Urn." The final essay of this early series, "They End in Speculation," argues that Keats used the word "speculation" as the equivalent of "contemplation," so demonstrating the unity of thought and sensation in Keats. The shrewd exegesis in this body of essays reminds us of Murry's capability for close reading as well as his gift for illuminating the poetic process itself through analysis of a particular poet. It was always easy for him to write conventional literary analysis; he chose instead to write unfashionably, to be the critic of negative capability.

Blake

When Murry published *William Blake* in 1935, his previous reputation was much diminished. People who had defended the religious enthusiasms of the *Adelphi* and *Keats and Shakespeare* were offended by Murry's "betrayal" of Lawrence in *Son of Woman* (1931). His espousal of Marxism in 1931 alienated other supporters. *William Blake* was sketchily reviewed and sold less well than previous books, although a review in the *Times Literary Supplement* called it "the most comprehensive study of Blake's genius that we have yet had."[39] The *Observer* review deemed it "profound and provocative" but criticized Murry's "arrogating mysticism,"[40] while *Scrutiny* predictably condemned its "loosely emotive language."[41] Critics have remained divided. In the sixties *A Blake Bibliography* warned readers of the "extra-Blakean thesis" but praised Murry's faithfulness to Blake's text and recommended him for help in understanding the contraries,[42] while the *New York Review of Books* condemned Murry's effort "to identify Blake's views with his own opinions on all subjects, particularly on the relation of sex to religion" and wondered "who thought of reprinting Murry at all."[43]

William Blake, then, like *Keats and Shakespeare*, is a mixture of good scholarly work, reflected in Murry's feat of tracing the symbolic system of Blake's prophetic poems (a task not undertaken so zealously before) and of emotionally charged revealings of prophetic truths suspiciously similar to Murry's own. It contains an element of forced admiration which makes the extravagent rhetoric less palatable than that of *Keats and Shakespeare*. Murry had poured light on those aspects of Keats with which he was most sympathetic, but his Keats was genuine, recognizable; we suspect his Blake of being partly fictive. Northrop Frye was probably thinking of Murry when he spoke of critics "who wish to find that Blake was a precocious discoverer of their own views."[44] There is a histrionic quality about Murry's veneration, a too-obvious construing of Blake to his own ends, which makes this a more blemished book than his other major critical works. To approach it we must review the circumstances of its composition.

Murry worked on Blake during most of 1931 and 1932, a period when his biographer declares that Murry hardly knew what he was doing. He had married his housekeeper, Betty Cockbayne, in 1931, only two months after his second wife, like Katherine Mansfield, had died of tuberculosis. His revulsion from that macabre repetition of events plunged him into a hasty sensual relationship with an uneducated country woman whose simple "gaiety" promised him uncomplicated happiness. As his friends foresaw, it was a tragic misalliance, and life with Betty was neither simple nor gay. Murry's notorious obtuseness toward other people's emotions aggravated his marital predicament, for he always blundered badly in human relationships, but Betty's temper was well known before he married her, and there is unanimous testimony that she was shrewish, vindictive, violent, and irrationally jealous. Her abuse of Col and Weg, Murry's two children by Violet, is recorded in Colin Middleton Murry's *I at the Keyhole*, and Richard Rees, a frequent visitor, says, "I am a connoisseur of domestic infelicity . . . , but I have never seen anything to equal the misery of the life at the Old Rectory; and the only similar case I have read of which is at all comparable for intensity of suffering is the later years of the Tolstoy ménage."[45]

The disillusionment and self-questioning provoked by even a few months with Betty sent Murry hunting in several directions at once. "Am I attracted only by two kinds of women—one that I kill, the other that kills me?" he asked himself.[46] Writing of the gulf between his daily life and the "calm, impersonal world of spirit," Murry reflected that he had lost all the "vital energy of illusion."[47] His search for a revitalizing cause led briefly to the notion of taking orders in the Church of England, although Murry had always been heterodox and disapproved of the effects of institutionalization on what he regarded as the vital metaphors of Christianity. In the event, his conversion was to a species of Christian Marxism rather than to Anglicanism. He joined the Independent Labor party late in 1931 and published *The Necessity of Communism* in 1932, both events coinciding with his Blake studies. It is not surprising, then, that Murry found Blake "a great communist" who anticipated Marx's discovery that "the inevitable outcome of economic individualism within the nation was economic individualism between the nations."[48]

The political bias of *William Blake* elicits this pronouncement, which is accompanied by a stress on Blake's anarchism and his apocalyptic expectations of a new world order arising from the French Revolution, both elements manifestly present in Blake, if less emphasized by other commentators. The Marxist influence is finally less bothersome than Murry's interpretation of Blake's religion and his doctrine of sexuality. Murry makes Blake a far less orthodox Christian than more recent commentators have. He interprets Blake's mysticism as a mysticism of descent, which rejects all supernaturalism and makes Jesus only man—man in a state of fully realized being. When Blake's poetry supports these ideas, which approximate Murry's arguments in *Jesus: Man of Genius* and *God: An Introduction to the Science of Metabiology*, Murry applauds; when Blake voices a less compatible theology, Murry is disposed to label him "mistaken." Blake's spiritual exploration he reads as a search for resolution of the elemental struggle of man and woman in the marriage relationship, a conflict between female jealousy and literal-mindedness and masculine spiritual endeavour. There is, of course, considerable textual support for these interpretations, but the exclusiveness of the critic's interest narrows the poet's range and distorts the tone. Murry gives little sense of Blake's lyricism and joyousness. When the matter leads away from discussion of his favorite topics, Murry does clarify Blake, but his remarks are never particularly acute. We can say of *William Blake*, as we could not of Murry's other major criticism, that its most valuable insights could have come from any competent critic.

Murry's claim to a special relationship with Keats is credible; when he implies special understanding of Blake only because he, too, has enjoyed a mystical revelation, he seems to be taking advantage. "These motions of the mysical mind may seem very arbitrary to the man without mystical experience. Even the ordinary religious mind knows little of that strange convulsion of the total man which leaves behind it a condition in which the difficulty is not to believe in the imminence of cosmic revolution, but to disbelieve in it."[49]

The difficulty, perhaps, is that he has an air of using Blake. The impassioned, prophetic tone can be convincing when the critic is genuinely captivated, but Murry's consonance with Blake is mostly intellectual. He was prompted to write the book by an attractive offer of the William Noble Fellowship at Liverpool University for a study of Keats and Blake and by the urging of his friend, Max Plowman, who had written an unmemorable book on Blake himself and greeted the project by announcing "A great event. Murry has been seduced into reading Blake. . . . I've been waiting years for this to happen. The result will be beyond expectation."[50] Although Plowman was loyally enthusiastic about the book, he also wryly noted that Murry "trimmed the borders of Blake's singing robes in order to make them conform to the pattern of [his] understanding."[51]

In the first chapter Murry confesses his difficulty with Blake's elusiveness and an initial sense of a "serious confusion lurking in his thought."[52] Murry resolved the latter issue by sympathizing with Blake's confusion when his doctrine contradicted Murry's own, but behind the complaint of elusiveness lay Murry's dissatisfaction with the abstractness of Blake's private idiom. Recognizing his own weakness for intellectualizing feeling and turning to metaphysical abstraction in place of "experiencing" life, Murry reserved his deepest praise for poets with a spontaneous affinity to the natural world and for those who crystallize sensory experience so that the originating feeling-thought is accessible. Shakespeare's poetry is naturally, instinctively, tied to life experience; Milton's is not. Similarly, Murry ranks Shelley as inferior to Keats and Coleridge to Wordsworth because the former poets lack organic immediacy. Their observations were artificially, arbitrarily, imposed by the intellect; they miss the living essence.

Like Northrop Frye, Murry defends the complexity of Blake's symbolic system by arguing that Blake could not have said what he had to say more simply, but save for a few lyric passages, Murry respects the thought, rather than the form, of Blake's poetry. On the issue of naturalistic art, the poet and his critic are at odds. Quoting Blake's denunciation of naturalistic art as false art, "a pretence of Art to destroy Art," and his accusation that "All the Copiers or pretended Copiers of Nature, from Rembrandt to Reynolds, Prove that Nature becomes to its Victim nothing but Blots and Blurs," Murry suggests that Blake's belief that his was the only true imaginative art reflects "unconscious equivocation" and concludes that "in this matter one must say openly that Blake was abusing his own doctrine, and suborning the truth of Imagination to the uses of the Selfhood."[53]

Two axioms from Keats define his position. "We hate poetry that has a palpable design upon us," Keats declared. "Poetry should be great and unobtrusive, a thing which enters into one's soul, and does not startle or amaze it with itself, but with its subject," Later Keats commented, "If poetry comes not as naturally as the leaves to a tree, it had better not come at all."[54] (By "natural" Murry takes Keats to mean intrinsic and organic rather than superimposed or asserted—not, or course, ease of composition.) With these precepts Murry contests Blake's definition of the "imagination," pointing out that naturalistic art has a "signal advantage" because "its spiritual function is fulfilled unconsciously. . . . there is a psychological resistance against art which carries an ulterior meaning, even though that meaning may be of supreme importance to ourselves, as was Blake's, and expressible by no other means."[55] Even in the epilogue devoted to justifying Blake's necessary obscurity and his need to "create a system" if he was not to be "enslaved by another man's," Murry rebukes Blake's aesthetic philosophy. Blake wrote, "Allegory addressed to the Intellectual powers, while it is altogether hidden from the Corporeal Understanding, is my Definition of the Most Sublime Poetry." To which Murry retorts that Blake's is a legitimate personal preference, but "it is opposed to the practice of most of those whom we regard as the greatest poets—the succession from Homer and the Greek tragic poets, through Virgil, to Chaucer, Shakespeare and Milton."[56] Despite his prophetic message, Blake stands below Keats and Shakespeare on Murry's scale because he is too abstract and abstruse to evoke spontaneous response in the reader.

Nonetheless, Blake offers a "vast and simple synthesis" which, Murry claims, makes him the "greatest, as he was the most isolated, prophet of the modern world."[57] His theology resolves the dilemma so troublesome to romantics of how imperfect multiplicity can be resolved to perfect unity. We may summarize Murry's interpretation of Blake's teaching: Eternity is a continuing potentiality of the Now. When man liberates his Identity (the true unconscious being) from the prison of the Self (the self-conscious ego), he is Free to know Eternity, to become God. The contraries of corporeal life are redeemed, the duality of estranged body and soul are resolved, by Annihilation of the Self and rebirth to original Identity. The man who possesses his Identity passes beyond good and evil to a knowledge of Oneness, a universe in which each part contains the whole. Jesus achieved divinity, in the same sense that any person may achieve it, by undergoing this process of spiritual resurrection. However, Christian doctrine itself cannot accommodate these truths, for it is founded in false moral law which views sexuality as purely carnal, the root of original sin, rather than in its true manifestation as an archetype of joy, a gateway to Eternity. Sexual revolution, like political revolution, signals progression toward a society unified in Body and Soul in which all men will annihilate Self and gain Identity and will thereby govern themselves with love and true desire.

Self-annihilation, Murry points out, is a continuous process. No rebirth is final. The shifting perceptions of Blake's prophetic books reflect his spiritual struggle and growth. His highest achievement is the great expansive vision of *Jerusalem*, in which Blake's supreme mission is revealed as the regeneration of Christianity. The orthodox doctrine of the fall from Paradise is distorted, according to Blakean theology, for the fall consisted of the birth of Selfhood, which caused division between the original androgynous spirit as well as between body and soul (reason and instinct) in the separated man and woman.

> For Los said: 'When the Individual appropriates Universality
> He divides into Male & Female: & when the Male & Female
> Appropriate individuality, they become an eternal Death.[58]

Regaining Eternity, then, includes a reunion of the Male and the Female, a merging of spirits in creative union. Human marriage is the path to the perfected spiritual life. Each partner must travel separately the path of Self-annihilation before attaining mutuality and unity, a state of Eternity in which the distinction between Man and Woman is erased.

The utility of this construct to a man involved in this sort of strife Murry experienced with Betty Cockbayne was immeasurable. Moreover, Blake's sexual doctrine furnished an answer to Lawrence's denigration of the spiritual in favor of the physical being, the perspective Murry had contested for years.

> The difference between Lawrence and Blake in this respect is singular and revealing. Both preached with impassioned sincerity a doctrine of sexual regeneration: of regeneration of sex and regeneration through sex. But in Blake the doctrine flows out of a larger doctrine from the beginning: all that is implicit in the experience and the conviction of the living unity of the Body and the Soul. Therefore Blake was proof against the error, into which

Lawrence not seldom fell, of asserting the Body and denying the soul. And
when he does this Lawrence drives division deeper; in Blake the division is
transcended from the beginning. For all their startling resemblances the
doctrine of Blake belongs to a higher order.[59]

Lawrence's sexual doctrine was at once so potent and so threatening to
Murry that he reviewed the point again and again, reiterating in his last
book, *Love, Freedom and Society*, the wholeness of Blake's and Keats's love
doctrines and asserting the partialness of Lawrence's.

Thus far I have suggested the multiple ways Murry used Blake's moral
theory to support his own preconceptions. It is even more interesting to
see how Blake acted on Murry. He became a pacifist in direct response to
Blake and used Blakean terminology to align political and sexual theory,
regarding the relation between the sexes as a microcosm of all societal
relationships. Murry expanded the latter idea into a strange, possibly
neurotic, conviction of "a correlation between [his] personal condition
and that of the world,"[60] a peculiar egocentricity which distorted his
thought on a number of issues.

The conversion to pacifism was a reversal of life long conviction. Murry
had disdained the movement since the First World War, when he reacted
against the group centered around the Morrells' Garsington Manor; he
was so vehemently opposed to pacifists that when he joined the Independent Labour party in 1931 he told Geoffrey Sainsbury that the pacifist
wing "ought to be extirpated."[61] Toward the end of 1932, while completing the Blake manuscript, he made a volte-face, arguing that socialism
must be nonviolent in terms drawn directly from his explication of Blake's
Jerusalem:

> I discover that my antipathy to violence in the cause of Socialism is absolute.
> It contravenes the very realisation of which made me a Socialist—namely
> the realisation of Eternity. . . . since the realisation of Eternity is potential in
> every living man, it is a crime against Eternity to take a man's life. The
> realisation of Eternity is the highest joy. It was in order that the crass
> obstacles which the human selfhood interposes between man and the attain-
> ment of that joy [be removed] that I became a Socialist. For a little while, it is
> clear to me, I lost the end in the means.[62]

The parallel passage in *William Blake* reads:

> The man who has been possessed by the Imagination which is Eternity can
> no longer kill a man, nor cause a man to be killed. . . . every man has the
> potentiality of being possessed by the Imagination of Eternity, and he
> cannot be robbed of his birthright. It is an impossibility for one member of
> the Divine Family to murder another.[63]

Murry's absoluteness proved nonabsolute. He wavered on the pacifist issue several times and declared after the outbreak of the Spanish Civil War that "one must fight: it is pure self-deception to believe that violence will not take us, cannot take us, to a Socialist society. . . . violence will take us to a society that may become a Socialist society—and that is what we are fighting for."[64] Three months later Murry reversed again, formally announcing his pacifism and joining the Peace Pledge Union, with which he was associated until the end of World War II.

The really telling point is that the political waffling precisely paralleled the motions of his marital life. Whenever Murry renewed his commitment to the formidable Betty he advocated pacifism and the supremacy of the love principle; when he left her, as he did several times, his pacifism collapsed. The connection between the public and private acts is explicit in a 1936 letter in which Murry describes socialism as issuing in struggle against the cruelties of the world, even at the sacrifice of love. Pacifism demands death in the service of love. Saying that he had chosen to love his wife, who would destroy him, Murry declared himself destroyed and reborn "into the knowledge that there is no power, no life, no future, no anything, except Love."[65] It was no accident that Murry joined the Peace Pledge Union on the same day he returned to Betty.

This messy blending of ideology and private trauma is responsible for the chaotic imbalance of Murry's political writings in the thirties, which invades some of his criticism as well. He justified the intermingling by proclaiming himself "all of one piece" (the man inseparable from his ideas), but it is precisely because Murry was personally unstable at the time that his convictions were liable to disintegrate in a moment.

In *William Blake*, Murry is quite evidently seeking a solution to the unhappiness of his marriage. Blake did not empower Murry's imagination as fully as Keats or Shakespeare. Consequently, the subjectivity is more impure, more flawed. Murry's idiosyncrasies as a critic are not sufficiently balanced by superior insight and intuitive sympathy. *William Blake* is clearly the least successful of his major critical works. Because he is more sympathetic to the Blakean doctrine than to its poetic mode, his untwining of the system of symbols has an air of laborious duty, and his enthusiasm for Blake's mysticism seems, in contrast, too fervid. This quality Collis pinpointed when he called *William Blake* a "passionately uninspired book."[66]

Shakespeare

In a discarded preface to *Shakespeare* (1936) Murry described the work as a "book of glimpses and half-lights," far from the book on Shakespeare he once proposed to write. But, he continued, "it is no use deluding myself any longer with the hope that one day I shall be free to write it as I once desired. . . . the book is nothing more than the record of some tentative gestures towards an Act that could not be."[67] Although the prefatory note he actually used omits this passage and stresses his effort to convey the "sensation" of Shakespeare, the rejected passage discloses his uneasiness. Murry had intended to "empty" himself "so that that which is greater may take possession," as he had with Keats. *Shakespeare* never assumed such a form because Murry was distracted by his marital tangle and by multiple political activities—but more importantly because Shakespeare was still too immense to assimilate in that way. The confrontation with Shakespearean immensity actually worked in Murry's favor. It contained his self-identifying impulse and begat clarity. His favorite expository method was to trace the motions of his own mind. When his conclusions are based on intuition only, his "proofs" abjure logic. Shakespeare drove him to use his considerable intellectual faculties. "Shakespeare," Murry noted, "seems always to bring to the true Shakespearean critic a liberation from himself."[68]

Murry's Shakespeare criticism is of Coleridgean lineage, and he defends Coleridge's excesses, terming him the "greatest of all critics of Shakespeare."[69] However, Murry's more direct tutelage came from A. C. Bradley, whom he credited with great imaginative sensibility and the gift of retaining the experience of a poet while analyzing him. (That was Murry's gift, too, although his analytic control was more variable than Bradley's and his intuitions finally less impressive.) Murry called Bradley's *Shakespearean Tragedy* "the greatest single work of criticism in the English language" and ultimately elevated him above Coleridge. "Bradley exposes whole what Coleridge gave glimpses of."[70] G. Wilson Knight was Murry's successor in this critical line, a disciple of sorts whose complex interpretations puzzled Murry. He considered Knight too intellectual and schematic and termed his pattern tracing a "self-proliferating growth" leading to "strange conclusions."[71] Knight, for his part, generously acknowledged his debt to Murry for generating a "thought atmosphere" which encouraged consideration of the religious content of great poetry, as well as for specific approaches to some of the plays. Their most demonstrable likeness was being "interpreters" rather than "critics," clearly distinguishable roles in Knight's lexicon. His explanation of these terms echoes Murry's defense of "creative" criticism:

> The critic is, and should be, cool and urbane, seeing the poetry he discusses not with the eye of a lover, but as an object; whereas interpretation deliberately immerses itself in its theme and speaks less from the seat of judgement than from the creative center. It deliberately aims to write of genius from the standpoint not of the reader, but of genius itself; to write of it from

within. So, while the critic stands on his guard against the lure of the unknown and prefers not to adventure too far from home, interpretation, it must be confessed, is happiest among the vast open spaces of what is, nonetheless, a severely disciplined speculation.[72]

There were, of course, serious divagations. Knight and Murry respectfully disagreed with one another during three decades of correspondence and reviewing of one another's work. The difference, Knight concluded in a retrospective essay on Murry, was that Murry was bound by traditional religious valuation. Murry wrote from his own spiritual experience, trying to align the literature he loved with the personal truths garnered from his "one great experience. . . . At the limit he writes not as an interpreter of genius but as a critic; the final court of appeal is his own judgement." Knight, in contrast, affirmed personal immortality and a posttragic vision and defined himself as writing from imagination rather than experience. "Imagination is precisely the faculty for apprehending and accepting what is *not* covered by one's own experience."[73] Against that dictum we may place Murry's judgment that truth in art means "fidelity to human experience" and his consistent distaste for scientific criticism, represented in Knight's case by his elaborate metaphor tracing. "There remains," Murry declared, "an instantly felt discrepancy between Shakespeare and the application of a 'rigorous critical method.' "[74]

Murry had trouble with a final definition of Shakespeare precisely because all his ideas of the poet as prophet-hero cohere in him. Shakespeare was the prototypal poet of *The Problem of Style,* used to demonstrate the ultimate possibility of imagery, of metaphor so organic that it is transmuted to a mode of apprehension. Essays on Shakespeare appeared in every collection Murry published in the twenties, indicating how close he remained to Murry's center of concern. *Keats and Shakespeare,* we know, was to have been *the* book on Shakespeare, reformulated because Murry found the titan difficult to approach directly. In 1927-28 he settled down to concentrated study of Shakespeare, but from it issued only two short essays and some *Notes on Shakespeare* for the *Adelphi.* That is why, by 1935, Murry began to feel "a kind of desperation, a determination to get something said about Shakespeare before [he] became incapable of saying anything about him at all."[75]

Most of the early essays are very good, focused on specific problems which Murry elucidates gracefully and pointedly. "A Neglected Heroine of Shakespeare" (1922)[76] discusses Virgilia as the representative of domestic love by which Coriolanus should be measured. "Coriolanus" (1922)[77] augments that interpretation by treating Coriolanus as a Homeric hero consumed by pride. "The Creation of Falstaff" (1924)[78] is marred by a flowery introduction which demands our "surrender" to

Shakespeare, but Murry's argument that Shakespeare was compelled by popular demand to go on creating Falstaff after his creative interest in the character flagged is persuasive and his remarks on the nature of comedy stimulating. "A truly comic character cannot degenerate morally, for he moves completely outside the kingdom of moral law." "To Be or Not to Be" (1926)[79] is a closely reasoned exegesis of the soliloquy, interpreted as a debate between action and inaction. "The Mortal Moon" (1929)[80] argues for a psychologically plausible dating of the sonnets, interpreting the "mortal Moone hath her eclipse indur'd" (Sonnet 107) to be a reference to the Queen's illness of 1596, rather than, as Hotson had theorized, a reference to the Armada. In this, as in other technical matters, Murry has been largely upheld by later scholars. "Shakespeare's Dedication" (1931)[81] traces the use of the word "dedicate" from "Venus and Adonis" through the plays, demonstrating its transvaluation of meaning after the publication of the sonnets, its connection with perfidy and disillusionment in the middle plays, and its "decontamination" in *The Winter's Tale* and *The Tempest*.

The familiar essay, a form which discourages overwriting and over-earnestness, elicited Murry's most polished prose. Restrained by the genre from prolixity and gush, Murry achieved an authoritative tone, at once colloquial and urbane. The early Shakespeare essays are among the best of the lot, written with a penetration and sensitivity to nuance that betokens close, comprehensive knowledge. It is regrettable that they have not been issued in a separate collection, for they would surely enhance Murry's reputation as a critic of Shakespeare.

However, that reputation is based almost entirely on *Shakespeare*, the one book Murry published in the thirties which gained widespread attention and esteem. It has held up very well indeed, its general excellence attested to by the variety of the praise accorded it. E. M. W. Tillyard commends Murry on the history plays, particularly his treatment of the Bastard in *King John*, G. Wilson Knight his "Antony and Cleopatra;" others mention "Shakespeare's Method: *The Merchant of Venice*," a frequently anthologized piece,[82] and C. G. Thayer thinks Murry's discussion of *Hamlet* so "elegant, lucid and sane all the way through, so sound, so sensitive, so imaginative that it deserves anthologizing along with the better-known essays by C. S. Lewis and Maynard Mack."[83]

In *Shakespeare* Murry was trying to establish the poet's absolute ascendency in the English poetic tradition and to reassert Shakespeare as a cultural force in the twentieth century. The *Times Literary Supplement* reviewer commented that the book would "help the plain man to see more of the beauty and meaning of his [Shakespeare's] plays,"[84] and this comment actually defines better than most Murry's intent. Although he was entirely competent in the scholarly art of pitting one reading of a line against another's, his interpretation was really directed to the nonspecialist. Murry links Shakespeare's "supreme imaginative achievement" with spiritual achievement, as he did with Keats, and the terms "self-annihilation" and "submission to experience" that he applies to Shakespeare have a familiar resonance to readers of Murry's earlier work.

Organized chronologically, like *Keats and Shakespeare*, this study also endeavors to approach the poetic life through the work, and the method produces some cohering theories about Shakespeare's poetic growth. First, he convincingly argues that Shakespeare was troubled for a time by the need to reconcile his poetic self to the exigencies of the sixteenth-century theater and then, having accepted the necessities of the popular theater, attained the power to transform it. By imagining Shakespeare's role as a working dramatist, Murry demonstrates in play after play exactly how the poet's lyricism, imaginative reach, and dramatic sense worked to recreate the tradition within which he worked. His lack of condescension toward his audience separated him from his rivals, Murry says, arguing that "the compulsion the audience exerted upon his genius" was responsible for his becoming "the greatest dramatist in the world"[85]—rather than a limitation of his genius. Shakespeare satisfied the popular appetite, previously nourished by the drama of the mass, with secular melodrama. He mastered the form precisely because he knew the theater as Jonson and the University Wits did not. The insoluble psychological problems of Shakespeare's play arose because he was loath to risk plots that had not proven dramatically effective, but the obligation to renew old formulas helped foster his genius. "Out of that not wholly certain struggle with the intractable . . . comes the finally overwhelming sense of a unique and incomparable 'truth' in Shakespeare's total work: by virtue of that struggle, and the manner in which it was waged, his work becomes the counterpart of the unending struggle of consciousness against the unconscious, the ideal against inertia, which is life, as men know it . . . , both in themselves and in the world about them."[86] This exegesis of Shakespeare's conquest of the popular theater is the most valuable single motif of the book.

Murry finds the history plays bound together by Shakespeare's investigation of the theme of order in relation to the doctrine of the divine right of kings, and the progression from *Richard II* through *Henry V* is an evolution toward a character who can embody ideal kingship. In *Henry V*, Murry says, Shakespeare resolves the dispute between order and divine right by embodying "organic and creative order"[87] in the king. "Only in so far as a king does incorporate the brotherhood of a nation is kingship justified. . . . He personifies the nation: if unworthily, he is a mere abstract symbol of the unity of his people; if worthily, it is because his effort is to bring that unity from an outward show to an inward reality."[88] Henry V is "king by right divine and by right of nature" because he "utters the soul of a people."[89] As Griffin points out, Murry defines Shakespeare as quintessentially English, celebrating an imaginative order which culminates in the "ideal Englishman."[90]

The theory of the "Shakespeare Man," the most original thesis of this book, also emerges out of the history plays. Murry argues that as Shakespeare developed the figure of the ideal king, he also gave expression to some element of the private self which produces a string of notably individual characters. Broaching the idea in his treatment of the Bastard in *King John*, Murry identifies this type in Berowne, Richard II, the Bastard, Hotspur, Falstaff, Prince Hal, Mercutio, Jaques, and Benedick and finds its consummate expression in Hamlet, who, he reminds us, Bradley called the "only character in Shakespeare's works who could have written Shakespeare's plays."[91] This hero figure in its various manifestations is a vehicle for the expression of Shakespeare's creative spontaneity, a "congenial incarnation of his impersonal self."[92] The danger is that these characters become too individually powerful and interesting, threatening the dramatic design and creating a hiatus between Shakespeare's imaginative truth and historical fact or theatrical necessity.

> Speaking roughly, when Shakespeare is most in control as an "artist," there the Shakespeare man is absent. He manifests a constant tendency to dissolve, so to speak, into Shakespeare the "artist" . . . where Shakespeare's liberty—which is a less responsible thing than his spontaneity—is most in evidence, the Shakespeare man tends to emerge. He represents something that the more deliberate, the more "artist" Shakespeare has to control. . . . He is the utterance of something which seeks to be uttered less personally, less diffusedly; when he appears he tends to sap the life which should be impersonally spread through the whole drama.[93]

In *Hamlet* Shakespeare renders the Shakespeare man as the play itself, the center of the drama, and through this incarnation rids himself of the compulsion. Marking a "crisis of realization" on the part of its creator, *Hamlet* is the consummate expression of Shakespearean sadness, his chafing against "outrageous fortune," and of a penultimate reconciliation with experience, of—in Murryian (and Keatsian) terms—"dying into life."[94]

This set of ideas is so obliquely expressed that it is intelligible only to readers familiar with *Keats and Shakespeare*, where Murry's philosophy of self-annihilation and rebirth through acceptance of all experience (the key phrase is Keats's—"the principle of beauty in all things") is fully articulated. Murry says too little here to convince us that this creation is Shakespeare's rather than his own. Familiarity with the context of the idea renders it more, rather than less, suspect, since we know its connection with Murry's ruling philosophy. His discovery of this crisis in Shakespeare, though suggestive, is too neatly partisan.

Although, as I've shown, Murry's poetic-biography approach leads to some pregnant insights, I cannot altogether agree with Griffin's belief that this approach works well to keep Murry in close touch with the work he is discussing.[95] As too many Shakespeare scholars have discovered, the scanty biographical data cannot bear a scaffolding of assumptions about the man Shakespeare. Murry was by temperament and critical method peculiarly vulnerable to the vice of speculative biography. Although he quite fairly tells us when he is dealing in surmise, he expends considerable time on conjecture. When he deals directly with the major biographical questions, he treats them gracefully and economically, supposing the "hero" of the sonnets to be Shakespeare's patron, the earl of Southampton, and the rival poet to be George Chapman. But he affirms too quickly his "soul knowledge" of the poet. The provocative biographical intimations of the sonnets lead him to emotional self-identification, as in his bathetic discussion of Sonnet 107 ("Not mine own fears, nor the prophetic soul"):

> I see no reason whatever to doubt that Shakespeare's heart had remained loyal to his patron-friend, as he claimed. The realization that his hopes had been inordinate, and that the social gulf between them was too vast to be bridged by genius, would not have changed the heart of the man I feel Shakespeare to have been. He would have considered that the fault was his, for having indulged in a dream. He was, as I read him, the kind of man who, so soon as he was in a position of some security, outward and inward, would take upon himself all the blame for what had been untoward in the relation. And that is what I find in the masterly group of sonnets in the midst of which Sonnet 107 occurs.[96]

Similarly, Murry's trait of connecting personal harmony or disorder with the macrocosm is transferred to Shakespeare. "To a man of his condition, a personal disaster is of universal significance; it comes to him as the quality of life made palpable in his own suffering. It is not he, but Man, who winces and is disquieted."[97]

At times Murry's reconstructive method falls into proven error. He identifies a cluster of images linking dog-candy-flattery and then associates them with an imagined incident in Shakespeare's life "when he was standing before the table in an Elizabethan hall, watching the hounds wagging their tails, licking the hands of a pompous company, gobbling up the rich and sticky sweet-meats thrown to them."[98] Armstrong condemns Murry's use of this "seductive device," noting that Murry's fictive scene is based upon a manifestly false legend about Shakespeare's deerstealing in Sir Thomas Lucy's park, calling the method illegitimate because if the associative linkages become "the subject of unthrifty inference the truth which they reveal will be submerged in a sea of specious error."[99] Nonetheless, Griffin points out that some of Murry's intuitions, such as his deduction from a series of similes in *Henry IV, Part II* that Shakespeare was building or renovating a house in 1597, have proven accurate.[100]

The more reputable side of Murry's interest in imaginative reconstruction appears in his vivid evocation of the privations of an actor's life. Recalling Thomas Hardy's story of the eminent nineteenth-century actor Edmund Kean, who walked into Dorchester with his wife, pushing a baby in a perambulator, Murry uses the anecdote to emphasize the "horrible precariousness" of Shakespeare's life as a strolling player during the plague years and the staggering importance to his art of the economic security he gained as an actor-playwright with a life interest in his own work.

The most compelling reason for criticizing Murry's reconstruction of Shakespeare's odyssey is that the approach obligates him to deal with every phase of the poet's career. The task he imposed upon himself was enormous, and intermittent chapters of *Shakespeare* betray haste and a sense of obligation to glance at all sections of the canon without evincing real interest in them. "The Pupil Age," for instance, treats the relationship between the early plays and the contemporaneous poetry superficially. Murry's eloquence about the growth of variety in Shakespearean blank verse does not atone for the descriptive, rather than analytic, discussion of parallel passages. The manner is pleasant, appreciative, gentlemanly; the matter calls for a weightier tone. Similarly, chapter 10, "The Shakespeare Man," attempts to deal with several distinct topics and to cover a great deal of ground. It becomes a hodgepodge of half-articulated ideas, enigmatic because the concepts are sufficiently provocative to interest us very much, perplexing because they do not lead to reasoned deduction. Murry speculates about the character of Shakespeare's audience (more country squires than courtiers, he says, although his reasons for thinking so are inadequately argued); he briefly discusses the positive force exerted by the Queen, against the middle class, on behalf of the Elizabethan theater, and turns to disquisition on the barrier, "which no effort of the sympathetic imagination can wholly bridge"[101] between us and Shakespeare as he appeared to the audience of his time. In treating the problem comedies, Murry again covers material too rapidly. His thesis that the psychologically unconvincing situations of plays, such as the marriage consummation tricks of *All's Well That Ends Well* and *Measure for Measure*, arise from the folklore tradition from which Shakespeare drew his material, is provocative, but because he is too impatient to examine the relation between fettered plot and Shakespearean ingenuity, Murry simply hands us the idea to work out for ourselves.

Generally, Murry needed the discipline of a contained subject to elicit his highest critical intelligence. When he moves from the particular to the general, the originating thesis continues and enriches the material; when he begins with a generalization, he too seldom returns to the particular or expands his illustrations enough to solidify a point. His theory of the development of Shakespearean imagery ("Imagery and Imagination") is ill supported by example and strays off into mystical conclusions. The advance in diction, he claims, is an intellectual and spiritual development, "the outward and visible sign of an inward and spiritual grace," itself the consequence of Shakespeare's "increasing power of identifying himself imaginatively with his characters."[102] The cohering point, that poetry is a fusion of thought and emotion, is muddied by familiar Murryian maxims about submission to life. It is interesting that he made the same point far more cogently in *The Problem of Style*, where his discussion of imagery was founded in Shakespearean example.

The most interesting chapters of *Shakespeare*, which give Murry his real standing as a Shakespeare critic, are those which deal with single plays, of which the essay on *The Merchant of Venice* is perhaps the most conceptually original. Defining it as a "pure melodrama" and so essentially a "fairy tale," Murry calls the play an "almost perfect example of the art which being prior to art itself, most evidently and completely satisfies the primitive man in us all."[103] Shakespeare's dramatic method, he explains, "consists, essentially, in the humanization of melodrama."[104] The situation precedes the characters, and Shakespeare was compelled to adhere to the familiar material. So Shylock must embody irrational hatred, even while he functions in other ways as a credible human being. "He is neither of these things to the exclusion of the other," Murry argues, since "at critical moments he is given dignity and passion of speech and argument to plead his cause to us and to himself. His hatred then is represented as deep, irrational and implacable, but not as mean or mercenary. It is then a force of nature—something greater than himself." The definition of *The Merchant of Venice* as a problem play is erroneous, since it is by nature anti-realistic. Modern criticism "seeks for psychological motives where none were given or intended." The play's appeal is "elemental," its morality "not of the formulable kind." Murry's conclusion is provocative. "It is worthy of more than passing notice that the two perennially popular plays of Shakespeare—*The Merchant of Venice* and *Hamlet*—are the two of which we can say, most definitely, that his freedom to alter the action was most limited; and that they are also the plays in which the nature of the chief

character is most disputed."[105] The analysis is specific, infinitely suggestive; it is the kind of criticism which inevitably expands our reading,
whether we accept its major premises or not.

On *Macbeth* Murry is specific and effective. Explicating the repeated
phrase "the time has been" and its resonance with the "Tomorrow, and
tomorrow, and tomorrow" soliloquy, Murry describes Macbeth's horri-
fied contemplation of the *human* time before the murder and the *inhuman*
time which follows, on the unannihilable distinction between what *has been*
and *what is*. Too few critics have remarked on the considerable virtue of
this short essay; it deserves to be better remembered.

Murry's treatment of *Hamlet* is so astute and disciplined that no brief
summary can do it justice. Establishing a focus on the tragedy by a
disquisition on the "To be or not to be" soliloquy, Murry covers this
well-trod ground without a hint of imitativeness or superfluity. He begins
by examining and disagreeing with Dr. Johnson's characterization of the
speech as asking "which is nobler, to suffer evil or to risk death in resisting
it."[106] The issues Murry raises revolve around the meaning of nobility and
cowardice in the context of this play. He argues that Hamlet has been
frightened by the ghost into contemplation of the terrors of the afterlife.
Hamlet's problem is to conquer his fear of an unknown futurity. The
discrepancy between Hamlet-in-thought and Hamlet-in-action which
orders the action is attributable to this new fear exerted upon a man who
has lost his center of certainty, his idea of order. The issue is resolved
when Hamlet is able to reintegrate his divided self; the triumph of the play
is that Shakespeare makes us believe in it.

In treating individual plays at length, Murry exchanges his conjectural
spiritual-biography method for the kind of analysis through characteristic passages which he advocated in "A Critical Credo." His essay on *Othello*,
too, is marked by a valuable particularity, since he begins by examining
the word "wonder" in connection with Desdemona's handkerchief, but
his theme leads to tiring maxims about human and divine love, and this
chapter is less substantial than others. The major failure in this group of
essays is the "heretical" chapter on *King Lear*, which argues that *Lear* is
inferior to the other great tragedies because it lacks imaginative control
and poetic intensity, these flaws being the result of Shakespeare's struggles with an obsession: a revulsion against sexuality and a bitter vision of
humanity "self-destroyed by its own animality."[107] His judgments were
clearly off target and Murry himself later humbly recanted this view of the
play in his preface to the new edition. "The treatment of *King Lear* in this
book is confessedly unsatisfactory. I recommend those who, like myself,
are dissatisfied with it, to read a notable book by Mr. John Danby: *Shakespeare's Doctrine of Nature: A Study of King Lear*. . . . I feel that however
honest, it was preposterous in me to say that Shakespeare was out of his

depth, when the evidence stares me in the face that I was out of mine."[108]

In my judgment, the essay on *Antony and Cleopatra* represents a unique pinnacle of achievement for Murry, a moment when he used apostrophic language in precisely the right way, to the right end. What might so easily be gush, what verges on hyperbole, issues as sustained eloquence. Murry's own language catches fire in the reflected radiance of the poetry of this play. As Thayer suggests, extravagance represents, in this case, the right approach.[109] The essay is an extended commentary on the word "royal," into which is gathered up, as Murry shows, the essence of the play. The necessity of measuring the conceptual reverberations of "royal" keeps Murry firmly tied to the poetry, which, he asserts, is "the ultimate and enduring structure of the play. . . . its life, its inward progression, derive from the response of poetry to poetry."[110] The concentrated language encourages him to eschew scruples against the "sacrilege of anatomizing."[111] As Heath points out, Murry actually applies here the method he had outlined years before in "A Critical Credo"[112]—that is, he approaches the play through consideration of a passage which reflects the work as a whole and acts as a vehicle for the critic's response. Analyzing the significance of the word "royal" by context does, in fact, display the essential quality of the author and simultaneously reveals to us the processes of our own awareness of poetic effect. Murry demonstrates how the concept of royalty is knitted to the basic imagery:

In *Antony and Cleopatra* the word "royal" is royal because it is made royal. Therefore it crowns the close—twice in a dozen lines.

> Now boast thee, death, in thy possession lies
> A lass unparallel'd. Downy windows, close;
> And golden Phoebus never be beheld
> Of eyes again so royal.
>
> • • • •
>   [V.ii. 317–21]

Then the music rises again. Somehow, by the words "golden Phoebus" Cleopatra herself is suffused with the majesty of the heavens. The order of the words is magical. It gives point and meaning to Coleridge's definition of poetry as "the best words in the best order". . . . This order is such that every significance is gathered up into the one word "royal." Now we know what "royalty" means—it means all that has gone before—all that was gathered up, before, into the "lass unparalled'd"—all this, moreover, bathed in the majesty of "bright Phoebus in his strength."

> His face was as the heavens; and therein stuck
> A sun and moon, which kept their course, and lighted
> The little O, the earth.
>   [V.ii. 76–80]

Poetry is not a matter of crude equivalents and equations; and I am not
suggesting that the sun and moon, which were the eyes of the Antony of
Cleopatra's vision, *were* also Antony and Cleopatra. But a flicker of that
suggestion is there: enough to bring a new depth, and add a new glancing
reflection to the final "royalty." Cleopatra is moon to Antony's sun, while
they are alive together. When the sun is set, then Cleopatra leaves the
moon—

> "the fleeting moon
> No planet is of mine—"

to take upon her the strength and majesty of the sun. And so what we have
called her final royalty is totally suffused by the glory of "golden
Phoebus."[113]

The method of significance gathering is not unique—Murry used a
similar technique in his studies of *Macbeth* and *Hamlet*. However, *Antony
and Cleopatra* risks parody because the critical rhetoric is impassioned by
the poetry; the effect is, genuinely, to render the "sensation" of Shakespeare—and to increase our wonder. He powerfully conveys the quality
of the poetry: "The potency of language which can cram imperial Rome,
its arenas and its aqueducts, its roads and its provinces, into a single phrase
and topple it over—'let the wide arch of the ranged empire fall'—has won
the challenge in a dozen words."[114] Even here, Murry occasionally verges
into familiar, tired language, again quoting Keats on poetry coming
"naturally as the leaves to a tree," but the essay as a whole exemplifies
impressionistic criticism at its best.

In the final chapter Murry succinctly discusses Shakespeare's influence
upon his successors and the loss of contact with the whole Shakespeare
caused by separation of the poet and the dramatist. "Part of him de-
scended into the playhouse; part of him ascended into the library; and no
one has ever quite succeeded in putting him together again."[115] The point
is well taken, and we are convinced at the end of this volume that Murry
has written the sort of criticism which will help reunify him.

Before concluding, I may as well say that the epilogue is a blot which
Murry ought to have had the taste to excise. This imaginary conversation
between Murry and Shakespeare about the economics of being a legend
and Shakespeare's consorting in a poet's paradise with Keats and Chatterton is dubious in conception; in execution it seems frankly silly, particularly in the closing passage, which grates upon us, as some of Murry's
Adelphi essays did, by its excessive sentimentality and hints of secret
significances truly understood by Murry alone. Murry's decision to retain
the epilogue in the 1955 edition of *Shakespeare*, despite good advice to the
contrary, indicates how deep-rooted the mawkish side of his personality
was. And despite the lapses this trait engendered in even his best books,

Murry's perseverance commands respect. He never feared ridicule, and his misjudgments arise from his peculiar integrities, not from sloth or waning of intelligence.

Shakespeare is Murry's most successful treatment of a major poet. At its best, and that I view as the treatments of *Hamlet*, *Macbeth*, and *Antony and Cleopatra*, *Shakespeare* shows the range and sensitivity of Murry's critical intelligence and suggests the kind of reputation he would have built had he not been tempted into other endeavors. It is the last full-length critical work that Murry was compelled to write by his own quest for values. His study of Swift was undertaken late in his career in an altogether different spirit and was never invested with the moral seriousness Murry brought to his spiritual heroes. When we consider the condition of his life when it was composed—his wrecked domestic life, his distracting political involvements—it seems surprising that it was written at all. Far from being a flawless book, *Shakespeare* has virtues much weightier than its failings. Murry's observations cast light on a score of fundamental matters and many more minor ones: his best essays stand among the best there are. His romantic receptivity is more an asset than a deficit in this work, for it enhances his responsiveness to the Shakespearean sensibility and shows what impressionistic criticism of the best order can accomplish. It is difficult to disagree with Thayer, who said: "If he allowed himself to be ravished by Shakespeare, one can hardly accuse him of bad taste."[116]

Chapter Four

KATHERINE MANSFIELD AND THE ANTIPODES:
D. H. Lawrence and T. S. Eliot

Katherine Mansfield

The romantic attitudes which govern Murry's approach to Keats, Blake, and Shakespeare grew out of the theories he and Katherine Mansfield developed during their ten-year collaboration. It is impossible to say who sponsored which idea, for they constantly echoed one another's phrases and judgments, shared the same heroes and enemies, and assured one another that they alone were concerned with fostering a literature morally adequate to their time. They constructed an ideology together. When they met, Katherine had little sense of working within a literary tradition or of her relation to her contemporaries, and Murry was aflame with postsymbolism. Their unanimity grew out of shared experience and mutual admiration; both cast away earlier models to reach the accord; for both the alterations were fruitful.

Although their private life was blemished by forced separations, by misunderstandings, by temperamental debilities on both sides which frustrated sustained intimacy, they concurred in believing that "love" must become the final faith of their age. So Katherine, writing to Dorothy Brett, said: "It seems to me there is a great change come over the world since people like us stopped believing in God; God is now gone for all of us. . . . Therefore love today between 'lovers' has to be not only human but divine today. They love each other for everything and through everything and their love is their religion. It can't become less supreme because it is an act of faith to believe."[1] Murry said the same thing and was still saying it more than three decades later when he reflected on the achieved fulfillment of his last marriage:

It seems to me that is the one thing of permanent value and significance I have achieved: the one thing worth listening to that I have to say: that man-woman love is the supreme felicity, and that it is attainable. . . . Before I knew Keats, I wrote about Katherine: "Lo! I have made love all my religion, Nothing remains to me if it be gone." Keats wrote the same: "Love is my religion, and you are its only tenet." And this sense of love as complete religious fulfillment is what fills my consciousness as I go to sleep with Mary at night and wake with her in the morning. I am in a new dimension of being, quite simple, quite real, quite familiar, yet every day absolutely new. And because of that I need no "religion"; I *have* all that "religion" promises, all that God could give.[2]

Murry's and Katherine's theme, the placing of ultimate value in the love relationship, is the idea Murry lived out; it connects his various literary, religious, and political postures and lends coherence to apparent contradiction.

The English romantics and the Russian novelists were their models, bulwarked against the modernist currents of their day. Again, both made the point explicit. Murry wrote to Katherine: "You and I are English, and because we are truly English we are set apart from our generation. That has gone a whoring after strange gods, and only you and I and Wordsworth and Coleridge, Lamb, Keats and Shelley abide." He concludes by describing Katherine to herself as "the perfect flower of England—the thing that Shakespeare dreamed, and almost embodied in Cleopatra."[3] (Murry was defining an idealized Katherine's literary/spiritual identity, but his interpretation of her quintessential Englishness is idiosyncratic, since Katherine's *social* sense of self was crucially bound up with the fact that she was an "outsider" in England, the little colonial. Moreover, her finest stories, as it proved, grew out of nostalgic recollections of her New Zealand childhood.)

Katherine was often cutting about her English contemporaries, and her occasional viciousness about Virginia Woolf is edged with rivalry, but her judgments, like Murry's, arise from a keen sense of a separate purpose. "It seems to me . . . that you and I are in some way *really different* from other writers of our time. . . . Other people—I mean people today—seem to look on in a way I don't understand. I don't want to boast. I don't feel at all arrogant, but I do feel that they have not perhaps lived as fully as we have. . . . but *who is* living . . . as we mean life? Dostoevsky, Tchehov and Tolstoy. I can't think of *anybody else*."[4]

Her prophecies for Murry, like his for her, are linked to a romantic identity poised against cynicism. "It's so difficult not to find a sneerer," she complains. "What's the good of sneering? . . . There's your mighty pull over your whole generation. . . . One has the feeling that you are out to discover, to explore literature in the name of Life."[5]

Murry wrote relatively little about Katherine's art. His primary role was to edit and publish the posthumous stories and poems, the journals and letters. He was widely criticized in the twenties for making a cult of Katherine, for exploiting her. (She asked in her will that her remaining papers be destroyed; Murry published them instead.) More recently, he has been attacked for "censoring" her journals and for constructing a falsely refined portrait which began the myth of a rarefied, ethereal sensibility and excluded the interesting flaws of Katherine's complex personality. No one now questions Murry's rightness in disregarding the instructions of the will; the material he saved has proven invaluable. If his rush to publish Katherine in the *Adelphi* (and the *Yale Review* in America) was guided by an excess of sentimentality, it was surely understandable. He was ridden by guilt, feeling that a more decisive husband would have imposed upon her a stay in a sanatorium and would have restrained her from the restless pilgrimages to the perfect place, the miraculous cure, which hastened her death. Establishing Katherine's place in literary history was an atonement for failing to aid her cure and for the conviction that their intensity of spiritual love had literally killed her. Few writers have had such an advocate, and Murry's zeal is undeniably responsible for her international reputation.

The censorship issue is more complex. From the beginning Murry idealized Katherine. In *Between Two Worlds* he claims: "From the first to the last Katherine appeared to me as a totally exquisite being. Everything she did or said had its own manifest validity. I do not think it ever entered my head, at any time, to criticize her in any way."[6] His account is borne out by the extant correspondence. Murry's tone is always generous, wholly admiring. The Katherine whom Strachey sourly criticized as a "foul-mouthed, virulent, brazen-faced broomstick,"[7] whom Gordon Campbell's wife, Beatrice, recalls as sometimes hysterically self-dramatizing, "putting on acts"—for example, weeping and wailing, "I am a soiled woman"—that left the impression she was secretly enjoying herself,[8] simply did not exist for Murry. He learned of the sexual escapades of her early years in London from Alpers's biography, not from Katherine, who cherished the "innocence" of her relationship to Murry and shielded him from knowledge of her past. The bitchy fussiness of her last years, her use and mistreatment of her lifelong friend Ida Baker, distressed and confused him. Years later, after completing the long-deferred and emotionally lacerating task of editing her letters to him for publication, he explained the unpleasantness to himself as an aberration of her disease, but he hadn't been able to face looking at those letters until he'd achieved real personal serenity and had borne her accusations unquestioningly for years, unable to think the unthinkable—that the fault lay in Katherine rather than in himself.

In that psychological context the accusation that he omitted material from her journal referring to adolescent experiments with lesbianism and toned down other sexual passages, although just, is too stringent.[9] Editing the material only five years after her death was at once an act of exceptional devotion and a masochistic exercise. In 1927 Murry's second wife, Violet, had been diagnosed as tubercular. He was incapable, then, of publishing material that seemed to him essentially not Katherine. The more telling criticism came from Katherine's devoted friend Koteliansky, who claimed that Murry "left out all the jokes, to make her an English Tchehov."[10] Murry brought to Katherine, as to his other idols, the vice of overearnestness. In the end he did publish her unexpurgated letters to him, which disclosed all the faults and ambivalences, letters few husbands would have been willing to print at all. Although they have helped to revise the popular belief that Murry "betrayed" Katherine (one reviewer commented that "pity for her gives way to an even greater pity for Murry: her need for him was so relentless"),[11] for the most part he sacrificed his reputation to hers by his self-abasement in *Between Two Worlds* and by publishing her letters without publishing his own. As Benet suggests, the vividness of Katherine's personality and capacity for self-expression have perpetuated injustice to Murry. "It is a tribute to the peculiar magic of Katherine Mansfield's style, and to the compelling aura of her personality, that Murry is now unquestioningly believed to have failed her, and that what he contributed to her art and her reputation goes unnoticed."[12] The truth is that Murry provided a center that steadied Katherine's concentration and enlarged her conception of herself as artist, just as she stabilized and fruitfully criticized Murry.

In the decade following Katherine's death, Murry brought out eight volumes of her work: two collections of short stories, the poems, the journal, the two-volume edition of letters, and a collection of her *Athenaeum* book reviews. His commentary during the first ten years provided factual exposition of Mansfield's attitude toward her work and background information about circumstances of composition. In only one essay, written in 1924, did he assess her place in literary history, calling her "the most perfect and accomplished literary artist of the generation to which I belong."[13] It was the 1933 biography by Mantz and Murry that really presented a mythic, sentimentalized Katherine. Murry certainly approved this version of her life, although Mantz did most of the research and writing and Murry's name amounted to a courteous addition. Nonetheless, Murry's introduction specifically assimilates Katherine to the English romantic tradition and the Keatsian sensibility, which he also ascribes to Blake and to Jesus. Art, he says, is "the utterance of Life through a completely submissive being," the result of "self-purgation, of self-refinement into that condition of crystal clarity for which Katherine

Mansfield unconsciously struggled and towards the end of her life consciously prayed." Leading a life of "sensations rather than thoughts," Katherine gained purity and "organic simplicity," and her art, though tiny in scope, possesses a serenity which eluded D. H. Lawrence, despite his apparently greater achievement.[14] Once articulated, this version of Katherine's significance became one of Murry's articles of faith. It is repeated and expanded in the posthumously published essay in *Katherine Mansfield and Other Literary Studies*. This second version stresses her likeness to Keats more emphatically, asserting that her life and work, like his, are a "single whole" and finding special significance in the letters of both. "There was no difference in kind between her casual and deliberate utterances; her art was not really distinct from her life; . . . every major advance in the art corresponds to a progression of some sort in the human being."[15]

Murry really had little to say about the stories themselves. His theory of her development, summarized in the essay published in *Katherine Mansfield and Other Literary Studies* and accepted and enlarged by later critics, is that her most significant writing was the body of stories about her New Zealand childhood. Murry states that her rebellion against New Zealand turned to recaptured innocence as she grieved over the death of her beloved younger brother, Leslie. The event provoked "profound self-knowledge," a "spiritual rebirth,"[16] through which she learned a new self-abeyance and reconciled herself to experience. The alternating joy and hopelessness of her stories are blended, in her best, into wisdom born of accepting the "compulsion of experience." Elsewhere, Murry agrees with other critics that her semisophisticated stories about London love affairs, such as "Bliss" and "Marriage à la Mode" are the weakest and notes that Katherine did not, as some claim, imitate Virginia Woolf but that she could not write well about Woolf's milieu.[17] The closest he comes to specific judgments of Katherine's work is naming "Prelude," "The Daughters of the Late Colonel," and "Je Ne Parle Pas Français" as significant stories. At another time he cited "The Doll's House" and "The Fly."[18]

It is interesting that while Murry used Keats and Katherine as his models of the artist, he avoided discussion of their work and focused instead on the personality behind the work. His real criterion is spiritual maturity. Katherine, like Keats, Blake, and Shakespeare, is interpreted by the pattern of her progress from conflict between idealism and disillusionment to a comprehensive vision of "beauty in all things." The doctrinal measurement works well enough in cases where Murry is sympathetic to the writer's pattern of development. In other cases, like Lawrence's, Murry's hostility to the artist's message engenders bad misjudgments about the art and so severely limits his critical range.

D. H. Lawrence

As Katherine Mansfield embodied the artistic sensibility for Murry, so D. H. Lawrence embodied the vatic. Murry's alternating pattern of resisting and succumbing to Lawrence was a cohering theme of his life. In his last work, *Love, Freedom and Society*, he was still striving to assimilate Lawrence's message to the uses of Christianity and civilization. Dealing with Lawrence as a spiritual explorer rather than as an artist, Murry denied him the status of artist-heroes like Shakespeare and Keats, whose consummate art emerged out of a reconciled vision. To the end, Murry contended that Lawrence was a major prophet of our time but a prophet of half-truths, because he upheld the flesh at the expense of the spirit and so never integrated his genius and his art. I explored Murry's dividedness toward Lawrence in chapter 1 in terms of its influence on the men's personal relationship; here I am concerned with tracing Murry's public attitudes and Lawrence's impact on his ideology.

Murry's writing about Lawrence was powerfully influenced by his complicated personal involvement, and he swerved between ardent praise and excoriation in synchrony with the private interaction. The inconstancy of his reactions means that his commentary is never wholly trustworthy although always interesting. Describing Lawrence in superlatives as "the starry genius of our time," "a major soul," and "a symbolic and prophetic man" even while he denounced his false doctrine, Murry took Lawrence absolutely seriously, and the intensity of his response made Lawrence important to others. Martin Green has shown how Murry's writing made Lawrence a "big figure" in British culture as he was not in American culture.[19] Until his role was preempted by F. R. Leavis in the mid-fifties, Murry was the chief purveyor of Lawrence to the English public.

When Lawrence and Murry met in 1912, *Sons and Lovers* was first being published, and their quick friendship owed something to Murry's candid admiration of the novel and his instant perception of Lawrence's genius. In later years Murry confirmed his first judgment by calling *Sons and Lovers* "the most remarkable novel produced by any living Englishman under forty" and declaring it the most artistically pure of Lawrence's novels.[20] By 1915, when *The Rainbow* was being published, Murry had recognized how deeply Lawrence's sexual doctrine conflicted with his own romantic religion of love, and *The Rainbow's* "promiscuity of flesh" repelled him. He "disliked it on instinct,"[21] as did Katherine Mansfield, who was sometimes interestingly prudish. (Katherine's sexual adventurism and wicked talk was "naughty," not "erotic.") Though neither

Murry nor Katherine openly confessed their distaste, Lawrence felt betrayed by their lack of enthusiasm; his bitterness deepened after Murry
rejected his second offering to the *Athenaeum*.

Murry's first review of Lawrence appeared in 1920, at a time when
Lawrence was sprinkling his letters with enraged references to the
"Murry-worms" and Murry was angry at Lawrence's gratuitous cruelty to
Katherine. The review of *The Lost Girl* reflected this dissonant background in the shrill tone and extreme language. Accusing Lawrence of
"corrupt mysticism and a falsifying theory," Murry said his characters
were like animals. "Mr. Lawrence would have us back in the slime from
which we rose."[22] His remarks about *Women in Love*, which he labeled a
"desperate abnormality,"[23] are similarly vitiated by his exaggerated repudiation of the sexual theme. Lawrence, he said, is confessing reverence for
"protozoic god"; his theory is "subhuman" and "bestial"; his characters
"writhe in a frenzy of sexual awareness of one another" and "grope in
their own slime to some final consummation."[24] These first reviews are not
totally undiscerning, since Murry clearly distinguishes between the conventional structure and unimaginativeness of *The Lost Girl* and the "power
of natural vision" of *Women in Love*, but the very aptness of his judgments
about other elements of the novels confirms one's sense that his animus
against *The Rainbow* and *Women in Love* is a product of psychological
defensiveness about the sex theory rather than a genuine inability to
comprehend Lawrence's achievement. His claim not to understand is
advanced with a spurious air of being allied with a standard of normality
which Lawrence is flouting. Lawrence may have "gone beyond us," but we
are "the sons of men, and we must be loyal to the light we have." This
half-admission of Lawrence's prophetic nature has the effect of paying
tribute to the power of the alternative vision while sidestepping the issues
it raises. It does, however, acknowledge the seriousness of Lawrence's
rebellion against civilization, something no other critic apprehended at
the time. In calling Lawrence "the outlaw of modern English literature,"
Murry was recognizing the profundity of his challenge.[25]

With his conversion to *Fantasia of the Unconscious* in 1923, Murry re-
tracted his former description of Lawrence as an "enemy of civilization"
and proclaimed him the essential prophet of the age, the "only writer with
something new to say."[26] It seemed to him that here, for the first time,
Lawrence was acknowledging the balance of spiritual and sensual elements of the unconscious as the ground of true identity. Moreover, he was
aligned with Lawrence in hostility to Freudian theory. He believed that
psychoanalysis produced a mechanistic revision of personality rather
than organic renewal. Lawrence, he rhapsodized, shows the way to a "new
order of being . . . and so succeeds where psychoanalysis has failed."[27]

This conversion to Lawrence promptly issued in the founding of the *Adelphi*. Murry not only serialized *Fantasia* but also defended Lawrence's religious views aginst readers' protests in two succeeding essays, arguing that Lawrence's religion was genuinely governed by a "passionate search" for a way of life in harmony with his deepest experience and that Lawrence was attacking not religion but faith (that is, belief in the divinity of Christ). He concluded that "faith must be offended if we are to have any real religion in this generation."[28]

For a few months Murry enthusiastically enacted the role of Lawrence's John the Baptist, which he had refused nearly a decade before, ignoring their historic divisions and persuading himself that Lawrence would take up his prepared role as an English Jesus, fighting for a revivified England from within the society. This was the model of action which Murry had chosen for himself as part of his spiritual renascence and from which he never thereafter deviated, although he advanced his creed under different banners at different times. Announcing in the first issue of the *Adelphi* that he merely stood in locum tenens for a better man, Murry entreated Lawrence to return to England from New Mexico.

Meanwhile, he effusively reviewed *Aaron's Rod* as "the most important thing that has happened to English literature since the war . . . , more important than *Ulysses*" and declared that this novel showed serenity, "the calm after the battle," a Lawrence freed from the "maelstrom of his sexual obsession."[29] This new novel confirmed Murry's belief that *Fantasia* marked the emergence of a new Lawrence with whom he could share a destiny. The grounds for his appreciation of *Aaron's Rod* are only implicit in the review. Later, in *Son of Woman*, Murry described Lawrence's struggle with his psychic insufficiencies as symbolic of his age and characterized *Aaron's Rod* as a great novel because in it Lawrence described his contradictory sexual yearnings—for a homosexual relationship to supplement an incomplete heterosexual relationship—and acknowledged the futility and self-delusion of that path.[30] No doubt Murry was also sentimentally affected by the obvious parallels between his friendship with Lawrence and the Lilly-Aaron relationship of the novel, parallels extending to a fictionalized recollection of Lawrence's nursing Murry through influenza.

Lawrence, the mood that engendered *Fantasia* and *Aaron's Rod* long spent, was unenthusiastic about the early issues of the *Adelphi* and distrustful of Murry's allegiance. When he did arrive in England late in 1923 he was in a sour state of mind, at odds with Frieda and jealous of the sexual undertone he discovered in her relations with Murry. He reacted against all that he saw. The effect of the trip was to strengthen his determination to stay away from England and build a community of followers in New

Mexico. He alarmed Murry by contending that England was doomed, played out, and that the only true function of the *Adelphi* was "to attack everything, everything; and explode in one blaze of denunciation."[31] Murry's nascent confidence in Lawrence's leadership withered.[32]

The developing tension between the two men which culminated in the famous betrayal scene at the Café Royal in 1924 most blatantly involved sexual rivalry. Thus Murry later claimed in his journal that he refused to go to New Mexico because "if I had gone with Lawrence and Frieda, Frieda would have become my woman."[33] Despite its element of supererogatory vanity, the statement is founded in a fantasy shared by Lawrence, who early in 1924 wrote a series of ill-tempered short stories satirizing Murry. The most unpleasant of the lot, "The Border Line," depicts a marriage between characters who are palpable images of Frieda and Murry and are being destroyed by the vengeful haunting of the ghost of the woman's first husband. The ghostly figure triumphantly reclaims her at the very moment when her present husband dies "wearing the sickly grin of a thief caught in the very act."[34] The other stories, "Smile," "Jimmy and the Desperate Woman," and "The Last Laugh," mock Murry's self-pretensions, his childish infatuations, his callow spirituality. In the last of the three he is killed by Pan.

Even without the sexual complication, one doubts that Murry would have gone to New Mexico. In the end, of the throng of admirers gathered at the Café Royal party only Dorothy Brett actually made the pilgrimage to Taos. To go with Lawrence meant commitment to a wholly foreign enterprise, which represented to Murry running away from the world, rejecting the hope *Fantasia* had engendered, abandoning manly purpose. "If the birth of the nucleus of a new society depended upon people having money enough to go to New Mexico, and a profession which would comfortably maintain them there, then it was hardly worth thinking about."[35] Fundamentally optimistic, as his successive embracing of new creeds shows, Murry never relinquished the hope of reforming civilization, and his utopian schemes always employed an English, rather than a cosmopolitan, model. He was always suspicious of prophets who retreated from their own land and criticized Schweitzer's retreat to Africa as he did Lawrence's effort to build a private commune in New Mexico. This attitude is responsible for a marked insularity in Murry's thought in comparison with Lawrence's, although it is accompanied by a corresponding depth of loyalty to an ideal England.

Deciding not to go to New Mexico, Murry also decided not to print Lawrence's diatribe against the "fear, impotence and malice of Englishmen contained in 'On Coming Home.' "[36] Criticism of Murry for his refusal to publish this essay in a magazine purportedly founded for Lawrence ignores Lawrence's decisive rejection of the *Adelphi* and

Murry's heightened determination to prove to Lawrence that it was worthwhile. Lawrence's embittered denunciation of his homeland was at odds with the magazine's philosophy, and Murry had chosen England and the *Adelphi* over Lawrence and New Mexico. Lawrence was surely inviting Murry to a test he expected him to fail in offering the essay at all. Had Murry gone with Lawrence then, there might actually have been a New Mexico community, and Lawrence's later career would inevitably have been quite different. Murry was masterful at getting things done and said himself that his job would have been to create the commune, that he would have done it. Frieda later confessed that Murry was the only one she was afraid of—for he would have made the commune happen—when she wanted only to be alone with Lawrence.

After this break both men were resigned to their failure to agree and to nourish one another. Lawrence adopted tones of remote well-wishing and reaffirmed his rejection of Murry's path in letters from New Mexico: "I feel it's a betrayal of myself, as a writer of what I mean, to go into the Adelphi, so I'd rather stay out."[37] Murry's marriage to Violet le Maistre, a replica of Katherine Mansfield, signaled his retreat from Lawrentian thought adventure to the safety of idealized love. Murry's reviews again treated Lawrence as a strange, inimitable genius, immune to the judgments of the kingdom of art. Although Murry was not alone in his puzzlement at that flawed novel *The Plumed Serpent*, his attitude toward the poems is telling in its insistence on dissociating Lawrence from all other men. Labeling him "a creature of another kind than ours, some lovely unknown animal with the gift of speech," Murry claims that Lawrence is endowed with a sixth sense which enables him to reenter the "womb of nature." But "Lawrence's wisdom seems to us absolute foolishness—a repudiation of the nature of things."[38]

A note that surfaces in this review suggests that Murry is telling Lawrence how to be saved from himself. Lawrence's hatred of love, Murry tells us, appears "perilously like a violation of his own nature," while his detestation of the intellectual consciousness dismisses the only hope we have of achieving harmony between the conscious personality and the unconscious. "Of such a solution Mr. Lawrence gives no hope; he has no use for the intellectual consciousness at all. That is well enough for him, with his sixth sense; but for the rest, who have only five, it is suicide—a suicide that we neither will nor *can* commit."[39] This revival of the old arguments continued in the review of *Lady Chatterley's Lover*, in which Murry deems Lawrence the "prophet of a half truth" and questions his thesis that "the only awareness we need is in the sexual mystery."[40]

Murry's loyalty was not to the doctrine of *Lady Chatterley*, but to *Fantasia*, from which he appropriated ideas in 1929 for an essay on "Modern Marriage." The piece asserts the importance of the sexual relation and blames the pervasive problems of modern marriage on the Christian doctrine of original sin, which perverts sexual feeling into morbid maternal possessiveness of the son in the woman and into a false quest for a reflection of the mother in the man.[41]

Fantasia, Murry insisted, acknowledged the truth denied in Lawrence's subsequent work, that psychic health depended on the harmony of body and soul. So in *God* Murry again attacked Lawrence for leaving out the spiritual and argued that Lawrence lacked self-knowledge. He needed to confront Jesus, the prototypal explorer of spiritual identity, in order to understand himself. Lawrence "exalts the body because he's afraid of the nature of the soul."[42]

Shortly after these words were written, Murry heard that Lawrence was seriously ill and wrote a reconciling letter, but Lawrence put off the suggested visit: "It is no good our meeting—even when we are immortal spirits we shall dwell in different Hades. Why not accept it."[43] These were Lawrence's last words to Murry; he died less than a year later. Murry, hurrying to Vence to pay his last respects to Lawrence, found himself having his long-deferred affair with Frieda. They were seriously attracted to one another, but of course Murry had left a tubercular wife and two small children in England, and he returned to his responsibilities while Frieda chose Angelo Ravagli and ultimately went back to Taos. They saw each other only once in the succeeding years, when Frieda came to England to do battle with Lawrence's sisters over the will; by then Murry was married to his ill-chosen Frieda surrogate, Betty. They ceased even to write for some years, until the fifties, when Murry instigated a nostalgic correspondence exploring the meaning of their love affair and probing the reasons for his arguments with Lawrence.

Despite its brevity, Murry's affair with Frieda accounts for the tone of *Son of Woman*. On the one hand, Lawrence's death freed him to say what he could not say while Lawrence lived; on the other, Murry was able to revolutionize his own life, to revise his own sexual being in response to Lawrence as he could not have done in the context of a living rivalry. Frieda yielded to him the secret of Lawrence's impotence, which Murry made the focus of *Son of Woman*. She was the "one living soul" whom Murry counted on to understand the necessity of his betrayal,[44] although Frieda was, in fact, so distressed by the book that she burned it and sent the ashes to Murry.[45]

Immediately after the affair Murry began to publish a series of reminiscences of Lawrence in the *Adelphi*, setting down the record of their turbulent friendship and portraying Lawrence's warmth and vitality and contrariness. These memoirs were harmless enough, although they are infected with the vice of overexplaining his own motives which later marred Murry's autobiography, *Between Two Worlds*. But Murry had to lay

Lawrence to rest, and that meant making up his mind about him in print. He needed to explore Lawrence's message. *Son of Woman*, published in 1931, is neither biography nor literary criticism but an effort to place Lawrence's prophecy, and to explain him genetically, by tracing the path of his thought formation.

Murry's thesis is that Lawrence was a spiritual-mental being who vainly strove for sensuality, falsifying his doctrine by exalting an animality he didn't feel. Because Lawrence was Oedipal-fixated, he was psychically and physically incapable of gaining the liberation through sex he proclaimed. By trying to disclaim his true nature, he denied his spiritual self and became a false prophet instead of the hero of humanity he might have been. Only in the halcyon interlude of *Fantasia* did Lawrence acknowledge that true unconsciousness is gained through the integration of flesh and spirit. Before and after he denied his own tenderness and extolled the dark gods. Jesus-haunted in his closing years, Lawrence still fought off the Christian model, mistaking the false idealism that overlay Jesus' message for the essence, refusing to believe that love of mankind could be genuine. Lawrence's tactic toward Jesus was to invalidate his spiritual triumph through death by creating a Jesus made whole by a sexual consummation after death. *The Man Who Died* and *The Escaped Cock* show that Lawrence was seeking a miracle, a fleshly resurrection, dreaming of a sexual consummation he could not find in life. It is, Murry says, a "childish" fantasy.

Murry voices these "revelations" in the explicit guise of Judas (Judas seen as the essential disciple who betrays his master into true self-revelation) and so portrays his "betrayal" as a belated act of courage, that which he failed to do for Lawrence during his life. "I have betrayed you. . . . This 'betrayal' was the one thing you lacked, the one thing I had to give, that you might shine forth among men as the thing of wonder that you were."[46] The wondrous qualities he finds in Lawrence—his extraordinary sensitivity, his life adventure, his symbolic embodiment of the conflict between the animal and the spiritual—are far less emphatic in *Son of Woman*, than is Lawrence's self-deception, his posturing to himself "as a bloody and brutal savage, a born hunter, a perfect male, a man of 'power,' " and the significance Murry finally names is negative. Lawrence is a "paradigm of disintegration,"[47] a false prophet who shows the way not to be followed, a man who could have changed the path of human destiny but lacked the strength to suffer to the end of self-knowledge and so fails us and himself. It is not a generous portrait.

There is, of course, more to *Son of Woman* than a spiteful denigration of Lawrence's sexual nature. Even when he is bolstering a wrongheaded verdict about a novel, Murry is perspicacious about specifics, and of course the essentials of Murry's analysis of Lawrence's psychology have stood. It is an important book about Lawrence but by no means a wise or balanced one. Murry was far too enmeshed with him to bring any objectivity to bear.

Putting aside the undertones of malice which provoked T. S. Eliot's remark that "the victim and the sacrificial knife are perfectly adapted to each other,"[48] one doesn't doubt that Murry did truly regard himself as an essential revealer and that he saw Lawrence as a genius, a man who became "an object of spiritual knowledge for his fellow-men."[49] But the approach diminishes Lawrence by divorcing him from his art. By concentrating on the most strident doctrinal elements of the novels, Murry disregards major significances. Reading Son of Woman, we receive no hint of the beauty and richness of Lawrence's sensory imagination. Lawrence's authenticity is tied to a tentative, exploratory reading of life; in his world the verities of a moment are continually altered by experience; so Murry battles Lawrentian doctrine which was never proffered as fixed truth and ends by attacking artifacts of his own construction.

It is of this interpretative method that F. R. Leavis complains in relation to Women in Love. Like Murry, Leavis dislikes the "Excurse" chapter of that novel. The difference is that Murry makes the "suave loins of darkness" passage the center of Lawrence's message, while Leavis regards it as a faltering of the major vision.[50] The most telling remark on Murry's evasion of Lawrence's artistic power was made by E. M. Forster, who noted that Murry complains when Lawrence's imagination puts a spell upon him, whereas "most of us are thankful when it does."[51]

Indeed, Murry's specious justifications for disregarding Lawrence's art are very revealing. He claims that "the necessary conditions of great 'art' are lacking in our age" because we don't have an organic society and the artist cannot take "elemental things for granted." Lawrence recognized this, Murry says, and "at bottom he was not interested in art." His dismissal of Lawrence's novelistic talent is astonishingly casual: "The 'pure passionate experience' of which he speaks in his preface does not include that passionate exercise of the disinterested imagination in the creation of human characters which is probably the perfection of the art of literature. It is not that Lawrence was incapable of it; though I do not think his capacities were very great. Certainly, he seldom cared to make use of them."[52] But if Lawrence deliberately gave up the pretense of being an artist and made the novel express his own thought adventures and his poems immediate experience, his achievement makes mere formally perfect and concentrated art seem "frigid and futile," for he was a "major soul" who could not be content with the "irremediably minor" art of his day. Although these remarks offer Lawrence some special status, they mark a refusal to test him against major literary traditions. Murry's definition of twentieth-century art as minor is arbitrary, and formal perfection was never a criterion he imposed on Keats, Blake, or Shakespeare. It was Leavis who finally awarded Lawrence the status of a major novelist, and of his treatment Murry complained that making Lawrence into a classic, "as it were the great successor of George Eliot," meant putting him on the shelf. "Lorenzo is an *experience*, not a classic."[53] One must put Murry's equivocation on this issue down to the terrible potency of his feelings for Lawrence, which accounts for his reluctance to see him primarily as a writer of books, and, as Martin Green suggests, to his desire to avoid confronting Lawrence in "areas where Murry took himself with professional seriousness."[54]

Son of Woman provoked deep hostility and charges of betrayal from Lawrence's admirers, and reviewers spoke of its revengefulness and "ghoulish dexterity." Aldous Huxley pithily called it an exercise in "destructive hagiography."[55] As Rees points out, "a book must have a good deal of truth in it to provoke that sort of reaction,"[56] but in fact the initial effect of Murry's book was to provide Lawrence's enemies with ammunition. The *New York Times* reviewer, for instance, judged Lawrence to be neither poet nor novelist and suggested dismissing the "vagaries of a mind so evidently distorted."[57] The most formidable detractor was T. S. Eliot, who praised *Son of Woman* as a "brilliant book," Murry's best, applauded the accuracy and justice of his quotations, and then used Murry's formulations to find in Lawrence the record of "spiritual pride, nourished by ignorance." Although Eliot did concede that Lawrence was a "great tragic figure," he condemned the impurity of his art and diagnosed his "relapse into pride and hatred" as the result of his rejection of Christian discipline and asceticism. "The false prophet kills the true artist," Eliot concludes; we feel "poisoned by the atmosphere of his world and quit it with relief."[58]

Despite the myopia of Murry's treatment, *Son of Woman* did finally enhance, rather than diminish, Lawrence's reputation; its power is attested to by the numbers of subsequent critics who have been constrained to argue with it. The storm of protest it aroused bewildered Murry, who had characteristically ignored the possible effects of baring Lawrence's soul. His combative instincts were finally aroused when Catherine Carswell published a memoir of Lawrence in which Murry figured as major villain. He succeeded in having *The Savage Pilgrimage* withdrawn from publication on the grounds that it slandered him and countered Carswell by publishing his own series of reminiscences from the *Adelphi*, accompanied by his published reviews of Lawrence and point-by-point refutations of her charges. *Reminiscences of D. H. Lawrence* thus added to the storm raised by *Son of Woman*, and most spectators found the whole affair distasteful; "a depressing example of the depths to which literary controversy can sink when personal animosities are so extensively involved," one reviewer commented.[59]

However, writing *Son of Woman* had been, as Murry claimed, an act of self-liberation, and his subsequent writing about Lawrence is substantially less defensive, more certain and balanced. This change of tone is first evident in the series of articles "On Marriage" written for the *Wanderer*, a little journal for private subscription which Murry published in 1933-34. Lawrence was right in seeing the man-woman conflict as the major issue of our time, he says, because the old order of male authority is atavistic, and new organic bonds between men and women must provide the foundation for a new social order. Lawrence was the great prophet of marriage, and his own marriage struggle was symbolically significant, although he never personally achieved the state of absolved manhood he conceived of. Since Murry was in the throes of socialist enthusiasms at this time, he criticizes Lawrence for finding no "point of fusion between the revolutionized individual and the social process" and suggests that Lawrence was defeated in his marriage struggle because his quest deteriorated into a corrupt "freedom to be himself." The creative power of disinterested male action was missing. His relation with his wife became a battle of self-assertion, without the religious/spiritual dimension which leads to a bond beyond ego.[60]

Despite the tacit suggestion that Murry, as a revolutionary socialist, has found the point of fusion Lawrence missed, the articles are more searching than any of his previous commentary. They contain a valuable interpretation of the extraordinary meaning of Lawrence's marriage for his work and a penetrating description of Lawrence and Frieda's struggle, recognizing Frieda's emancipation, her experience of "male authority in disintegration," her dismissal of the "man's world" except in so far as it tended toward "the increase of the female," against which Lawrence could pose only "his self-evident daimon, his prophetic genius." "On Marriage" is evidence of Murry's real grasp of Lawrence's erotic theory and of an authentic conversion, if not a capitulation. Lawrence is no longer the prophet of the negative way, but a man of genius who "sticks fiery off indeed" [*sic*] from the other writers of his time, one who points to the paths, if he could not follow them himself.[61] Murry has transformed himself from the disciple of necessary betrayal to the apostle of completion, who sees his life's task as supplying what was lacking so that Lawrence could be brought to serve ordinary life.

Murry returned to the Lawrence theme in *Adam and Eve* some ten years later. By this time his own Lawrentian marriage battle had painfully ended, and he had had his first taste of real sexual happiness with Mary Gamble. His private felicity allowed him to confront Lawrence with increased assurance. The arguments are familiar: the key to a regenerated society is regenerated marriage, marriage built on egoless love compounded of the physical and the spiritual, but the propositions carry the certainty of felt experience. His sexual theory acknowledges the corruption of purely spiritual, idealized love and so represents an accommodation to Lawrence, an admission that he was right about Katherine and

Violet. But Murry's experience of Betty has validated his disbelief in Lawrence's way ("I discovered on my pulses he was wrong")[62] and accounts for the confidence in his own solution.

The most interesting ideas of *Adam and Eve* arise from Murry's effort to relate his grapplings with Lawrence to a theory of civilization by taking Lawrence and Aldous Huxley as representatives of the divisions forced by historical Christianity:

> Both were driven to an individual and personal mysticism; Lawrence to a mysticism of the flesh, Huxley to a mysticism of the spirit. These mysticisms . . . were complementary, but irreconcilable, as it were thesis and antithesis, of which the synthesis was adumbrated only by Lawrence. The emergence of this thesis and antithesis . . . was the re-emergence after four centuries of a specious solution by Protestantism, of the fundamental conflict between the religious-ascetic and the secular-sexual which had divided historical Christianity from the time it became the religion of a civilization.[63]

The synthesis adumbrated by Lawrence is, of course, the doctrine of *Fantasia*, which Murry explicated and supplemented. The synthesis Murry arrives at is a composite of the revelations of Jesus (who represents the possibility of selfless love but gives no direction about the man-woman relationship) and the revelations of Lawrence (who showed that the new Adam and the new Eve were prerequisite to a new society). Lawrence went wrong, Murry says, in seeing an opposition of the flesh and the spirit; the real opposition is between the spirit and the self. The tenderness of genuine human love schools spirituality and enables us to follow the Jesus pattern of submission to crucial experience. This book, then, insists that Lawrence's life values are commensurate with the Christian love ethic, although Lawrence had insisted that they were not.

Murry was thinking about Lawrence right up to the end of his life. His last work, *Love, Freedom and Society*, adds little to his prior interpretation, since it still ruminates on Lawrence's relationship to Christianity and strives to incorporate him with the Christian humanist tradition, but the perspective is broader. Beginning with *Adam and Eve*, Murry tried to place Lawrence historically and contextually. In an essay published while he was writing *Love, Freedom and Society*, Murry compared Lawrence and Rousseau, remarking the affinity of attitudes toward the primitive, their like enmity toward the pure intellect, their wish to promote a "renascence of the religious sense based on pure feeling." Rousseau marked the beginning of the age of Romanticism; Lawrence marks its end, he suggested. "As Rousseau was the prophet of democracy to be, Lawrence is the prophet of its doom."[64] These abbreviated remarks are preliminary to the more sustained effort of *Love, Freedom and Society* to show Lawrence in relationship to significant contemporaries—Albert Schweitzer and T. S. Eliot.

There is, as Murry says, an "obvious congruity" in confronting Lawrence, the last romantic, with Eliot, the definitive twentieth-century classicist. The relationship to Schweitzer is more obscure, and the juxtaposition reflects Murry's desire to deal with Schweitzer more than it demonstrates intrinsic parallels between the two careers. He finds Lawrence and Schweitzer significant religious figures who rejected traditional Christianity, foresaw the end of Western civilization, and proclaimed the opening of new modes of love to be the salvation of humanity. Schweitzer, the rationalist, and Lawrence, the irrationalist, both abandoned their native societies and succumbed to historical pessimism and radical skepticism about human progress. They became, therefore, inveterate individualists. Their ethical modes depended upon separation from society, an isolationism which Murry criticized in both.[65] In an earlier book, *The Challenge of Schweitzer*, Murry had argued that a meaningful ethical philosophy must be capable of operating within society, and that Schweitzer's absolutistic doctrine of "reverence for life" is not serviceable, since it depends upon people's following him outside civilization. Murry's centering faith in the ethical progress of mankind is expressed as belief in the evolution of democratic society by "explicit thought and by the trial and error of social and political adjustment, towards a future in which justice is ever more closely permeated by love."[66]

Murry had, of course, criticized Lawrence's despair of democracy in similar terms. In this work he finds both Lawrence and Schweitzer fragmented by the cleavage between feeling and thought and resurrects Keats as the standard of wholeness and ethical maturity. Since his use of Keats rests on the solitary maxim that suffering schools "an intelligence to make a soul," it is a manifestly shaky foundation for the meaning Murry heaps on it, and we have the sense that he makes Keats express his own views to lend them greater weight against the eminence of Lawrence and Schweitzer.

His treatment of Lawrence-Eliot is far more productive, in part because his comparison is made through an analysis of *St. Mawr* and *The Cocktail Party.* He argues that Lou of *St. Mawr* and Celia of *The Cocktail Party* are women in a similar spiritual condition, each with a vision of salvation. The oppositeness of their visions reveals the antithetical philosophies of their authors. Lawrence's Lou cherishes an image of a man with whom she could find a vital love relation, while Eliot's Celia carries no hope of human love. Only Christ can offer salvation. The Lawrentian vision of regenerated sexuality is simply not available to Eliot. The discussion elucidates the ways in which Lawrence and Eliot "repudiate" each other and ends with Murry's explicit endorsement of Lawrence. "I am profoundly with Lawrence rather than Eliot."[67]

We can summarize Murry's work on Lawrence by saying that up to and through *Son of Woman* his extravagant tributes carried an undertone of fascinated hostility. Afterward that note disappears, replaced by a vision of Lawrence as a cathartic hero, a purifier, an annihilator, against whom Murry stands as an "ordinary" man. He once called himself "abnormally normal"[68] and represented himself as offering a standard of sanity against the excesses of genius.

Several commentators have attempted to categorize the difference between Murry and Lawrence which accounts for their valuableness to one another. Beer, pointing to Murry's links with an earlier generation of intellectuals, shows how Murry represented ideas which Lawrence fought to discard. He describes them as postmental and premental, respectively, viewing the "long contention between the autonomic nervousness of Lawrence and the sympathetic nervousness of Murry" as a paradigm of the "major split within the psyche of European man."[69] Murry had used this sort of terminology to describe his early disputes with Lawrence, but in his later phase, of course, he claimed to be representing integration. Griffin's analysis traces the pattern of mutual attraction and repulsion in the terms set forth in Lawrence's play *David*. He identifies Murry with Jonathan, the sympathetic friend who cannot relinquish the old order, even for love of David, and Lawrence with the David figure, who is compelled to fulfill the prophecy and pass beyond the old dispensation.[70] This approach has the virtue of moving beyond the starker Rupert-Gerald opposition of *Women in Love* to suggest what Lawrence made of Murry later on. Significantly, however, Murry did not recognize himself in either Gerald or Jonathan.

Against this background, F. R. Leavis's approach to Lawrence, which involved displacing Murry as primary interpreter, is particularly interesting, for Leavis made Lawrence an English artist, embodying national standards of sanity and normalcy. He accused Murry of distorting Lawrence by stressing his vatic qualities and eccentric doctrinal elements. Of course, Leavis was also annoyed by Murry's impressionistic mode of criticism and castigated the lack of critical sensibility in *Son of Woman* as a "defect of intelligence."[71] But the point I am making here is that Leavis located in Lawrence the "English" values which Murry identified with himself and defended against Lawrentian radicalism. Murry and Leavis each accused the other of not understanding Lawrence. Murry claimed that Leavis looked at Lawrence without his daimon, and Leavis explicitly refused the Murryian version by declaring that Lawrence's greatest attribute is a "transcendent intelligence," that his intelligence worked as the "servant of the whole integrated psyche," that there is "no profound emotional disorder" in him.[72] Elsewhere, Leavis objects to Harry Moore's acceptance of Katherine Mansfield's account of Lawrence's cruel letter ("stewing in your consumption") and insists that the story is certainly false. His genius, Leavis says, "manifested itself in sympathetic insight and an accompanying diagnostic intelligence, and cruelty was not in him."[73] One can imagine the spleen Murry would have vented in response to these remarks. He was, however, dead when the essay was published.

If we consider that Leavis saw Lawrence's best as *Women in Love* and that Murry saw it as *Fantasia of the Unconscious*, we must grant that Leavis is right, but his picture of Lawrence is won by excluding the fanatic and discordant elements which were for Murry major truths, part of the fabric of his personal experience with Lawrence. Leavis's accusation that Murry employs biographical reductionism and misses the impersonal themes in Lawrence is just. The equivalent truth is that Murry's aim was to make Lawrence a living force capable of acting on other lives as he had acted on Murry's—and that Murry in some measure succeeded.

T. S. Eliot

At least one observer has called the debate between John Middleton Murry and T. S. Eliot, which began in 1923 and lasted until Murry's death, "the most serious intellectual controversy in England during that period."[74] If the contest does warrant that claim, it never gained the attention it merited, probably because Eliot's greater prestige fostered the assumption that all the plaudits fell to him and none to Murry. Moreover, the classicist/romanticist labels Eliot and Murry applied to themselves in the twenties have obscured the wider issues both men insistently explored. Their center of concern was identical: the necessity of spiritually replenishing twentieth-century society. Eliot, the Anglican convert, argued that a renascence could occur within existing institutional frameworks via the truths of Christian dogma; Murry, the agnostic mystic, endorsed individual spiritual questing and rebellion against fossilized institutions, making Jesus into the same type of spiritual explorer as Keats, Blake, and Shakespeare. On Murry's side the divergence was sharpest on the treatment of human love. When, at the end of his career, he defined himself as antipodal to both D. H. Lawrence and T. S. Eliot, his distinction was based on his antipathy to Eliot's asceticism and his feeling that Lawrence wrongly excluded the spiritual. Eliot objected to Murry's unregenerate romanticism, the undisciplined "inner voice" which led him on so many unpredictable pilgrimages, and to his lack of critical stringency.

However, one is struck by the synchronous pattern of their opposition, the way in which Murry and Eliot repeatedly concurred on the diagnosis and differed on the cure. Murry's parents attended a Unitarian chapel and Eliot's family were New England Brahmins whose Unitarianism inspired their liberal causes and social activism. Both Murry and Eliot rejected that kind of liberalism, Murry because of its emotional austerity, Eliot because of its dismissal of Christian dogma. Thus, responding to Murry's essay on "Christ and Christianity," Eliot wrote: "It seems to me that one must either ignore the Church, or reform it from within, or transcend it—but never attack it. . . . You see I happened to be brought up in the most 'liberal' of Christian creeds—Unitarianism: I may therefore be excused for seeing the dangers of what you propose, more clearly than I see the vices of what you attack. If one discards dogma, it should be for a more celestial garment, not for nakedness."[75] The two men's rejection of the same creed for opposite reasons is typical of the kinds of polarities they established. Both endorsed Shakespeare and rejected Milton, but Eliot objected to Miltonic technique and craftsmanship, Murry to the Miltonic temperament (that is, his "inhumanness" versus Shakespearean spontaneity).

Their social criticism displays some remarkable similarities. Both Eliot and Murry believed twentieth-century machine civilization to be a decayed culture which threatens all humane values. Both located the organic, integrated society in the peasant culture of medieval Christianity, where life was naturally tied to the soil and where class hierarchies protected man's spiritual relation to nature. Eliot's response was to affirm Christianity as a mode of establishing value, Murry's to endorse, for a time, revolutionary socialism, and later, to establish a community farm as an experiment in true agrarianism. At the time he wrote *The Free Society*, after World War II, he briefly espoused a social theory of which Eliot approved.

Murry functioned as the heretical outsider, while Eliot identified himself with orthodox institutions; Eliot espoused integration through the doctrinal truths of Christianity against Murry's radical individualism, his definition of truth as an ongoing intuiting through experience. Finally, Murry upheld sexual values and marriage as an article of faith and criticized the sterility of Eliot's doctrine of Christian renunciation. Temperamentally the men were opposites: Murry, the enthusiast, displayed his personality as part of his thought, in contrast with Eliot's classical reserve, his personal austerity and elusiveness.

Their personal relationship was always warm, if never intimate. (Eliot always resisted intimacy.) They took one another very seriously and repeatedly helped one another. In the beginning Murry was able to offer more assistance to Eliot. Most of the essays in *The Sacred Wood* first appeared in the *Athenaeum*. He kindly reviewed *Ara Voc Prec*, and Eliot's review of *Cinammon and Angelica* provoked his first remarks on the condition of contemporary drama. (Eliot described Murry's play as a "Promethean effort to revitalize the afflicted verse drama, though not an entirely successful one.")[76] The mutual regard of the early relationship is documented by Eliot's writing Murry, "You must realise that it has been a great event to me to know you, but you do not know yet the full meaning of the phrase as I write it,"[77] and Murry's writing Katherine that Eliot was "the only critic of literature I can think anything of."[78]

Virginia Woolf, who was piqued by Murry's low rating of her work, claims that Eliot shared her view of Murry's "badness." She records a conversation with Eliot about Murry's failings which concludes: "I think indeed his opinion is black at all points; & he knows him and his methods better than we do. . . . I think its true that Eliot had wished us to open our eyes about Murry. He certainly agreed to all criticisms, & made me feel that he could stress them & add facts if he chose."[79] Her remarks ring false when one hears Eliot welcoming Murry's offer of support on the beginning of the *Criterion*, writing: "Your support will certainly be of the greatest value. . . . I think I am safe in believing that you will be in sympathy with the paper's aims."[80] Eliot's confidence in Murry's agreement with the *Criterion*'s classicism was misplaced, but not in his personal sympathy. The next year, hearing of Vivien Eliot's illness, Murry wrote affectionately:

> My dear Tom,
>   I have been looking for news from you these last few days most anxiously. No news worries me. Will you send me a wire: Is there *anything* I can do that will help?
>   Dear old boy, I don't know what to say to you. I never do. But in my way believe me I love you—I think of you and feel for you continually. And there is this queer feeling that you and Vivien and I are bound together somehow.
>   John[81]

In September, Murry took Vivien to Freiburg, Germany, for medical treatment. He continued to sponsor Eliot professionally, too, using his influence to gain him an invitation to give the Clark Lectures of 1924—this after their romanticism/classicism debate was well under way and the *Criterion* and the *Adelphi* had established their ideological rivalry.

Eliot responded in kind. In 1927, when Murry told him that he needed money, Eliot asked Marianne Moore, then editor of the *Dial*, to solicit some reviewing from Murry, adding "it would in fact be a personal favor to myself."[82] The "abyss," which Murry finally acknowledged between their ideas after his essay "Towards a Synthesis" failed to resolve their debate never affected their personal cordiality, and their parallel activities as editors and literary and cultural critics meant that their paths frequently crossed. So in the thirties both were members of that group of religious and social thinkers called "the Moot"; both spoke at the Malvern Conference called by the archbishop of York, where Murry denounced the Anglican establishment. ("The church fails in leadership, because it shows no sign of having known despair; no evidence of having been *terrified* by its own impotence.")[83]

As Murry retreated further from the centers of influence, his personal contacts with Eliot were more sporadic, but their fitful correspondence picked up in the fifties, both men expressing a desire to renew the old friendship, and after their last meeting in November 1956, four months before Murry died, Murry recorded in his journal that "it was as it used to be between us 35 years ago," while Eliot recalled that visit as "particularly happy."[84]

The private amiability behind Murry's and Eliot's ideological postures places their debate in a decorous intellectual framework as a civilized, Apollonian exchange which never encroached on the self of either man. Murry's controversies with Lawrence were always more crucially impassioned because they involved a radical shift within the person, a giving over to other values. That is why Murry's tone toward Lawrence is often defensive and even hysterical.

But it is time to trace the explicit terms of Murry's and Eliot's public stances toward one another. As I showed earlier, Murry positively accepted Eliot's influence during the *Athenaeum* period, employing an Eliotic critical mode in *The Problem of Style*, even trying a feeble version of Eliot's "Prufrock" style in a few poems. Moreover, Murry had a sense of kinship based upon Eliot's similar distance from Bloomsbury, a feeling that Eliot "lived in the same kind of isolation."[85] Notably, the period when Murry most approved of Eliot coincided with the interval of greatest alienation from Lawrence. The early sense of affinity with Eliot was disturbed by Murry's dismay at the "nihilism" of *The Waste Land* and "The Hollow Men," by Eliot's defense of tradition and classicism, and by his Anglican conversion.

Murry commented on *The Waste Land* in a 1926 essay, "The Classical Revival," at a stage in the classicism-romanticism debate, long after the poem had begun to revolutionize the direction of modern poetry.[86] Murry's attack, which is joined to a negative appraisal of Virginia Woolf's *Jacob's Room*, is really a protest against the "universal skepticism" of both works. Murry was unwilling to admit that the only emotion possible to the

modern world was the "cry of grinding and empty desolation" of *The
Waste Land*, although he was also critical of the "prodigious intellectual
subtlety" employed to produce the effect of a "final futility." His aesthetic
judgment, that *The Waste Land*, is "overintellectualized," lacks "spontaneity," is "over-ridden with calculated subtleties," and "fails to produce any
unity of impression," is not unreasonable, and he recognized the seriousness and impressiveness of the work, but his discomfiture with its nihilistic
tone blinded him to the poem's impact. "Fifty, ten years hence, no one will
take the trouble (no small one) to read either of these works, unless there
should be some revolutionary happening in their authors—some liberation into a real spontaneity—which will cause these records of their
former struggles in the wilderness to be studied with the sympathy and
curiosity which a contemporary now bestows upon them."[87]

Woolf and Eliot, Murry acknowledges, are endeavoring to create something "adequate to the welter of dissatisfaction and desires which has
invaded the sensitive mind during and since the war"; they are expressing
the "modern consciousness—a complex state of mind, a spiritual atmosphere which exists now, and has never existed before."[88] But Murry could
not endorse a literature without affirmation and believed that *The Waste
Land* marked a transitory state of mind, a divorce between Eliot's understanding and his being which issued in a contradiction between his poetry
and his thought. To Murry, who admitted no separate standards for art
and life, the division within the man defined the incomplete, strained,
blasphemous quality of the art, its "unconscious cynicism," and marked
Eliot as an "unregenerate and incomplete romantic . . . If he believed his
classical principles, he wouldn't have published his poetry. . . . For classicism, of the fundamental kind which Mr. Eliot professes, imposes moral
obligations. It is not something to which one can give intellectual assent
and ethical repudiation."[89]

If Eliot was to remain a classicist, he would have to submit himself to an
ordered system of thought, and the sort of system Eliot was attracted to,
Murry rightly adduced, was not that of the Augustinians but of the
Catholic tradition. Murry presciently argued that because Eliot "is in a
Godless condition and suffers from it," he would have to make a choice to
free himself from the dilemma. "The one more obviously indicated is that
he should make a blind act of faith and join the Catholic church." But, he
continues, the Catholic solution is not available to the twentieth century:
"The condition of mind of Dante and Milton has been lost." Therefore, "it
is not possible for a man so sensitive and scrupulous as Mr. Eliot to reach a
belief in God by the grand old ways."[90] The thrust of Murry's argument is
to convince Eliot to renounce his classical principles, acknowledge his
romantic impulses, and so free himself for spontaneous exploration with-

out binding himself to the external spiritual authority implicit in classical tradition.

When Eliot made his Anglican conversion five years later, Murry was disappointed. "Mr. Eliot has made his decision, and I am sorry that it was what it was. With very few of my contemporaries have I felt myself, at one crucial moment or another, more deeply in sympathy than with Mr. Eliot; so that it had seemed to me that we had the same realisations, but that by some trick of destiny or idiosyncrasy, the effect of these realisations upon us was antipodal."[91] Eliot's embrace of institutional Christianity is a significant emblem of the intellectual chasm separating him from Murry, who reflected that he, Lawrence, and Katherine Mansfield shared an order of moral concern in which Eliot did not participate: "None of us was, or ever could have become, capable of accepting dogmatic Christianity as Eliot did."[92] It is typical, too, of the two men's divergence on social theory. Eliot's stance was preservational and quietist, a holding action against the forces of machine culture; Murry continually investigated modes of revolt against industrial forces and engaged in acts of enthusiastic commitment to alternative social models, organizing people in experimental societies at the Adelphi Center and later at the community farm, while Eliot, through his publishing and editorial activities, aligned himself with the centers of influence and power.

The issue of institutionalization versus allegiance to individual exploration is the core of the classicism-romanticism debate as well. The controversy was set off by a 1923 essay in the *Adelphi*, "On Romanticism," in which Murry declared that "in England there never has been any classicism worth talking about. . . . All our classics are romantic." Connecting the strength of the English romantic tradition to Protestantism ("in religious terms, the English tradition is that the man who truly interrogates himself will ultimately hear the voice of God, in terms of literary criticism, that the writer achieves impersonality through personality"), Murry described Catholicism and classicism as concurring in the "principle of unquestioned spiritual authority outside the individual" and ends by praising the romantic mode. "Romanticism is the discovery and discrimination of inner reality. . . . Therefore, it is not libertarian or egalitarian. . . . it demands a complete surrender . . . to achieved completeness in others."[93]

Eliot attacked these precepts in "The Function of Criticism" in the *Criterion*. The essay characterized Murry's "inner voice" as "whiggery" and acerbically established opposing meanings for the romanticist-classicist labels. "The romantic is deficient or undeveloped in his ability to distinguish between fact and fancy, whereas the classicist, or adult mind, is thoroughly realist—without illusions, without day dreams, without hope, without bitterness, and without an abundant resignation." Classicists, Eliot said, "believe that men cannot get on without giving an allegiance to something outside themselves."[94]

In his answer, "More about Romanticism," Murry reasserted the tenets of his earlier essay, defining romanticism as an ethical attempt

> to solve the problem of conduct by an exploration of the internal world. If this exploration is complete it will result in an immediate knowledge of what I may and may not do. The implication of the certainty of this knowledge is that at some point in this non-intellectual exploration of the self a contact is established between the finite soul and the infinite soul of which it is a manifestation. . . . the more resolute romantic accepts the reality of the external universe and finds the cause of its contradiction with the internal world . . . in a limitation of the human consciousness. He believes that the human consciousness has not yet reached the point in its own development where it is capable of apprehending reality.[95]

That rejoinder added little to Murry's side, and he tried to bolster his position with a third essay, "Romanticism and the Tradition," which Eliot published in the *Criterion*. Exploring the relation between religion and literature more fully, Murry called romanticism "something that happened to the European soul after the Renaissance" and asserted that the foundation of the modern consciousness is the willingness of the individual to "take his stand apart and alone, without the support of any authority."[96] The last essay provoked some response from *Criterion* readers, but Eliot himself did not pursue the point. However, Vivien Eliot, under the initials "F. M.," ridiculed Murry for using the word "golly" ("revealing his sensitiveness to the living soul of the language") and scornfully reviewed his last novel, *The Voyage*. "One has the sensation of having strayed into a little company composed of neurasthenics and imbeciles, who circle painfully around their complexes and neuroses weaving a tangled web from which there is no escape but physical or mental suicide."[97]

There the matter rested for several years until Murry reignited it with a 1927 essay, "Towards a Synthesis," published in the *Criterion* and intended to effect a resolution, rather than a renewal, of the debate. Murry's hope for an accommodation with Eliot involved a rather strained redefinition of terms. He argued that "Classicism may be applied to that moment of the soul life in which the movement is towards cognition; romanticism to that moment in which the movement is towards a revivification of the conceptual hierarchy by immediate and concrete experience. Classicism and Romanticism, in this sense, are moments, constantly recurring in the full soul life of the complete man." But Murry's definition rigorously excluded the possibility of founding a "new classicism" on Thomistic epistemology, of returning to the pattern of pre-Renaissance thought, for "the important elements of educated experience are no longer intrinsically the same." The new synthesis arises from resolving the antinomy between intuition and intelligence; it cannot arise from the old opposition of faith and reason. Instead, Murry sought to transcend the Classicism/Romanticism issue by subsuming the terms "intuition" and "intelligence" in a new concept of reason as the product of both, generated, as it were, by the friction between them. "This opposition between intuition and intelligence cannot be resolved by the victory of either (which means death to both): it is by their incessant action and reaction that reason, the faculty of true objective synthesis, is operative."[98] We might say that Murry was offering Eliot another version of the Lawrentian doctrine of polarity, the fruitful struggle of opposites producing a creative, ongoing synthesis.

It was an option which Eliot predictably declined, 1927 being the year in which he affirmed his allegiance to categorical truth by making his conversion. He evidently decided to put an end to Murry's effort at a counterconversion once and for all, decisively burying Murry's vitalistic synthesis with a flurry of *Criterion* articles, of which he wrote one himself and translated two others. The barrage opened in the September *Criterion* with essays by Father M. C. D'Arcy and Charles Mauron, the first arguing that Thomistic thought did contain the intuitive element Murry described, the second attacking Murry's very definition of intuition. "Intuition, far from explaining anything, is nothing but a catch-word applied to all the mental phenomena of which we have no clear idea."[99] The next issue contained "A Note on Intelligence and Intuition" by Ramon Fernandez and "Mr. Middleton Murry's Synthesis" by Eliot. Fernandez accused the romantic spirit of trying to extract thought from the ineffable instead of "disposing this ineffable in an intelligible perspective" (as the classical spirit does), while Eliot insisted that the Thomistic system of intelligence remained believable. T. Sturge Moore's "Towards Simplicity," which derided the artificiality of Murry's synthesis, concluded the counterattack.[100] Murry's last, lame response, "Concerning Intelligence," was a half-hearted defense against these combined polemics, and he signaled the end by writing Eliot: "All my hopeful feeling when I undertook that frightful essay ["Towards a Synthesis"] has evaporated. . . . It seems that there really is some sort of abyss between us—not humanly thank goodness—but in respect of our ideas and convictions."[101]

Eliot had been the more able disquisitionist, but he was finally less serious than Murry, who didn't indulge in ridiculing or belittling his opponent. One has the impression that Eliot was never engaged with the debate in the sense of being ready to enlarge his own perspective as Murry was. Hence Eliot's contributions were more clever, Murry's more conscientiously reflective and sincere. The controversy lasted too long, ending by increasing the distance between the combatants, and the positions both held at the end characterized their occasional commentaries on one another over the next thirty years.

Eliot's difficulty with Murry is capsulized in his review of *Son of Woman*, which he gifted with backward praise by calling it "a definitive work of critical biography . . . so well done that it gives me the creeps." But Murry is implicitly condemned for adopting the Lawrentian heresy, that is, "using the terminology of Christian faith to set forth some philosophy or religion which is fundamentally non-Christian or anti-Christian." Eliot's definition of "true education" brands Murry, as much as Lawrence, with being "ignorant." "What true education should do . . . is to develop a wise and large capacity for orthodoxy, to preserve the individual from the wholly centrifugal impulse of heresy, to make him capable of judging for himself and at the same time capable of judging and understanding the judgements of the experience of the race."[102]

The narrow demand for orthodoxy meant, of course, that he and Murry, though pursuing the same ends, inevitably continued to disagree. Eliot found in Murry's life of Jesus "the familiar gospel of Rousseau: the denial of original Sin" and satirized the fuzziness of Murry's theology. "I find it terribly hard to believe, with Mr. Murry, that man is 'the son of God' and also that he 'must be God.' "[103] In a later commentary he sarcastically accused Murry of confusing Marxism and religion. "It is better to worship a golden calf than to worship nothing; . . . My objection is that it just happens to be mistaken."[104] He did praise Murry generously when he found grounds to do so. His review of *Shakespeare* was among the most laudatory to appear in 1936, acknowledging Murry's genuine capacity to be receptive before he became active and crediting him with an understanding of the nature of poetry "more penetrating than that of most scholars and men of letters, and more comprehensive and catholic than that of most poets."[105]

Eliot accorded respect in other areas as well, acknowledging his debt to Murry's *The Price of Leadership* in *The Idea of a Christian Society*, although the social programs set forth in those two books are significantly different. (Murry emphasizes eradicating the class system and building an educated democracy through a revivified Christianity, while Eliot's model invokes the doctrines of a ruling class and a hierarchical state church. Both, however, prescribe cures for the diseases of secular society and describe the normative community as rooted in the soil and unified by traditional ties to a particular place.) Murry's last political conversion, from the pacificism of the war years to the neo-orthodoxy of his attack on Russian totalitarianism in *The Free Society*, evoked Eliot's praise, although he still disputed, as he had for twenty years, the legitimacy of Murry's calling himself Christian. Shortly before Murry's death Eliot wrote that he thought their friendship "all the more valuable because of differences in temperament and point of view,"[106] and his final estimate of Murry's accomplishment was very high indeed. John Middleton Murry, he said, was an original literary critic who had a "solitary eminence in his generation." He distinguished Murry as the rarest sort of critic, one whose "primary creative act is criticism," who informs his work with a "significance of personality" and concludes that the writers Murry treats are "important to us because they were important to Murry, and because we are interested in what happened to Murry's mind and sensibility when they came in contact with literature that he found important."[107]

Murry, for his part, pondered the significance of his division from Eliot over the years, and his criticism persistently centered on the limited moral vision of Eliot's Anglicanism, the denial of life values in his ascetic creed. Without disclaiming Eliot's genius or his stunning impact on twentieth-century literature ("single-handed, he seems almost to have formed the sensibility of a whole period—to have given the note to poetry, the method to literary criticism, and a new birth to poetic drama),"[108] Murry decried the direction in which Eliot had led his contemporaries. In a 1937 essay he suggested that because Eliot was an American he had no real experience of the spiritual annihilation of the First World War; his ironic disillusionment with machine culture is not equivalent to the British experience. Because he began with a different cultural experience, the influence he has exerted has stultified young English poets, who could not follow him into the Church of England. Eliot is "able to busy himself with blotting out three centuries, precisely because he never knew the necessity of blotting out four years."[109]

Murry's commentaries on Eliot's poetic drama clarify the terms of the religious divergence: it is because Eliot cannot conceive of the redemptive value of human love that his moral resolutions are partial and unsatisfying. The Augustinian mysticism which pervades Eliot's drama and later poetry, Murry says, belong to a venerable tradition, one that has cost Eliot to hold to. But this traditional spirituality will no longer serve—"Too much is breaking, or has broken. The man whom the Christian tradition assumes no longer exists"—and Eliot has been incapable of making a new assertion in another direction. His themes of celibacy, renunciation, and self-sacrifice lead to sterility because they distance him from the familiar things of the earth, from human affirmations. In Eliot's world, all ecstasies must be converted to the love of God or "dwindle into resigned acceptance."[110] Eliot defines the human condition as a continuous "expiation of an undefinable and omnipresent and all-defiling sin."[111] Because Eliot cannot conceive of the salvational possibilities of sexual fulfillment and human love, he never attains the whole vision of the great artist. He cannot speak prophetically to us. "Admiration of Mr. Eliot's poetic and dramatic achievement will always be tempered by a sense that the super-human difficulty of so much of his writing is causally connected with his almost inhuman detachment from the most exalted experience that falls to the lot of the common man."[112]

The alternative Murry posits is the "beginning of a new tradition of spirituality," which he locates in Lawrence's vision of regenerated man and woman creating a new kind of marriage and so a new kind of world. It is Lawrence's "tension of a vital relation to the world" that leads Murry to his clear choice: "I am, profoundly, with Lawrence rather than Eliot."[113]

Significantly, Murry's definition of the antithesis between Eliot and Lawrence and his contention that one must choose one or the other parallels F. R. Leavis's position. Both critics viewed picking Lawrence and rejecting Eliot as a moral issue with ramifying consequences for twentieth-century culture. Thus Leavis contrasts Lawrence's "health" and "affirmation of life" with Eliot's "standing-off from life" throughout *D. H. Lawrence: Novelist*. He maintains that Lawrence possessed a "true moral sense . . . that ministers to life" against Eliot's distaste and disgust, his "ignorance of the possibilities of life," and argues that Eliot's plays "force us to recognize how little the genius of his personal poetry carried with it major creative powers—the creativity of a great creative writer. They exhibit something like a Flaubertian intensity of art: there is the slow meticulous labour of calculating judgement that clearly went to the doing; and, on the other hand, there is the sick poverty, the triviality, and finally, the nothingness of the done—the human and spiritual nullity."[114] This statement is strikingly similar to Murry's stance toward Eliot, although he never adopted so severely disputatious a tone and was never so much on Lawrence's side against Eliot's as Leavis was.

Late in his life Murry wrote that he and Eliot "lived in the same *kind* of isolation." "Not that I could really enter his world, or he mine; but there was a strange feeling of kinship between us."[115] Griffin's discussion of the consonance between Murry and Eliot and their separation from "scientific" critics shows exactly where that kinship lay: "Their ways were different," he says, "but they were both Christ centered in their attitude to life and literature. . . . both approaches were ethical in that they chose and knew their choice; in this commitment lies their main distinction from much of modern criticism." Northrop Frye, a representative scientific critic, took Eliot to task for approving of Murry's taking of definite positions, remarking, "There are no definite positions to be taken in chemistry or philology, and if there are any to be taken in criticism, criticism is not a field of genuine learning." That, as Griffin shows, is exactly the point. Neither Murry nor Eliot regarded criticism as "*primarily* a field of learning."[116]

But, Murry realized, despite his deep sympathy with Eliot, despite their shared realizations, "the effect . . . upon us was antipodal."[117] In the end, Murry saw himself as standing between and apart from both Eliot and Lawrence. "They are antipodal to one another; my something—a veritable *nescio quid*—is friendly antipodal to each of them; much in the way of a saturated solution that either of them can precipitate into the certainty 'Thou art not that!' "[118] Many facets of Murry's career, and particularly his compulsion to repeat himself in writing, can be attributed to his sense of apartness from them and his knowledge of their greater talent and the difficulty of making his voice heard over theirs. The most telling comment he made on the situation appears in an essay on William Godwin's relationship to Shelley, in which he says of Godwin, "There are few harder fates for a man of some genius than to be intimately associated with a man of more. He is remembered, but in such a way that it seems better to be forgotten."[119]

Chapter Five

VICES AND VIRTUES OF AN AUTOBIOGRAPHICAL CRITIC

Murry and the English Romantic Tradition

The degree to which Murry's thought was rooted in the English romantic tradition can be demonstrated by noticing how searchingly he explored it and how comparatively little he wrote about other literature after the early twenties. This concentration meant that he paid little attention to the literature of other nations. He acknowledged American literature only with a brief comment on Melville's *Billy Budd* and one long essay on Whitman, and he more and more ignored the French and Russian literature he had once explored. He had little interest in contemporary British writers other than Lawrence and Eliot, both of whom he tried to reform and persuade back to the central romantic line. English romantic literature embodied for him the essential post-Renaissance revelation—the means of establishing value after the fall of the old order.

The romantic principle he embraced was what Langbaum calls the doctrine of experience: the discovery through experience of the "empiric ground for values," values always tentatively formulated with expanding potentiality for insight and refinement. Concurrently, it treats immediate imaginative apprehension as primary and succeeding analytic reflection as "secondary and problematic."[1] This attitude is the source of Murry's habit of pronouncing a new truth on the grounds that "I felt it on my pulses," a practice which cost him a great deal in an age of analytic criticism. But it is important to see that this criterion of felt truth was for him a fundamental model for establishing societal, as well as individual, values—the key to rebuilding a humane civilization.

Debating the meaning of romanticism with Eliot, Murry found in it the habit of mind which engendered democracy's assertion of the supreme value of the individual and the Protestant belief that "the man who truly interrogates himself will hear the voice of God."[2] Ethically, Murry said, romanticism "attempts to solve the problem of conduct by an exploration of the inner world. . . . at some point in this non-intellectual exploration of the self a contact is established between the finite soul and the infinite soul of which it is a manifestation."[3] The point of fusion he envisioned is visible and communicable in its highest moral/aesthetic form in the moments of "plenary apprehension" of great art.

Murry's sense of the romantic spirit as the shaping force of English history and culture was allied with a deep attachment to the English soil. He explicitly accepted the Wordsworthian premise that a life cut off from nature is spiritually stunted, and his diverse social schemes turned on modes of ameliorating twentieth-century urbanization and mechanization, of recreating the connection between the individual and the land. His own life warped by a sense of division from living tradition, constructed, he says, out of "broken patterns," Murry thought it axiomatic that social theory must work toward reincorporating man and his machine into the cycle of nature. Spiritual renewal depends upon rebuilding the fulfillment in daily work which once made the craftsman's life a "lived religion."[4]

Because Murry's studies of the romantic strain of English literature employ a variety of critical voices, we can form a clearer sense of what is best and worst about his impressionistic approach by examining some representative statements. His handling of rhetoric is closely related to his stance toward his material—determined by the degree of his self-projection and his anticipation of the reader's assent or dissent. He tended to lose control, for instance, when he was uneasy about the reception of an idea, or when it was invested with moral urgency. His most readable, pleasant essays are appreciative rather than argumentative. He is least strained when constructively "placing" a writer or identifying the positive qualities of a minor figure. The tone of his best essays is intelligent and temperate, and although it becomes occasionally *too* relaxed, a whimsical belles lettres manner, it is more often penetrating and eloquent.

In this vein one thinks, for instance, of the essay on Spenser in which Murry's responsiveness to the "song" of English poetry works to rekindle the reader's forgotten delight in the infinite modulations of Spenserian verse.[5] Adroitly reminding us of Spenser's most melodious lines, Murry also shows why he has become neglected. He lacks the intrinsic interest-ingness, the quality of depicting human nature, which Chaucer and Shakespeare possessed. Spenser's supreme quality is the aesthetic perfection and purity of his poetic line, the instrument he "devised and shaped, and inlaid and polished" which taught successive generations of poets the craft of poetry. This essay is an almost perfect specimen of Murry's qualities as an appreciative critic.

His treatment of Chapman has the same accomplished air. Detailing the ways in which Chapman was overshadowed by Shakespeare, his greater contemporary, Murry suggests the special quality of his flawed verse. He was, Murry thinks, "a man more conscious than others of the strangeness of the age in which he lived . . . his choice of themes is that of a man who is aware of the Renaissance as a European happening . . . , the half-conscious *vates* of an era when an old great order had crumbled and the emergence of a new seemed doubtful."[6] The perceptions of this essay are deliberately unscholarly, unprofessional, and they demonstrate the advantages of the nonspecialist in gracefully placing a secondary writer.

One of Murry's significant contributions to English letters is his restoration of interest in such minor romantic poets as Anne of Winchelsea and John Clare. In editing and introducing the poems of Lady Winchelsea, Murry directed attention to her "exquisite sense of nuance" and "simple felicity" of expression and established a small place among the precursors of the romantics for a talent that had been admired by Wordsworth and Hunt but had fallen into obscurity.[7] The three essays on John Clare, a contemporary of Keats, do more than simply build a sympathetic case for Clare's inclusion in the canon on the basis of his unique powers of song and "sheer natural vision."[8] Murry locates a special individuality in Clare's naivete, his remarkably childlike response to nature, but acknowledges that he is indisputably a minor poet, without the center of "disciplined experience" found in Keats and Wordsworth. Clare's inability to order his perceptions into a "dominant thought-feeling" were magnified, Murry observes, in a life full of trials and troubles into an "inability to master his own moral experience." However, Clare's more universal significance, his visionary quality, is his sensitivity to the changes brought by enclosure of the old English common lands. "In Clare's poetry, as nowhere else in our literature, we can see and feel the transformation of the countryside and the disruption of the old village community which was involved in that great and pitiless social revolution."[9] Enlisting our response to the innocence of Clare's love of nature, and our sense of his personal disintegration in the face of change he could not assimilate (he ended his life in a mental institution), Murry makes him an emblem of the process of disinheritance from the soil which has been the history of England since the Renaissance. It is regrettable that none of the John Clare essays were included in the *Selected Essays*, where they would be more accessible, for, as Griffin says, "all that was best in the amateur quality of Murry's criticism comes out in them."[10]

When we scrutinize the set of companion essays on Keats and Shelley and Coleridge and Wordsworth contained in *Katherine Mansfield and Other*

Literary Portraits, we can see more clearly the sources of the marked unevenness of Murry's criticism. When Murry assumes a prophetic voice, he loses his poise. Judiciousness is lost to the imperatives of truthtelling. The argument of "Keats and Shelley," in which Murry asserts his preference for Keatsian life involvement and receptivity to experience over Shelleyian Platonism and mental ideality, is solid enough. Murry as the man of letters is suggesting what he responds to and what he doesn't. Shelley fails to satisfy him, he says, because he seldom offers the concentrated aesthetic/intellectual vision of Keats. He connects his dissatisfaction with real confusion in Shelley's absolutes (the intermixing of the concepts of eternity and the immortality of fame, for instance) and with his dividedness toward life. "At one moment he accepts and glorifies Existence, at another he rejects and denigrates it. At one moment Life is the utterance of Love, at another it is the dull, dense Matter that clogs the feet of Spirit."[11] Keats represents the opposite relation with experience, a "capacity to absorb everything that Life may bring."

In many respects the essay is perfectly satisfactory. The quotations Murry uses to demonstrate the two poets' contrasting sensibilities are apt, his thesis that Shelley is abstract where Keats is concrete is fully validated, and nowhere else, I think, does Murry use self-confession quite so attractively and modestly. "I fear that if I had written poetry it would have been poetry of the Shelley kind: abstract, intellectual, metaphysical. But my heart demands something different" (p. 240). What goes wrong in this essay, and often goes wrong with Murry, is a distortion of the original purpose by an anxiety that we won't agree with him. At one moment he is the genial man of letters, inviting our participation in his discovery of some private truths through some familiar poetry. In the next he is the man with a mission, requiring our ratification of his discovery that Keats is the bearer of supreme truth. This discontinuity between appreciation and prophecy unbalances both argument and rhetoric, breeding archaic syntax ("Let not the lover of these beautiful lines condemn me for sacrilege because I seek to understand them" [p. 232]) and irrelevant nonsense. "I am not blaming Shelley for not having known Keats. He would not easily have understood him if he had. Keats was wise in holding himself aloof. Shelley's Keats is Shelley, as no doubt he had to be; and Shelley knew it" (p. 236). Murry's besetting sin as a critic was this loss of control when he wrote about what moved him most deeply. It is the quality that Katherine Mansfield criticized in him from the beginning. "When a book really engages your passions you are dangerous."[12]

The second essay I am considering here, "Coleridge and Wordsworth," is longer, complex—and more deeply interesting. Murry's preliminary thesis, presented with admirable clarity and specificity, is that although Coleridge and Wordsworth had a complementary relationship, Wordsworth's poetry was far more masterful. His lifelong intimacy with nature produced a "reciprocity" between himself and the natural world which the city-born Coleridge never possessed. The difference, embedded in the very texture of their poetry, corresponds very closely to Wordsworth's distinction between the fancy and the imagination. "Coleridge's observation of nature is rare, and precise with an almost scientific precision," Murry suggests. It is essentially artificial. Wordsworth possessed, in Coleridge's own term, "esemplastic power," while Coleridge had only the "power to organise his dream" to tell a "strange and fascinating story" and bathe "imaginary events in a glamourous supernatural light."[13]

These remarks lead to a long interpretation of Coleridge's "Dejection: An Ode," a poem Murry describes as deceitful, equivocating, and treacherous. In it Coleridge claims to have lost a "shaping spirit of imagination" which, Murry insists, he never possessed. By attributing his loss to personal unhappiness, Coleridge implies that Wordsworth owes his continuing poetic power to private happiness, not, as he claimed, to a spiritual achievement, a mutual interaction with nature. Coleridge defines the creative power as simply a projection of the self upon the world. This is, Murry adds, a false, narcissistic point of view, closely related to Coleridge's personal fault of using people and objects as a focus of association for "obscure feeling" (p. 67). "Dejection" is guilty of what Coleridge himself defined as the most disgusting species of egotism: "not that which leads us to communicate our feelings to others, but that which would reduce the feelings of others to an identity with our own" (p. 70). Murry notes that in earlier poems ("The Aeolian Harp," "Fears in Solitude") Coleridge had presented himself as experiencing authentic nature-rapture, whereas the state he described is really an ordinary, undifferentiated sensation of passivity and tranquillity. He never, like Wordsworth, exhibits a "truly responsive soul" which recognizes "one Being of which itself and the world beyond are modes" (p. 70). He therefore lies to himself in representing his experience as akin to Wordsworth's and equivocates by denying the real source of Wordsworth's genius.

The problem with Coleridge, Murry continues, is that he had "an altogether amazing hiatus at the core of his being. . . . no other man of genius that I know of [has] so little sense of [his] own personal identity as he. He seems to have experienced himself chiefly as a negation; and he was continually groping after some means of communicating to others the strangeness of his own experience of himself" (p. 76). Relying heavily on other people, on an "atmosphere of affection," to maintain a sense of his identity, he shrank from the condition of aloneness with the universe which leads to the "authentic mystical passing from isolation to communion." Coleridge never had geniune religious experiences: his Neoplatonism and mystical musings were all intellectually based. The shallowness of his religious feeling is paralleled by his self-centeredness. "Coleridge did love, where he loved, very intensely. But it was for all its intensity, a diffused love which spread a kind of circumambience, or veil, over the thing or person loved. It was a love which shrank from seeing the object as it was and loving that" (p. 81). In accordance with this analysis of Coleridge's character deficiencies, Murry castigates him for leaving his wife and two small children alone while he accompanied the Wordsworths to Germany and blames him for the death of a child in his absence. Proof of his accusations is a passage from Dorothy Wordsworth's diary on Coleridge's love for Sara Hutchinson. "His love for her is no more than a fanciful dream—otherwise he would prove it by a desire to make her happy. No, he liked to have her about him as his own, as one devoted to him, but when she stood in the way of other gratifications, it was all over" (p. 67).

Coleridge's collapse after his break with the Wordsworths was due, Murry says, to Coleridge's fatal confusion of Wordsworth's experience and his own; his identification with Wordsworth confirmed an "unconscious habit of intellectual and moral duplicity in a matter of all things most vital to his own true life." Thereafter "Coleridge lost the thread of his own being. . . . he never afterwards knew what the truth was" (p. 87).

"Frost at Midnight," Murry argues, is the only meditative poem that contains a moment of genuine illumination, for it implicitly acknowledges the profound difference between Wordsworth and himself: "For this moment, he was veritably the voice of Nature—not Wordsworth's Nature, but the Nature of his own experience: a starved and lonely childhood, a passionate longing for affection, but all bitterness resolved in an utterly unselfish desire that his babe so beautiful shall be rich where he is poor" (p. 89). Coleridge could not be loyal to his self-knowledge; he denied his inner truth and began to decay. "Within five years he was a broken man, and the fire of his genius glowed seldom through the ashes" (p. 90).

There are many singular elements in this essay. What strikes one first is the modernity of Murry's viewpoint. Norman Fruman's psychoanalytic biography, *Coleridge: The Damaged Archangel* (1971), similarly emphasizes Coleridge's role playing and prevarications, drawing the same conclusions from the same evidence. Fruman, too, says that Coleridge's early nature poetry "manipulates emotions and 'recollections' which were not and could not have been genuine" and calls the explanation of the poet's failing powers in "Dejection" "an elaborate masquerade." The critics concur on a variety of seminal points, seeing "Frost at Midnight" as his most successful meditation poem, agreeing on the dividedness of the poet's personality and his habit of self-deception. Clearly Murry's essay, startlingly unorthodox in 1949, anticipates much more recent scholarship, assembling data others ignored until long after.

The difference between Murry's judgments and Fruman's is that Murry ascribes Coleridge's flaws to an impaired moral sense, an inability to truly love, while Fruman deduces specifically sexual conflicts. For

Murry the real issue is that Wordsworth had a genuine mystical experience, while Coleridge had not. Because he never faced the "implacable otherness of the universe," he never experienced "the condition which leads to the authentic mystical passing from isolation to communion" (p. 80). (That is why Murry argues that Coleridge might have been a genuine poet had he not been supported by Wordsworth. At the crucial time he was not forced to be alone.)

All Murry's judgments about Coleridge are negative in this essay. Reading it in the light of Murry's own biography shows that self-identification is fully at work. Murry tellingly says that " 'the story of Coleridge' fascinates me; and I wish it did not. I lean over him to read his heart, and I find myself forever discovering things that I do not want to discover" (p. 88). The explanation for the unrelentingly condescending and sometimes hostile tone is that in Coleridge Murry identified his own "younger" self—a self he wished to condemn and eradicate.

There are any number of obvious biographical parallels between the two men: both were city children and students at Christ's Hospital, both left the university before gaining a degree and engaged in multifarious journalistic, social, and utopian enterprises, aside from the obvious congruence of their interests as literary critics. Indeed, the most salient difference is that Coleridge was an achieved poet and Murry a failed one. It is telling that Murry attacks the poet Coleridge, not the critic Coleridge, whom he here ignores but elsewhere esteems.

The psychological traits Murry attributes to Coleridge are more interesting than the biographical coincidences, however, and it is significant that near the beginning of the essay, although nowhere else, Murry explicitly identifies his own childhood experience with Coleridge's account of watching the fire in "Frost at Midnight." Like his famous predecessor at Christ's Hospital, Murry has sat lonely at school, longing for a visitor. The note of empathy is confined to "Frost at Midnight." It is the only Coleridge poem he fully endorses.

There is an amazing correspondence between Murry's version of Coleridge's psychology—his uncertainty of his own identity and dependence on other people—and his self-portrait in *Between Two Worlds*. "I was beset by an unconscious urge toward a peculiar intensity in my personal relations. In these alone my isolation was overcome. Only when I was surrounded by the safety and warmth of an intimate personal affection could I breathe freely, or suffer myself to be off-guard."[14] The comparison of Coleridge's barren intellectual mysticism with Wordsworth's organic responsiveness is reminiscent of Murry's description of himself in relation to Lawrence, while the statement that Coleridge loved "diffusely," loving his image of a beloved more than the actual person, echoes Katherine's accusation that Murry loved being in love with her rather than loving *her*.

Perhaps the most interesting accusation is that Coleridge consciously or half-consciously betrayed Wordsworth by misinterpreting him and "reducing [his] feeling to an identity with [his] own." If this is Murry's judgment on his own interpretation of Lawrence, it is a significant index of his self-hatred and explains why he was compelled to condemn himself in the guise of Coleridge.

"Coleridge and Wordsworth" brands Coleridge with Murry's own most hated traits. It repudiates an earlier personality which Murry defeated by virtue of an integrative mystical experience (which he denies Coleridge had) and by his conversion to a life-embracing, body and spirit uniting creed. Murry's perspective is not wholly just to Coleridge, but it leads to penetrating truths and exhibits the rewards and dangers of Murry's manner of feeling his way into a writer. The underlying factor of psychic compensation is betrayed in the rhetoric and in part explains why it has been undeservedly ignored.

Heaven—and Earth, written two years after *Shakespeare*, is an unusually far-reaching study which moves beyond appreciation and soul reading to strenuous juxtaposition of ideas. It contains the fullest, most satisfying statement of Murry's theory of modern civilization presented by studies of twelve key figures representing different epochs of English/European thought. (The book's American title is *Heroes of Thought*.) More than one person thinks it Murry's best book,[15] a judgment with which I concur if one considers the whole, although individual chapters of *Shakespeare*, for instance, surpass individual chapters of *Heaven—and Earth*.

Although most of the "heroes" of this work are democratic heroes, and Murry is explicitly antitotalitarian, he is as much concerned to detail the failures of democracy as to defend its potentialities. Since the Renaissance, English and European civilization has grown progressively more rootless and unstable, Murry argues. The harmonious medieval world order collapsed. The Protestant doctrine of individuality which replaced it gave rise to the prodigious expanding impulse toward political liberty, nationalism and imperialism, exploration and conquest, science and invention, which have culminated in the present "machine-age" society where, paradoxically, the individual has been effectively abolished as a real power in the world. The end of individualism, Murry says, is the destruction of the individual. His vision of the twentieth century is apocalyptic. "It is fundamental to my view of life that if the blind creative process is suffered to continue upon a purely natural, or 'scientific' level, it must end in a living death to individuals, and universal catastrophe to mankind."[16]

If these words bore a special resonance from being written on the eve of World War II, they can hardly be dismissed in an age of threatened nuclear catastrophe, although the salvationist doctrines which accompany

Murry's diagnosis of social chaos are embarrassing in their naivete: "If the distinction between Good and Evil is not to perish from the world, if humanity is not to 'prey upon itself like monsters from the deep,' the world must be redeemed by love." The aim of his book, he says, is to "commemorate the heroes of thought, the philosophers of 'heaven and earth,' who have striven to regenerate the world by the divine vision, in the spirit of selfless love."[17] The preachiness of the introduction, its abstractions and tired language, mislead the reader, for the main body of essays in *Heaven—and Earth* explicate the theme with convincing subtlety and clarity; Murry is not simplistic when he is engaged in defining the central passions of great men.

Cromwell, Milton, Rousseau, Marx, and William Morris emerge as the central prophets of European civilization in this study. The early chapters describe the passage from the "pleine felicity" of the Chaucerian village community to the tension of conscious individualism of the Renaissance. The growth of individualism led to gradual enlargement of democratic principle. Cromwell's revolutionary belief in the freedom of the individual to believe as he must was the driving force of the English civil war, and Murry depicts Cromwell as "the demiurge of the modern world, upon whose massive shoulders the private and individual man was heaved into the center of European history, for weal or woe."[18] With him stood Milton, the ardent spokesman of freedom of thought whose *Areopagitica* infused the Cromwellian religious vision with the ideal of the liberated human reason. The English civil war actually accelerated the process of secularization, despite its religious origins, for the doctrine that each man may interpret the scripture for himself ends in investing the self with divine authority. Milton was, Murry claims, "the pure and extreme case, a man in whom Puritanism was in fact operative, beneath its professions and appearance to the contrary, as a complete emancipation from Christianity and the incentive of a purely secular individualism."[19]

Rousseau, the next great democratic prophet, added the principle of political equality to religious equality, embracing the Greek premise that in order to become an ethical being a man must become a conscious political being. *The Social Contract,* Murry says, was the greatest attempt since Plato's *Republic* to create a "consciousness of the social whole," and he regards it as the founding document of the French Revolution.

Marx and Morris, the socialist visionaries, represent the final crucial evolution toward the modern world. Murry finds Marx a flawed prophet, for his demand for economic equality omits the demand for political liberty and violates Murry's maxim that "every great, creative revolution which begins from feudal society needs to reassert all that was positively asserted by previous revolutions that began from the same point."[20] Morris is Murry's socialist hero, an organicist whose economic precepts are joined with ethical vision. He preached Murry's own belief that "socialism begins, and can only begin, in a revolution in the heart and mind of man,"[21] and he linked social renewal to the integration of life and work, one of Murry's central themes. Ending with Morris, Murry brings the historical pageant of *Heaven—and Earth* full circle, since he made his life task relating the social model of the Middle Ages to the modern world. In his doctrines Murry finds the key solution to the twentieth-century dilemma.

As this summary suggests, *Heaven—and Earth* is an ambitious book. Its view of the tangled web of modern European history in terms of the thought of twelve great men is complicated by Murry's method (adopted from Lessing) of "approaching the doctrines of creative thinkers . . . along the path of the process of their own formation: genetically or historically." It is made still more intricate by Murry's demonstration of the intricate interconnections of ideas, his effort to show how "different revelations correct, complete and fructify one another."[22] A measure of his success is that any one of these studies can be read more profitably in the context of the whole than in isolation, although some studies are inevitably more valuable than others.

The section on Shakespeare tends to reiterate and emphasize favorite ideas, some of which have little bearing on the theme. Here, as elsewhere, Murry approaches Milton with an admission of distaste for the abstractness of his theology and his private inhumanity. Few would agree with his pronouncement: "I would give all *Paradise Lost* for the *Aeropagitica*. That may be Art; but this is Prophecy."[23] Wordsworth probably does not belong in this classification of heroes, and Murry's discussion merely expands an earlier note on Wordsworth, "On Faith in England," in *The Pledge of Peace*. He clearly wanted to say more about Blake but could not work him into the main scheme of the book, for digressions on Blake intrude on the treatment of Milton, Goethe, and Godwin. His Goethe study is modeled on Carlyle, but the discussion is vague and the conclusions fuzzy, probably because Murry was weak at the systematic philosophical classification which this approach requires. The most original and provocative studies are of Cromwell and Rousseau. The essay on Cromwell has been more widely praised; Murry himself was proudest of the Rousseau chapter, which more than other sections of the book contradicts received interpretations. He treats Marx by assuming understanding of and agreement with his attack on capitalism and stresses the deficiencies of Marxist theory. From Murry's account alone it would be difficult to see why Marx should be counted among significant creative thinkers, but the critique of Marxist theory is cogent, showing the philosophic elisions which led to the perpetuation of totalitarianism in his name.

A recurring weakness in Murry's attitude is equivocation of the private moral lapses of his heroes. He glosses over Cromwell's Irish massacre, refers to Rousseau's leaving his children at the foundling hospital as a terrible mistake (which, he assures us, Rousseau regretted), and explains how Godwin could not have prevented Fanny Imlay's suicide. The difficulty in all these cases is that Murry refuses to confront the human cost of idealism and so evades an important moral issue.

In other respects his analysis is admirably sane and balanced. He is impassioned, but disinterestedly so. We do not feel that he has twisted ideas to conform to a theory, and the links between the figures are intrinsic and unforced. The flawed element of the book is the proselytizing introduction and sermonizing passages tagged to the ends of chapters. The intrusion of this extraneous material betrays Murry's uneasiness. Having trenchantly demonstrated his ideas in the body of the essays, he is still impelled to shout at the reader.

Prophetic earnestness and all, *Heaven—and Earth* is impressive. Because Murry was an unfashionable and suspect pacifist when it was published, the book was not reviewed as widely or sympathetically as it deserved, and that relative oblivion has been its fate. Yet Beer's judgment—"It would be hard to name another book which succeeds in 'placing' so many important ideas in the evolution of European economic and intellectual history with such clarity and in such short compass"[24]—still holds up. It is an undeservedly neglected work.

The Objective Critic

At the end of his life Murry deliberately moved outside the circle of ideas associated with the English romantic tradition and undertook a more conventional criticism. This decision reflected the mature serenity of his private life after World War II, which allowed him the leisure to reexamine his career and to ponder, rather wistfully, the paths he had forsaken along the way. Art, he reflected, had taken second place to a search for reconciling values, to finding a creed to live by. "To this search for integrity—the reconciliation of Heart and Mind, Emotion and Intellect—I have sacrificed whatever talent for art I possessed. It was, probably, not much: but I think I had the makings of a good literary critic. But it was not really, or not wholly, a sacrifice: for criticism (as I wanted to practice it anyhow) depended on values—a determination of what is good for man. . . . And I had to find out."[25]

When Murry arrived at a new formulation of himself, he characteristically essayed a self-revision. The product of this definition of his career was the decision to write some standard criticism. A few months later he was writing Henry Williamson that he intended his biography of Jonathan Swift to be "the *nec plus ultra* of objectivity."[26] He had decided, he wrote in his journal, to make himself "for the first time, and for a final brief period, what I have never been—simply a professional writer—in my case, a professional literary critic, who sets himself tasks of appreciation, purged of all *arrière pensée*, uncontaminated (and uninspired) by any effort to save my soul, by discovering what I do, or ought, to believe."[27] Swift was deliberately chosen as a figure he could not conceivably identify with, someone the "very antipodes" of himself.[28] The antithesis of a love hero, Swift represented the man who had upheld reason at all cost—excluding inspiration and enthusiasm from his art as he excluded sexual passion from his life.

Approaching this study as a critical exercise rather than as a mind- and soul-absorbing quest, Murry wrote with academic decorum, without the gushy rhetoric and moral exhortation which had often meant that Murry on Keats, Blake, or Shakespeare was not taken very seriously. The restrained tone owes something to the moderation of age but set *Jonathan Swift* against its successor, *Love, Freedom and Society*, and it is clear that Murry was cultivating dispassion, as he claimed.

Murry's approach to Swift is more emphatically psychological than literary. He views the pride and sensitiveness bred by Swift's homeless, lonely childhood as responsible for his "singularities of character," for the contentions of pride and love which shaped his life.[29] Swift's difficulties with his early patron Sir William Temple were due to his search for a father, Murry argues. The frustrated quest for a paternal model accounts for the inconstancies of his friendships and the repetitive feuds and intrigues of his political life. Similarly, Murry traces Swift's misogyny and the oddities of his relationships with Stella and Vanessa to his embitterment at being refused by Varina, the bishop's daughter he courted as a young man. The pride with which Swift responded to this rejection led to a willful distortion of his own nature, a determined renunciation of love.

This interpretation of Swift's emotional life emerges in the course of a long, fundamentally conventional biography which many critics thought the most complete treatment of Swift to date. Murry painstakingly traces the evolution of Swift's early satires, as he does the perambulations of his London political life. Although literary comment is often overshadowed by the welter of facts and dates surrounding Swift's complicated dealings, when Murry does focus on the works his remarks are acute, as this engaging passage on the comic genius of *A Tale of a Tub* demonstrates:

> For the comic spirit, any cosmos is an illusion to be shattered; but . . . to be shattered gaily, not desperately, with the suggestion that the same force of genius which destroys the existing cosmos might easily create another and a better. . . . When this elemental comic spirit is at work, it is extraordinarily difficult to say how seriously its detailed manifestations are to be taken. It is difficult because one has the obstinate feeling that it is irrelevant. Seriousness in this sense of the word is always relative to a cosmos, a moral order, a

hierarchy of values, which is precisely what the comic spirit repudiates and overturns. Its specific seriousness lies in itself, in its own total significance. It is the evidence of a metaphysical potentiality, a reminder that any order is precarious.[30]

His discussion of *Gulliver's Travels* is long and thoughtful, one any student of Swift would find useful, although, as Bullitt points out, it suffers from a confusion of Swift with his created character and implicitly treats satire as self-expression.[31] It is, nonetheless, a distinctive individual interpretation of a literary masterpiece which commands a hearing. G. Wilson Knight considered that the treatment of *Gulliver* showed Murry "at his best, most revealing: the symbolism of the Houyhnhnms has never before been so admirably expounded."[32] Other reviewers were divided, some wishing that Murry's admirable analysis had been more extensive, others finding it biased and limited by Murry's disapproval of Swift's moral philosophy.

For it is on Swift's creation of the Yahoos and the scatological poems which followed *Gulliver* that Murry based his controversial treatment of Swift's "excremental vision." Swift's vision of man is distorted, he insists, by his neurotic desire to "annihilate the sexual relation, and with it every animal function of the body." His loathing for physical functions arose from his "deliberate and prolonged repression of the emotion of love in the name of reason."

> The impression made by his creation of the Yahoos is of an elemental upsurge giving demonic strength to an effort to annihilate the physical nature of humanity. . . . It is because the filthiness of the Yahoos is quite eccentric to Swift's satiric or moral purpose that we are compelled to ask why it is there at all, and why it is so dominant in the picture. If physical nastiness were an adequate and forceful symbol of moral corruption, we could accept it. But it is not. . . . This physical loathing of the human-Yahoo adds nothing to Gulliver's spiritual stature: it diminishes it. . . . In the last resort we must pronounce that his vision lacks integrity. Its profound spiritual truth struggles against the egoistic power that makes for its corruption, and the truth cannot wholly prevail. Neither Gulliver, nor his creator, can be reborn.[33]

Murry attributes Swift's growing horror of animal desire to a self-justification of his refusal to marry and suggests that Swift's conception of reason was warped by his revulsion from physical intimacy. Its function became not merely control, but suppression, of sexual passion. "Reason must be the mirror of a mind which abhors sexual love." The Houyhnhnms do not furnish an answer because they are not human.

"The human predicament—Swift's predicament—remains precisely where it was. His real answer is the Yahoo. Whether or not God intended men's passions to prevail over their reason, Swift's sentence is that it is an abomination if they do."[34]

Swift's personal imbalances shaped, but also limited, his genius. He achieved his satiric purposes by leaving his essential self out of his work, and in consequence he is less than complete—an antithesis to Shakespearean fullness. Murry hypothesizes that Swift underwent a psychological crisis after writing *A Tale of a Tub* which issued in a deliberate expunging of qualities which made him vulnerable to humiliation. He chose self-discipline and the ambitious pursuit of power over full exercise of his genius and so diminished himself. "Religion was discarded, and he was a clergyman; love was discarded, and he was hungry for intimacy and affection; inspiration was discarded, and he was a genius."[35]

In a pamphlet written for the British Council, Murry summarized this theme of *Jonathan Swift*, arguing that painful self-repression underlies all Swift's later work and that the destructive cost of containing the immense creative energy he feared increased as the years went on:

> Swift is forever assuming a mask. . . . One senses an underlying and less variable persona as a necessity of a tolerable existence; a deliberately adopted means of escape from an emotional nature that threatened to overwhelm him. Tender, generous, passionate, and perhaps also *malade de l'idéal*—these elements were to him so many sources of weakness that had to be stopped at all costs in one who would battle with the world. . . . He stood incessantly on guard against his affections and emotions which menaced the citadel of his rationality and would sweep him from the rock of self-control.[36]

In *Jonathan Swift*, Murry concludes that in his later years Swift was "radically infected by the corruption he universally discovers."[37]

When we look at the biography in relation to the rest of the Murry canon, some interesting patterns emerge. Murry's interest in Swift's relations with women brings this study into the framework of preoccupation with love and marriage. This motif is at once the best and the riskiest element of the book, it seems to me. Murry's preconceptions lead to formulaic interpretation, to an overly tidy assimilation of the life and the work. He accepts thin evidence when it supports his theory without fully acknowledging its shakiness. His belief that Swift proposed to Varina and was rejected rests on one letter, which may or may not represent a proposal. (Not many scholars believe it did.) He similarly accepts the tradition of a secret marriage to Stella, which most Swiftians regard as spurious. At the same time, his insights about Swift's relationship to Stella and its bearing on the life and art are the most original and valuable element of what would otherwise be an ordinarily competent biographical account. Whenever Murry gazes at the "woman" issue, he sees things other critics and scholars have overlooked. He suggests that Swift's habit of treating his women as younger than they were and his resolve never to be fond of children reveal the defenses he erected against sexual passion. He observes that the "little language" Swift used with Stella served as a barrier to real intimacy but also remarks on the positive side of Swift's determined celibacy: a genuine intellectual enjoyment of women unusual for his day. "He not only admired the feminine quality of a woman's mind, but he enjoyed the underlying sex attraction. . . . The little grain of the romance was the spice of life to Swift. It entered into his relations with young women and old."[38]

The quality of *Jonathan Swift* most revealing about Murry is that despite the claim that Swift represented the "very antipode" of himself, Murry emphasizes those elements of Swift's life and personality which most closely parallel his own—and interprets them as crucially important. That is, Murry stresses Swift's sense of homelessness, his estrangement at school, and his quest for a father. (Murry's childhood experience was obviously similar, and his series of attachments to heroes surely attests to a comparable psychic motive.) In the arena of relationships with women the correspondences are also interesting. Murry came to his "healthy" version of marriage after a series of personal disasters. His biographer informs us that his first two marriages were virtually nonphysical—far more affairs of the spirit than of the flesh. Murry employed his own "little language" with both Katherine and Violet—the letters overflow with "Wigs" and "Tigs" and "Boogies." His discovery that his pattern was to love "girl," not "woman," as well as his casting of Violet in the fantasy role of child wife parallels Swift's infantilizing of Stella. Murry, however, appears unconscious of these resonances and writes with apparent innocence that Lady Acheson "seems like so many of Swift's women friends to have been tubercular."[39]

This element of unconscious identification surely influences the conclusion that Swift's celibacy diminished his genius. Murry argues that if Swift had chosen marriage and normative healthiness—if he had, in effect, chosen a Murryian sort of self-revolution—he would have been a greater writer. So of Swift's proposal to Varina he writes, "Swift's love for Varina belonged to the heyday of the blood: it was directed, from the beginning, towards marriage as its right and natural consummation. It was the healthy natural love of a naturally passionate and naturally generous nature. Her rejection of it was probably as important in Swift's life as anything that happened to him."[40] Few would debate Murry's judgment that Swift was sexually unbalanced, that his later works suggest neurosis, but his assumption that Swift's self-repression crippled his art ignores the opposite possibility, that Swift's genius represented the creative inversion of neurosis. In short, Murry's belief in the healthiness of marriage prejudices him against admitting that celibacy could nourish art. Griffith's charge that Murry was temperamentally incapable of appreciating Swift's posture rings true, and we must agree that whatever Murry's intention, *Jonathan Swift* is not the nec plus ultra of objectivity.[41] He was not able to leave himself out of his work, nor would it have been all to the good if he had. No other critic has displayed so much acumen about Swift's relations to women. The study would have gained, however, from an acknowledgment of a certain psychic identification, which could have led to an open confrontation of ideas, as in Murry's criticism of Eliot.

Murry's conclusions were received according to the preconceptions of his readers, who were divided into contending camps. Murry is most aligned with what Denis Donoghue calls the "Swift-as-Heathcliff" view, the heritage of Thackerian horror of Swiftian scatology. This concentration on Swift's writings as the expression of misanthropy and "demoniacal malevolence" Donoghue identifies with Eliot, Huxley, and Shaw.[42] (One must also, in connection with Murry, think of Lawrence's allusion to Swift in *Lady Chatterly's Lover* and of F. R. Leavis's judgment that Swift's writings display "probably the most remarkable expression of negative feelings and attitudes that literature can offer—the spectacle of creative powers . . . exhibited consistently in negation and rejection.")[43] The other camp Donoghue represents with Sherburn's statement that "it is Swift's rhetoric rather than his life that is thrilling."[44]

According to some members of the first group, Murry failed to go far enough. G. Wilson Knight, for instance, says that because Murry is "reluctant to depart from traditional valuations in either religion or the psychology of sex," he doesn't fully depict the element of insanity and sexual abnormality in Swift's genius, while the *New York Times* reviewer regretted the academic conventionality of the book. "It would be churlish not to applaud the success of his Swift-like gesture in the face of the pundits who dismissed his earlier work as 'too emotional' or 'critically unsound.' But it is disappointing not to have from the author of *Keats and Shakespeare* an equally vivid and human portrait of the great dean of St. Patrick's."[45] Professional Swiftians, for the most part, thought it unsatisfactory, marred by mistaken hypotheses and factual errors and omissions. Murry's use of secondary sources for biographical data irritated more academic critics, and several scholars charged him with knowing too little of eighteenth-century religious and literary traditions. Murry interpreted Swift's religious sense very narrowly, suggesting that Christianity provided him a refuge from the precariousness of human affairs and arguing that Swift used Christian doctrine chiefly as a system giving "supernatural sanction of reason on which to depend."[46] His treatment of *Gulliver*, Herbert Davis suggests, shows his unfamiliarity with the tradition of Christian morality from which Swift's satires were drawn, and Bullitt notes that Murry lacked sophistication in the traditions and techniques of neoclassic satire.[47]

Despite the validity of these objections, *Jonathan Swift* possesses narrative vigor and acute commentary, which led most reviewers to more praise than faultfinding. V. S. Pritchett summarized the overall attractiveness of the book: "It is absorbing to read, it is continuously pliant and sympathetic in approach, gentle in handling a fierce character and mature in judgement. . . . He has conveyed the central fact—that Swift's life was a passion."[48] Murry himself was bemused by the sudden resurgence of his fame provoked by *Jonathan Swift*, although he was pleased by this evidence that he had achieved his purposes—of proving to himself that he was "at bottom a good literary critic" and of producing a "standard book on Swift for generations to come."[49] In comparison with Murry's other major works on individual writers, *Jonathan Swift* is more widely useful, but in the fullest sense less interesting, posing less of a challenge to future commentators.

The long essay on George Gissing published posthumously in *Katherine Mansfield and Other Literary Studies* is a better example of "objective criticism" than *Jonathan Swift*.[50] Here Murry's distinctive critical virtues—his responsiveness to the author behind the work, his sympathy with the themes—work inventively to produce new perspectives and fresh grounds for appreciation. Characteristically tying the novels to the life, Murry finds that the Gissing characters that involve self-portraiture inevitably depict men whose lives have been damaged by a past indiscretion, from whose effect they are never entirely free. He reminds us that Gissing became a social outcast and Grub Street journalist in consequence of his marriage to a prostitute. Murry suggests that a major strength of Gissing's fiction is the memorableness of his women characters. Gissing's second wife was, in Murry's words, "a vulgar shrew . . . of the pernicious sort who enchains a man by her sexual attractions." The virago type is a recurring figure in Gissing's novels, and his most interesting piece of literary criticism is an essay on the figure of the shrew in Dickens. Obsessed by the type, Gissing juxtaposed the demonic female figure against ideal women, who are capable of faithfulness and self-transcendent love but who usually prove unobtainable. Murry describes Gissing's fascination with these opposed female types as the consequence of disillusionment in a nature inclined to be impassioned and indiscriminately idealizing of women. His discovery that Gissing was never able to portray an ideal man as he did an ideal woman is equally perceptive.

Murry's sympathetic interest in Gissing's treatment of women is clearly attributable to his own experience of Betty Cockbayne. His third marriage parallels Gissing's life with Ellen Underwood, recorded in *The Year of the Jubilee*, even down to the detail of separation, a reconciliation producing a second child, and reseparation. The parallel experience serves, in this essay, to enhance Murry's perceptions about the springs of Gissing's creativity and to focus on an element that other critics, viewing Gissing in relation to sociological themes, had neglected. Murry explicates and clarifies without overstating his case or using Gissing for his own ends. The only remarks of which we might complain arise from wholly unconscious chauvinism rather than from a wrenching of Gissing. (Murry irrelevantly suggests that the preponderance of damaging wives over damaging husbands in literature reflects a genuine pattern in men-women relationships, without reflecting that the literature he speaks of was written by men rather than women.) The same unconscious bias probably accounts for Murry's dismissal of *The Odd Women*, a novel that now seems unusually perspicacious, as a "strange failure."

The qualities Murry most admires in Gissing and makes real to us—his idealism and fierce moral independence—reflect lived values in Murry's own career and expand the intrinsic convincingness of the essay. Murry's private experience enhances his capacity to enter the writer's emotional world and elucidate it for us. As John Gross says, his study of Gissing is "a narrow interpretation, but a compelling one."[51] It leads us to want to read Gissing again.

Murry and His Contemporaries

In his readiness to "surrender to his own temperament,"[52] Murry was related to the nineteenth-century romantics and to Carlyle; in his qualities as a moralist, he was a link between Matthew Arnold and F. R. Leavis. The combination of traits, Murry wryly acknowledged when he was analyzing the reasons for his neglect by editors and reviewers, made him "troublesome," "difficult to pigeonhole."[53] The difference between Murry and Leavis, for instance, is considerable, although the two have more in common than either would have been likely to admit. Both men regarded themselves as more fundamentally "serious" than other critics and cultivated a sense of their separateness from the cultural establishment, just as both located virtue in a lost organic society and disapproved of contemporary culture. But Leavis's moral dictums were applied in severely hierarchical terms; he consistently endorsed certain writers in a way that derogated others and imposed strict choices. He was averse to Murry's sort of eclecticism and, even when they agreed about the significance of a writer, as they did about Lawrence, charged that Murry's judgments arose from personal sympathy or antipathy rather than from a disciplined response to the total imaginative effect of a work. The key accusation was lack of discipline or rigor. Leavis repeatedly admonished Murry for writing in uncritical or precritical ways. For his part, Murry thought Leavis deprived great writers of their vitality by putting them on the shelf, making them classics rather than using them, as Murry did, to influence the actual conduct of life. His most polemical criticism of Leavis appeared in an essay on Fielding. In *The Great Tradition* Leavis said that Fielding "is important not because he leads to Mr. J. B. Priestley but because he leads to Jane Austen, to appreciate whose distinction is to feel that life isn't long enough to permit of one's giving much time to Fielding, or any to Mr. Priestley."[54] Murry's response was that Leavis "cannot appreciate something without depreciating something else," and his essay is designed to convince us that Fielding still matters. He had, Murry says, all the qualities Leavis praises in great novelists: "a vital capacity for experience, a kind of reverent openness before life, and a marked moral intensity."[55] *Tom Jones* is a great novel not only because it is full of enduring characters but because it upholds individuality and spontaneity and criticizes the forces repressive of these human qualities. In Fielding "good nature," in the sense of a capacity for "imaginative sympathy with the joys and sorrows of others," is the highest moral virtue, and it alone is capable of love. Fielding's morality is always on the side of life, for to him "tenderness, warmth, sympathy, gratitude, generosity" are the true virtues, and "cruelty, coldness, hypocrisy, ungratefulness, meanness" the cardinal vices. "In Defense of Fielding" exhibits Murry's flair for conveying the most attractive quality of a writer, for making us desire to read again the work he is describing, and it makes a telling point against Leavis, for if literary standards require excluding Fielding in order to establish Jane Austen's merit, they end in unduly narrowing our literary pleasures. The essay triumphantly establishes what Murryian appreciativeness offers against Leavisite stringency.

The more significant opposition is not that of Murry and Leavis but of Murry and the New Critics, whose scientific reductionism Murry viewed with alarm. From the 1920s on he saw quite clearly that the concentration on formal technique and the proliferation of a specialized critical vocabulary were inimical to the kind of criticism he thought important. The New Critics, he charged, leave out the only elements in our experience of literature which matter. Although he viewed his own disinclination for formal analysis as a shortcoming ("I am . . . always notoriously weakest in the examination of the technical side of a work," he told Katherine Mansfield), he refused to "treat art as a clever game."[56] In "A Reply to I. A. Richards," Murry ridiculed the sterility of Richards's description of the emotion produced by great literature as "an indication that all is right here and now with the nervous system"[57] and countered Richards's attack on the "revelationist theory of literature." Upholding the idea that "poetry, in its highest form, does actually reveal somewhat of the else hidden nature of reality," Murry argued that the unique quality of the artist is precisely his capacity to experience the "real" more profoundly than others and that our response to his statement involves enlarging our own "experiencing natures," coming closer to a perception of reality. We do not go to Shakespeare, Murry insists, to learn if our nervous systems are in order. "The words of the poem are the cause of the reaction to the poem only in so far as their possible meanings are circumscribed and governed by the reaction to the poem as a whole. Unless analysis observes this inward humility, it becomes incontinent; it not only brings us no nearer, but definitely takes us away from the goal of more intimate understanding."[58] A posthumously published review of books by Blackmur and Tate connects the proliferation of "arcane" criticism with the learned twentieth-century poetry of Yeats, Eliot, Pound, Stevens, and Auden and stresses the economic reliance of both on the university. This sort of poetry, he points out, "depends on the reality of words to carry all other reality"; it creates private worlds, and the academic criticism which strives to elucidate it, to make the private world public, ends in engendering "other private worlds which lack the freshness of creation, or the decisiveness of incarnation."[59]

These reactions to technical criticism, stretching across three decades, have in common a determination to resist the forces separating art and mass culture. A governing impulse of Murry's criticism was bringing literature out of the academy, to which it more and more insistently retreated during his lifetime, to the people. He wanted to make art a life force, not a subject of esoteric study. When we are tempted to deride Murry's enthusiastic rhetoric, his offenses against the decorum of intellectual exploration, it is wise to recall that he became, as he intended, an influential middle-brow writer whose books sold well even during periods of official unpopularity, whom people stopped on the street to talk about Shakespeare. I do mean to suggest not that Murry deliberately debased ideas in order to win popularity but that his catholic criterion allowed him to relate literature to the lives of people who might never otherwise have appreciated it. His criticism found an audience because it impressed people as being written out of deeply felt experience, not out of academic debate.

Murry's position as a middle-brow writer who substantially influenced the general reading public is analogous to Aldous Huxley's, and although Huxley was antagonistic to Murry, there are some interesting parallels in their spheres of ideology and activity. Both were, in Martin Green's sense, "undandy,"[60] operating aside from Bloomsbury and from academic circles. They were nonspecialists with wide-ranging interests that cut across the boundaries between literature, religion, and politics. Both were representative British thinkers who objected to the ethos of their time, focused on man's alienation from nature as a source of modern malaise, and proposed moral remedies. Both were magnetized by Lawrence. In fact, there is reason to suppose that Huxley's venomous portrait of Murry in *Point Counter Point* was prompted by some jealousy of Lawrence's feeling for Murry. In any case, listening to Huxley describe Lawrence, one has the sense that one might well be listening to Murry: "a being, somehow, of another order, more sensitive, more highly conscious, more capable of feeling than even the most gifted of common men . . . To be with Lawrence was a kind of adventure, a voyage of discovery into newness and otherness. For, being himself of a different order, he inhabited a different universe from that of common men—a brighter and intenser world of which, while he spoke, he would make you free."[61]

Huxley's infatuation with Lawrentian vitalism was shortlived. Lawrence had served to release him from the skepticism of his early novels, but he was temperamentally ill suited to living out life values, and the ephemeral humanism of *Do What You Will* gave way within two years after Lawrence's death to the mysticism and spiritual conversion recorded in *Eyeless in Gaza*. Thereafter Huxley preached an essentially ascetic doctrine of nonattachment which was far closer to Eliot (despite its non-Christian framework) than to Lawrence. Murry's "mysticism of descent" incorporated life values and was therefore more truly Lawrentian. Murry suggested the fundamental difference between them when he wrote: "The struggle of the Western man is not (in my experience) simply to be 'non-attached,' which is Mr. Huxley's favorite phrase; the struggle of the Western man is to *love*."[62]

Murry readily praised those works of Huxley with which he felt compatible. The social theory of *Ends and Means*, for instance, includes ideas Murry was exploring. As members of the Peace Pledge Union they had like concerns, but Murry did not deeply admire Huxley, and Huxley continued to speak of Murry in terms that reflected some personal antipathy. Certainly he failed to acknowledge the costing changes in Murry's personality since the *Athenaeum* days, and it seemed gratuitously unkind of him to write Mary Murry after John's death that John's "very power of appreciating other men's works of art and philosophy often resulted, it seems to me, in his becoming involved, under their influence, in real-life situations which he was temperamentally unequipped to cope with. It was as though one part of his mind—the part concerned with concepts—were trying to make him feel and believe and do things which the rest of his organism was not inclined to feel or believe or do."[63] In this, as in other relationships with men of larger reputation, Murry was the more generous.

But, in fact, by the end of his career, Murry had very few links with literary contemporaries, and none at all with the younger generation of artists and critics. Even during that brief period of editorial fame in the

twenties he operated outside coteries and was unimpressed by movements that figure largely in literary history. Ezra Pound he ignored
entirely. He criticized Yeats for constructing an unintelligible private
myth and never reconsidered him.[64] Acknowledging the genius of Proust
and Joyce, Murry did not like them, and he never altered the position he
took in a 1924 essay, "The Break-Up of the Novel," that their work led
toward a *"reductio ad absurdum* of subjectivity" which made literature
inaccessible. "The art of literature," he contended, "is based upon a
compromise. The writer who does not accept the condition may be a man
of genius, but he is an imperfect writer. As Goethe said, the writer who
writes without the conviction that he will have a million readers has
mistaken his vocation. . . . it is much easier to be complicated than to be
simple, to be mysterious than to be intelligible. . . . A truly great novel is a
tale to the simple, a parable to the wise, and a direct revelation of reality in
the light of a unique consciousness to the man who has made it part of his
being."[65] Not surprisingly, Thomas Hardy was his hero among the older
generation of novelists. Murry was among the first to appreciate Hardy's
poems as well as the novels and considered him the greatest living English
writer during the 1920s, for he alone was "adequate to the scrutiny of life"
which the war experience demanded.[66]

He praised Wilfred Owen and Siegfried Sassoon among the young war
poets but later made Lawrence the model for poetry, as for the novel, and
regretted that younger poets chose Eliot instead. He was fixedly unsym-
pathetic to all that tended to the arcane and consequently rejected people
like Auden and Wallace Stevens. As he grew older, he more and more
measured writers by the humanity of their vision, and it is interesting that
he chose to praise J. D. Salinger's *Catcher in the Rye* in his last radio
broadcast, "Generosity in Literature."[67] His only "discovery" among new
writers was his friend the novelist Henry Williamson, whom he mildly
overrated by calling him a "truly gifted artist . . . working on the grand
scale."[68] (He took pains to delineate Williamson's artistic defects, however,
and by no means upheld him as a new prophet.)

Murry's literary taste was sure. Nowhere in the long stream of literary
comment do we find his judgment absolutely wrong, as we find Leavis
wrong, for instance, in his applause of quite negligible writers. Of course,
Murry was not as aggressive a critic as Leavis. His primary impulse was to
praise artists who embodied positive values for him rather than to dispar-
age those he disapproved of. His concentration on great figures of the
past and his incompatibility with the main currents of twentieth-century
literature do result in an evasion of certain issues which Leavis con-
fronted. The absence of sustained, forceful comment on his contemporaries (always excepting Lawrence) limited Murry's influence and is
one of the reasons for his relative obscurity now. Since he primarily wrote

about literature that appealed to him empathetically, he never evaluated the literature of his own age in a way that stimulated his fellow critics or gave a new direction to young artists.

The Achievement

When we survey the prolific body of criticism that spans the years 1912 to 1957, it is clear that Murry stands among the important twentieth-century critics. His best criticism is among the best of this, or any, time. He shares with other good critics the gift of quickly penetrating to the essence of the work he is discussing and making observations about it that bear upon the whole canon. His extraordinarily responsive sensibility, what D. H. Lawrence called his "valuable inertia," enabled him to write, as it were, from within the work he was discussing, to make the author part of his own being. This quality, in combination with acute native intelligence, impressive erudition, and an absence of preconceptions, lends him real individuality. He gave literature an important cultural status by regarding it as the one surviving instrument of the spiritual life in the modern world, an attitude which lends dignity and weight to his judgments. His integrity as a critic was tied to his commitment to taking literature seriously, as a guide to conduct, and his perspective was unwaveringly humane.

His individual insights are consequential, but it is more in his attitude toward literature than in the particular piece of criticism that Murry made his mark on the century. He insisted on the value of subjectivity in an age that turned criticism into a technical vocation. Beginning in revolt against the genial laxness of Edwardian literary journalism, he stood by the middle of his career against the tides of scientism and intellectual formalization. To insist on the worth of Murry's voice is not to derogate the twentieth-century revolution in critical method but to suggest that by proffering unfashionable options he offered a healthy antithesis to the prevailing critical fashion—not least by upholding the romantics against the cult of metaphysical poetry sponsored by Eliot and his followers.

Much that he wrote was second-rate. No one has ever had trouble locating Murry's flaws. The entanglement of his personality and his criticism was damaging as often as it was beneficent. The urgency of his private search for personal harmony sometimes distorted his thought. It made him impatient with dogged reasoning, with thinking through to the logical heart of issues, and too eager to find the definitive idea, the redemptive hero. By projecting himself into his subjects, he enhanced his quality as a discoverer but sometimes imputed to the work he was discussing ideas he was exploring for himself or found a larger truth than the author will bear. This, it seems to me, is a difficulty with *Keats and Shakespeare.*

Self-annihilation became part of his creed because that was for him precisely the most difficult act; struggling with the exigencies of his own nature, he made a theatrical performance of conquering the ego, which included a confusing claim for achieving self-forgetfulness through personal confession. "Although it may seem paradoxical that the deliverance from egotism should express itself in an 'extravagantly egotistical' style, this is precisely one of the paradoxes which spiritual discrimination should find easiest to accept."[69] He suffered from an incessant need to reveal himself—to reveal, even, the processes of his own thought—as though the forms of introspection, rather than their issue, were salient in criticism. Katherine Mansfield, always his most cogent critic, attempted to discourage this trait, which she called his "sham personality . . . , this awful insidious temptation to show your wounds." She explicitly denounced its appearance in the preface to *Aspects of Literature*, where Murry candidly announced that he had revised none of the articles in this collection because he assumed his readers would enjoy seeing the progress of his thought. After reading this statement Katherine exploded: "My dear Bogey. How could a person say such a thing? It's so naive as to be silly, or so arrogant as to be fantastique. Suppose I wrote: 'I have dated my stories as I venture to hope my readers may enjoy tracing my development—the ripening of my powers . . . ' What would you think! You'd faint! It is indecent, no less, to say such things. And one doesn't think them!"[70]

Murry did continue to think, and say, such things. In a real sense he felt his own emotions and experience to be tremendously important. He intrisically viewed himself as a symbolic man—not a figure of genius, but "everyman." That is why he interpreted his own experience as crucial for others and recorded it so carefully. The positive side of this trait is that as a man of sensibility and intelligence he did diagnose the diseases of his own culture through dissecting his private conflicts. By taking his experience seriously he was empowered to speak about issues that concerned everyone in accents of deeply felt truths. Conducting literary criticism as a discovery of what he was thinking himself, he contacted what mattered most, the enduringly significant.

Murry's claim for himself is, on another level, simply preposterous, and the air of being a self-appointed messiah, in combination with his changeable discipleships and lack of forcefulness, is responsible for the accusations of fraudulence and charlatanism which circulated around him throughout his career. It is an index of his startling naivete that he never understood how this attitude alienated people, and his protestations that he was only a vessel for ideas greater than himself simply made the matter worse. In "The End of an Egoist," for instance, he says that since his mystical experience he has developed the faculty of regarding himself "impersonally." "From a certain point in the year 1923 I ceased to take responsibility for myself. The burden of that responsibility was put somewhere else. I personally ceased to bear it."[71] Such statements exasperated Murry's most ardent supporters, although Richard Rees testifies to the intrinsic accuracy of Murry's self-description. "The residue of his mysticism was a core of impersonality which gave me the impression that he genuinely and profoundly felt himself to be, not a free agent, but an instrument; and his *personal* success or failure in life was of no concern to him at all."[72]

There is an equivocal quality about all Murry's achievements. On one hand, the constant presence of the critic in the criticism makes his work strikingly individual, strikingly responsive. As Cranston says, "All his best books are *tours de force* which could not have been written by any other hand."[73] On the other, Murry hedges his subject by the perimeters of his own temperament and thereby misses much of interest. One may think of his *William Blake* in these terms. In *Shakespeare*, however, Murry retained his attitude of intimacy with the writer without pretending to encompass him fully and thereby offered a fresh version of his genius.

We see the worst side of his self-projecting impulse in the prose style itself. A naturally facile writer who worked with enviable rapidity, Murry refused to rewrite, in part because of his desire to reveal the motions of his own mind. This stubbornness was connected to central convictions about the tentativeness of judgments, "negative capability," the doctrine of experience. In practice, however, it meant falling into cliché and tired repetition, into archaism and flatulence and gush. The undisciplined rhetoric coincides with the vein of loose emotionalism in Murry to produce passages that disfigure the work of which they are a part, and no work of his is entirely unspoiled by this lack of control. Ultimately, such an attitude toward words indicates a lack of respect for them which is not easy to excuse in a serious critic. Kermode's severe judgment on the style is difficult to contest. "His prose is undistinguished, and often strangely like that of the litterateurs he despised and replaced. Really good criticism can catch quality from the work on which it attends. Murry's never does; therefore it lacks the one thing necessary to long preservation."[74]

All of these defects persuade us that Murry frequently wasted his talent: weighty ideas are cast out unballasted by careful exposition; months of research and meditation are squandered in a hasty article; fine perceptions are blemished by the vulgarity with which they are expressed. For it is chiefly form, rather than substance, that is objectionable in Murry. His was a personality perpetually on the edge of defeating itself. Thayer pithily described him as a "strange, eccentric, neurotic man—generous, impulsive, quixotic, mercurial, naive, nutty and bright—with enough problems to suit almost anyone."[75] His contradictoriness and contrariness proceeded in large measure from his profound social discomfiture—his sense of himself as unclassed and rootless. He quoted Katherine Mansfield's description of him as a "monk without a monastery" in explanation of his spiritual malaise, and it is tempting to speculate on the purer uses he might have made of his gift in another age, for he found his own time deeply uncomfortable.

All limitations considered, we are left with a great deal of value in Murry's work. His intense purposiveness and energy and the singular probity of his pursuit of values lent vitality to his criticism and made him a distinctive force in his society. Sir Richard Rees, who knew most of the substantial intellectual figures of England during the last fifty years, said that "Murry was the most valuable intellectual I have ever personally known."[76] The tributes from those who viewed Murry's career with interest contrast sharply with the trivial flippancy of the establishment attitude toward him. Hilary Corke's denigration of Murry as a "great lovable, pointless booby"[77] in 1960 is remarkable for not having provoked a rebuttal. The supercilious arrogance of this fairly typical attitude lends point to Jones's observation that Middleton Murry "has been openly and casually jeered at (for he was never any good at biting back) by people without half his talent or a tenth of his dedicated industry."[78] Murry commands our respect because he desired above all to be a good man, and his failings were honorable ones.

He was a man of extremes, whose criticism exposes his passions. He indicted the twentieth century for its inhumanity and impersonality and reminded us that art divorced from life is sterile, that what distinguishes great literature is its capacity to rejuvenate the reader and lead him to govern his life by the truths he discovers in it. Murry lived and wrote in accord with that principle. Surveying his career, one is led to wonder, as Reyner Heppenstall did by Murry's graveside, "*Why*, for so long, John Middleton Murry had not been lazy and indifferent like the rest of us."[79]

Notes

Introduction

1. Richard Rees, *A Theory of My Time: An Essay in Didactic Remembrance* (London: Secker and Warburg, 1963), p. 57.

2. *Ottoline at Garsington: Memoirs of Lady Ottoline Morrell, 1915–1918*, ed. Robert Gathorne-Hardy (London: Faber and Faber, 1974), p. 190.

3. Rayner Heppenstall, *Four Absentees* (London: Barrier and Rockliff, 1960), p. 67.

4. Dora Carrington to Gerald Brenan, May 31, 1923, in *Carrington: Letters and Extracts from Her Diaries,* ed. David Garnett (New York: Holt, Rinehart and Winston, 1970), p. 251.

5. Rees, p. 75.

6. J. S. Collis, *Farewell to Argument* (London: Cassell, 1935), p. 203.

7. Margaret Tims, "A Biography of John Middleton Murry," *Aryan Path* 31 (Jan. 1960), p. 34.

8. John Middleton Murry, Journal, Feb. 14, 1953, as quoted by F. A. Lea, *The Life of John Middleton Murry* (London: Methuen, 1959), p. 332.

Chapter 1

1. John Middleton Murry, *Adam and Eve* (London: Dakers, 1944), p. 37.

2. John Middleton Murry, Journal, April 28, 1948, as quoted by Lea, p. 7.

3. John Middleton Murry, *Between Two Worlds* (New York: Messner, 1936), pp. 287 and 315.

4. Lea, p. 14.

5. John Middleton Murry, "Coming to London—VIII," in *Coming to London,* ed. John Lehmann (London: Phoenix House, 1957).

6. Lea, p. 16.

7. Murry, *Between Two Worlds,* p. 106.

8. Ibid., p. 154.

9. Murry to P. Landon, Jan. 1911, quoted by Lea, p. 20.

10. Lea, p. 24.

11. John Middleton Murry, "Art and Philosophy," *Rhythm* 1 (summer 1911), pp. 9–12.

12. Cyrene N. Pondrom, *The Road from Paris: French Influence on English Poetry, 1900–1920* (Cambridge: Cambridge University Press, 1974), p. 54.

13. Ibid., pp. 10–11.

14. Murry, "Art and Philosophy," p. 12.

15. Murry, "Coming to London," p. 30.

16. Murry, *Between Two Worlds,* p. 184.

17. Murry to P. Landon, April 1911, as quoted by Lea, p. 24.

18. John Middleton Murry, review of *La Chute, Blue Review* 1 (May 1913), pp. 56–62.

19. Murry, *Between Two Worlds,* pp. 180 and 185.

20. Edward Marsh, *A Number of People* (London: Heinemann, 1939), p. 226.

21. Murry, *Between Two Worlds,* p. 262.

22. Ibid., p. 312.

23. Graham Hough, *The Dark Sun: A Study of D. H. Lawrence* (1956; reprint ed., Harmondsworth, England: Penguin, 1961), p. 264.

24. Murry, *Between Two Worlds,* pp. 316–17.

25. Anthony Alpers, *Katherine Mansfield: A Biography* (New York: Knopf, 1954), pp. 167–68.

26. Lea, p. 32.

27. Katherine Mansfield, *The Journal of Katherine Mansfield,* ed. John Middleton Murry (London: Constable, 1954), p. 263 (Jan. 2, 1915).

28. D. H. Lawrence to Mary Cannon, Feb. 24, 1915, in *The Letters of D. H. Lawrence,* vol. 1, ed. Harry T. Moore (New York: Viking, 1962), p. 322.

29. Murry, *Between Two Worlds,* p. 333.

30. Lawrence to Ottoline Morrell, Feb. 1915, in *Letters of Lawrence,* p. 321.

31. Murry, *Between Two Worlds,* pp. 334–35.

32. Lawrence to Cynthia Asquith, Aug. 15, 1915, in *Letters of Lawrence,* p. 362.

33. Murry, *Between Two Worlds,* p. 351.

34. Lawrence to Katherine Mansfield and John Middleton Murry, March 8, 1916, in *Letters of Lawrence,* pp. 441–42.

35. Frieda Lawrence to John Middleton Murry, May 1954, in *Frieda Lawrence: The Memoirs and Correspondence,* ed. E. W. Tedlock (London: Heinemann, 1961), p. 342.

36. John Middleton Murry, *Reminiscences of D. H. Lawrence* (London: Cape, 1933), p. 79.

37. Murry, *Between Two Worlds,* p. 412.

38. Murry, *Reminiscences,* p. 79.

39. Lawrence to Ottoline Morrell, May 24, 1916, in *Letters of Lawrence,* pp. 452–53.

40. Lea, p. 64.

41. John Middleton Murry, "The Condition of English Literature," *New Republic* 22 (May 7, 1920), pp. 340–41.

42. John Gross, *The Rise and Fall of the Man of Letters* (New York: Macmillan, 1970), p. 247.

43. Lea, p. 52.

44. Gross, p. 247.

45. Michael Holroyd, *Lytton Strachey: A Critical Biography,* vol. 2 (London: Heinemann, 1967), p. 350.

46. Lawrence to John Middleton Murry, Oct. 11, 1916, in *Letters of Lawrence,* vol. 1, p. 479.

47. Lawrence to S. S. Koteliansky, Dec. 15, 1916, in ibid., p. 492.

48. Lawrence to Katherine Mansfield, Nov. 1918, in ibid., p. 565.

49. Lawrence to John Middleton Murry, March 6, 1919, in ibid., p. 579.

50. Lawrence to Mary Cannon, Feb. 12, 1921, in *Letters of Lawrence,* vol. 2, p. 641.

51. Lawrence to Katherine Mansfield, Feb. 6, 1920, in ibid., p. 620.

52. Mary Katherine Benet, *Writers in Love* (New York: Macmillan, 1977), p. 50.

53. Alpers, p. 65.

54. Katherine Mansfield to John Middleton Murry, Feb. 23, 1918, in *Katherine Mansfield's Letters to John Middletn Murry: 1913–1922,* ed. John Middleton Murry (London: Constable, 1951), p. 181.

55. Murry, Journal, Aug. 3, 1956, as quoted by Lea, p. 110.

56. J. W. N. Sullivan, *But for the Grace of God* (New York: Knopf, 1932), p. 150.

57. Katherine Mansfield as quoted by Lea, p. 38.

58. Murry, *Between Two Worlds,* pp. 214 and 494.

59. Katherine Mansfield to Murry, Jan. 10, 1920, in *Letters to John Middleton Murry,* p. 475.

60. Murry to V. Bartrick-Baker, March 10, 1923, as quoted by Lea, p. 104.

61. D. H. Lawrence, *Fantasia of the Unconscious* (1922; New York: Viking, 1960), p. 180.

62. Lawrence to Koteliansky, June 23, 1923, in *Letters of Lawrence,* vol. 2, p. 747.

63. John Middleton Murry, "The Cause of It All," in *To the Unknown God: Essays towards a Religion* (London: Cape, 1924), pp. 13–24.

64. Ibid., and see J. H. Watson, "A Good Workingman and His Friends: Recollections of John Middleton Murry," *London Magazine* 6 (May 1959), pp. 51–55, for an account of Murry's special appeal to the working man.

65. Murry, "On Being Inhuman," in *To the Unknown God,* pp. 152–59.

66. Martin Green, *The Von Richthofen Sisters: The Triumphant and the Tragic Modes of Love* (New York: Basic Books, 1974), p. 295.

67. Richard Aldington, *Portrait of a Genius But . . .* (London: Heinemann, 1950), p. 272.

68. Catherine Carswell, *The Savage Pilgrimage,* rev. ed. (London: Secker, 1932), p. 203.

69. Murry, *Reminiscences,* p. 202.

70. John Middleton Murry, *Son of Woman* (New York: Cape, 1931), p. 366.

71. Lawrence to John Middleton Murry, May 20, 1929, in *Letters of Lawrence,* vol. 2, p. 1154.

72. Lea, p. 122.

73. Manuscript of John Middleton Murry, 1947, quoted by Lea, p. 144.

74. Murry, Journal, Aug. 12, 1953, quoted by Lea, p. 176.

75. Murry, Journal, Oct. 30, 1930, quoted in ibid., p. 176.

76. Murry, Journal, Sept. 16, 1931, quoted in ibid., p. 187.

77. Colin Middleton Murry, *I at the Keyhole* (New York: Stein and Day, 1975), p. 168. Also published as *One Hand Clapping* (London: Gollancz, 1975).

78. Ibid., p. 54.

79. Lea, p. 312.

Chapter 2

1. Murry, *Between Two Worlds,* p. 319.

2. Collis, p. 226.

3. Joyce Cary to Gertrude Cary, 1917, quoted by Malcolm Foster, *Joyce Cary: A Biography* (Boston: Houghton Mifflin, 1968), p. 155.

4. Katherine Mansfield to Murry, Dec. 1917, in *Letters to John Middleton Murry*, p. 105.

5. John Middleton Murry, *Poems: 1916–1920* (London: Cobden-Sanderson, 1921), p. 35.

6. Murry, 1913 Notes, quoted by Lea, p. 37.

7. Katherine Mansfield to Murry, Dec. 5, 1919, in *Letters to John Middleton Murry*, p. 430.

8. John Middleton Murry, *Cinammon and Angelica* (London: Cobden-Sanderson, 1920), p. 25.

9. S. P. B. Mais, *Some Modern Authors* (London: Richards, 1923), p. 131.

10. Ernest G. Griffin, *John Middleton Murry* (New York: Twayne, 1969), pp. 29–32.

11. Rebecca West, review of *The Things We Are*, *New Statesman* 19 (June 24, 1922), p. 326.

12. Katherine Mansfield to Murry, Dec. 5, 1919, in *Letters to John Middleton Murry*, p. 431.

13. Dorothy Brewster, *East-West Passage* (London: Allen and Unwin, 1954), p. 162.

14. John Middleton Murry, *Dostoevsky: A Critical Study* (London: Secker, 1916), p. 37.

15. Ibid., pp. 148, 173, and 247.

16. Ibid., p. 219.

17. Ibid., p. 254.

18. Murry, *Between Two Worlds*, pp. 368–69.

19. *Nation* 104 (Jan. 4, 1917), p. 23.

20. *Bookman* 44 (Nov. 1916), pp. 299–300.

21. Murry, *Dostoevsky*, p. 34.

22. John Middleton Murry, "The Honesty of Russia," in *The Evolution of an Intellectual*, 2nd ed. (London: Cape, 1927), pp. 16–29.

23. John Middleton Murry. "The Significance of Russia Literature," in *Discoveries* (London: Cape, 1924), pp. 45–80.

24. Ibid., pp. 54–55.

25. Griffin, p. 39.

26. Murry, *Between Two Worlds*, p. 314.

27. John Middleton Murry, "Thoughts on Tchehov," parts 1 and 2, in *Aspects of Literature* (London: Cape, 1934), pp. 76–90. Originally published in the *Athenaeum*, Aug. 22, 1919, and March 5, 1920; reprinted in *Selected Criticism, 1916–1957*, ed. Richard Rees (London: Oxford University Press, 1960).

28. Ibid., pp. 76–81.

29. Frank Kermode, "On the Frontiers of Criticism," *Manchester Guardian* (June 10, 1960), p. 8.

30. Murry to Katherine Mansfield, March 30, 1920, quoted by Lea, p. 22.

31. T. S. Eliot, Preface to the 1928 Edition, *The Sacred Wood* (1928; reprint ed., London: Methuen, 1969), pp. vii–viii.

32. Murry, "The Function of Criticism," in *Aspects of Literature*, pp. 1–14.

33. Eliot, "The Perfect Critic," in *The Sacred Wood*, p. 7.

34. Murry, "Poetry and Criticism," in *Aspects of Literature*, p. 180.

35. Ibid., pp. 132–33.

36. John Middleton Murry, "A Critical Credo," in *Countries of the Mind,* 1st ser. (London: Collins, 1922), pp. 240–41. Page numbers in text refer to this edition.

37. John Middleton Murry, *The Problem of Style* (1922; reprint ed., Oxford: Oxford University Press Paperbacks, 1960), p. 3.

38. Ibid., pp. 11–12.

39. David Lodge, *The Language of Fiction* (New York: Columbia University Press, 1966), p. 5.

40. Murry, *The Problem of Style,* p. 97.

41. T. S. Eliot, "Hamlet and His Problems," in *The Sacred Wood,* p. 100.

42. Murry, *The Problem of Style,* p. 17.

43. Ibid., p. 71.

44. Ibid., pp. 75–76.

45. Ibid., p. 85.

46. T. S. Eliot, "Tradition and the Individual Talent," in *The Sacred Wood,* pp. 53–54..

47. Murry, *The Problem of Style,* p. 129.

48. Ibid., p. 84.

49. William R. Heath, "The Literary Criticism of John Middleton Murry," *PMLA* 70 (March 1955), p. 53.

50. James R. Bennett, "The Problem of Style," *D. H. Lawrence Review* 2 (spring 1969), pp. 41–42.

51. W. K. Wimsatt, Jr., and Monroe Beardsley, "The International Fallacy," in *The Verbal Icon* (Lexington: University of Kentucky Press, 1954), pp. 3–18.

52. T. S. Eliot, Foreword to *Katherine Mansfield and Other Literary Studies,* by John Middleton Murry (London: Constable, 1959), p. x.

53. Heath, p. 56.

54. Kermode, "On the Frontiers of Criticism," p. 8.

55. John Middleton Murry, "Metaphor," in *Countries of the Mind,* 2nd ser. (London: Oxford University Press, 1931), pp. 1–16.

56. Murry, "The Nature of Poetry," in *Discoveries,* pp. 16–17. Page numbers in text refer to this edition.

57. Murry, Journal, Aug. 3, 1956, quoted by Lea, p. 110.

Chapter 3

1. John Middleton Murry, *Keats and Shakespeare* (London: Oxford University Press, 1925), p. 6.

2. Ibid., p. 129.

3. Ibid., p. 154.

4. Ibid., p. 95.

5. Collis, p. 204.

6. Murry, *Keats and Shakespeare,* p. 6.

7. John Keats to B. R. Haydon, May 10 and 11, 1817, in *The Letters of John Keat,* ed. Maurice Buxton Forman, 2nd ed. (London: Oxford University Press, 1935), p. 29.

8. Keats to Woodhouse, Oct. 27, 1818, in ibid., pp. 227–28.

9. Murry, *Keats and Shakespeare,* p. 53.

10. Keats to Bailey, Nov. 22, 1817, in *Letters of Keats,* p. 67.

11. Keats to Bailey, Aug. 14, 1918, in ibid., p. 368.

12. Keats to George and Tom Keats, Dec. 21, 1817, in ibid., p. 72.

13. Murry, *Keats and Shakespeare,* p. 55.

14. Keats to George and Georgiana Keats, April 15, 1819, in *Letters of Keats,* p. 72.

15. John Middleton Murry, "The Parables of Jesus," in *Things to Come* (London: Cape, 1928), pp. 157–76.

16. Richard Harter Fogle, "Beauty and Truth: John Middleton Murry on Keats," *D. H. Lawrence Review* 2 (spring 1969), p. 74.

17. Murry, *Keats and Shakespeare,* pp. 135 and 147.

18. Keats to George and Georgiana Keats, Dec. 1918, in *Letters of Keats,* p. 258.

19. Murry, *Keats and Shakespeare,* p. 116.

20. Keats to George and Georgiana Keats, Feb. 18, 1819, in *Letters of Keats,* p. 305.

21. C. M. Bowra, *The Romantic Imagination* (New York: Oxford University Press, 1961), p. 148.

22. Keats to Benjamin Bailey, Nov. 22, 1817, in *Letters of Keats,* p. 67.

23. Murry, *Keats and Shakespeare,* pp. 18–22.

24. Ibid., p. 75.

25. Ibid., p. 143.

26. Ibid., p. 92.

27. F. R. Leavis, "Keats," *Scrutiny* 4 (March 1936), p. 377; E. M. W. Tillyard, *The Miltonic Setting: Past and Present* (New York: Barnes and Noble, 1966), p. 29.

28. Murry, Journal, Jan. 11, 1949, quoted by Lea, p. 334.

29. Murry, *Keats and Shakespeare,* p. 72.

30. Ibid., p. 229.

31. Griffin, p. 86.

32. Murry, *Keats and Shakespeare,* p. 167.

33. Keats to George and Georgiana Keats, Sept. 27, 1819, *Letters of Keats,* p. 425.

34. Murry, *Keats and Shakespeare,* p. 215.

35. Tillyard, *The Miltonic Setting: Past and Present,* pp. 29–31.

36. John Middleton Murry, *Keats* (1955; reprint ed., New York: Minerva, 1968), p. 255.

37. Griffin, p. 95.

38. Unpublished manuscript, quoted by Lea, p. 344.

39. *Times Literary Supplement* (Oct. 26, 1933), p. 727.

40. Basil de Selincourt, "The Problem of Blake—Self and Its Annihilation," *Observer* (Oct. 1, 1933), p. 4.

41. T. R. Barnes, review of *William Blake, Scrutiny* 2 (March 1934), pp. 424–26.

42. G. E. Bentley, Jr., and Martin K. Murni, *A Blake Bibliography* (Minneapolis: University of Minnesota Press, 1964), pp. 23–24.

43. W. Blunt, "Blake and the Scholars," *New York Review of Books* 2 (Oct. 28, 1965), p. 280.

44. Northrop Frye, Introduction to *Blake: A Collection of Critical Essays* (Englewood Cliffs, N.J.: Prentice-Hall, 1966), p. 5.

45. Rees, *A Theory of My Time,* p. 62.

46. Murry, Journal, Aug. 16, 1931, quoted by Lea, p. 187.

47. Murry, Journal, Oct. 11, 1931, quoted in ibid., p. 186.

48. John Middleton Murry, *William Blake* (London: Cape, 1933), p. 316.

49. Ibid., p. 150.

50. Max Plowman to Mrs. Orgill MacKenzie, March 5, 1931, in *Bridge into the Future: The Letters of Max Plowman,* ed. D. L. P. (London: Dakers, 1944), p. 371.

51. Max Plowman, "The Key to Blake," *Aryan Path* 5 (July 1934), p. 465.

52. Murry, *William Blake,* p. 39.

53. Ibid., p. 339.

54. Keats to J. H. Reynolds, Feb. 3, 1818, and Keats to John Taylor, Feb. 27, 1818, in *Letters of Keats,* pp. 94 and 108.

55. Murry, *William Blake,* p. 353.

56. Ibid., p. 367.

57. Ibid., p. 275.

58. William Blake, *Jerusalem,* chap. 4:11, ll. 52–55.

59. Murry, *William Blake,* p. 125.

60. Murry to T. S. Eliot, Jan. 6, 1945, quoted by Lea, p. 163.

61. Lea, p. 196.

62. Murry to Max Plowman, Nov. 10, 1932, quoted by Lea, p. 200.

63. Murry, *William Blake,* p. 311.

64. Murry, Journal, Aug. 20, 1936, quoted by Lea, p. 232.

65. Murry to W. Wordsworth, Oct. 21, 1936, quoted by Lea, p. 232.

66. Collis, p. 231.

67. Lea, pp. 217–18.

68. John Middleton Murry, *Shakespeare* (London: Cape Paperback, 1965), p. 21.

69. Ibid., p. 22.

70. John Middleton Murry, "Andrew Bradley," in *Katherine Mansfield and Other Literary Portraits* (London: Nevill, 1949), pp. 110–22.

71. Preface to *Shakespeare,* p. xii, and review of *Wheel of Fire* by G. Wilson Knight, *Adelphi* 1 (Jan. 1931), p. 347.

72. G. Wilson Knight, *The Imperial Theme* (London: Methuen, 1931), pp. v–vi.

73. G. Wilson Knight, "J. Middleton Murry," in *Neglected Powers: Essays on Nineteenth and Twentieth Century Literature* (London: Routledge and Kegan Paul, 1971), pp. 359, 365–66.

74. Murry, *Shakespeare,* pp. xviii and 24.

75. Ibid., p. ix.

76. Murry, "A Neglected Heroine of Shakespeare," in *Countries of the Mind,* 1st ser., pp. 29–50.

77. Murry, "Coriolanus," in *Discoveries,* pp. 263–86.

78. Murry, "The Creation of Falstaff," in ibid., pp. 223–62.

79. Murry, "To Be or Not to Be," in *Things to Come,* pp. 230–39.

80. John Middleton Murry, "The Mortal Moon," in *John Clare and Other Studies* (London: Nevill, 1950), pp. 246–55.

81. Murry, "Shakespeare's Dedication," in *Countries of the Mind,* 2nd ser. pp. 97–112.

82. T. S. Eliot, "Books of the Quarter," *Criterion* 15 (1936), pp. 708–10; E. M. W. Tillyard, *Shakespeare's History Plays* (1944; reprint ed., Harmondsworth, England: Penguin, 1966), p. 233; Knight, *The Imperial Theme*, p. v; Kenneth Muir, Introduction to *Shakespeare: The Comedies: A Collection of Critical Essays,* ed. Kenneth Muir (Englewood Cliffs, N.J.: Prentice-Hall, 1965), p. 6.

83. C. G. Thayer, "Murry's Shakespeare," *D. H. Lawrence Review* 2 (spring 1969), p. 55.

84. Feb. 8, 1936, p. 101.

85. Murry, *Shakespeare,* p. 134.

86. Ibid., p. 140.

87. Ibid., p. 185.

88. Ibid., pp. 184–85.

89. Ibid., p. 183.

90. Griffin, p. 115.

91. Murry, *Shakespeare,* p. 231.

92. Ibid., p. 174.

93. Ibid., pp. 231–232.

94. Ibid., p. 234.

95. Griffin, pp. 110–11.

96. Murry, *Shakespeare,* pp. 103–4.

97. Ibid., p. 11.

98. Ibid., p. 37.

99. Edward A. Armstrong, *Shakespeare's Imagination* (Omaha: University of Nebraska Press, 1963), p. 170.

100. Griffin, p. 109, and see Armstrong, p. 34.

101. Murry, *Shakespeare,* p. 218.

102. Ibid., p. 276.

103. Ibid., p. 189.

104. Ibid., p. 200.

105. Ibid., pp. 194–211.

106. Ibid., p. 237.

107. Ibid., p. 340.

108. Ibid., pp. xvii–xviii.

109. C. G. Thayer, "Murry's *Shakespeare,*" *D. H. Lawrence Review* 2 (spring 1969), p. 57.

110. Murry, *Shakespeare,* p. 370.

111. Ibid., p. 359.

112. Heath, "The Literary Criticism of John Middleton Murry," pp. 54–56.

113. Murry, *Shakespeare,* pp. 356–59.

114. Ibid., p. 369.

115. Ibid., p. 427.

116. Thayer, p. 59.

Chapter 4

1. Mansfield to Dorothy Brett, Aug. 29, 1921, in *The Letters of Katherine Mansfield,* vol. 2, ed. John Middleton Murry (London: Constable, 1928), pp. 131–32.

2. Murry, Journal, Feb. 27, 1954, quoted by Lea, p. 326.

3. Murry to Katherine Mansfield, March 30, 1918, quoted by Lea, p. 62.

4. Katherine Mansfield to Murry, May 25, 1921, and Dec. 13, 1919, *Letters to John Middleton Murry,* 1913–1922, pp. 640 and 447.

5. Katherine Mansfield to Murry, Oct. 26, 1919, and Dec. 1, 1920, ibid., pp. 353 and 608.

6. Murry, *Between Two Worlds,* p. 209.

7. Holroyd, vol. 2, p. 538.

8. Lady Beatrice Glenavy, *Today We Will Only Gossip* (London: Constable, 1964), p. 70.

9. Philip Waldron, "Katherine Mansfield's Journal," *Twentieth Century Literature* 20 (Jan. 1974), pp. 13–15.

10. As quoted by Lady Beatrice Glenavy, p. 69.

11. Rosemary Paris, review of *Katherine Mansfield's Letters to John Middleton Murry, Furioso* 7 (winter 1952), p. 67.

12. Benet, p. 211.

13. John Middleton Murry, "Katherine Mansfield," *New York Evening Post Literary Review* 3 (Feb. 17, 1923), pp. 461–62.

14. Mary Mantz and John Middleton Murry, *The Life of Katherine Mansfield* (London: Constable, 1933), pp. 6–7.

15. John Middleton Murry, "Katherine Mansfield," in *Katherine Mansfield and Other Literary Studies* (London: Constable, 1959), pp. 72–73.

16. Ibid., pp. 83–84.

17. Murry, "The Isolation of Katherine Mansfield," in *Katherine Mansfield and Other Literary Portraits,* pp. 7–8.

18. Murry, "Katherine Mansfield," *New York Evening Post Literary Review,* p. 461, and "Katherine Mansfield," in *Katherine Mansfield and Other Literary Studies,* p. 87.

19. Green, p. 296.

20. Murry, review of M. Chevalley's *Le roman anglais,* in *Reminiscences,* p. 320.

21. Murry, *Between Two Worlds,* p. 351.

22. Murry, "The Decay of Mr. D. H. Lawrence," in *Reminiscences,* p. 218.

23. Murry, review of Frank Swinnerton's *Coquette,* in *Reminiscences,* p. 229.

24. Murry, "The Nostalgia of Mr. D. H. Lawrence," in *Reminiscences,* pp. 218–24.

25. Ibid., p. 220.

26. Murry, "Fantasia of the Unconscious," in *Reminiscences,* p. 240.

27. Ibid.

28. Murry, "Religion and Faith," in *To the Unknown God,* pp. 53–65.

29. Murry, "*Aaron's Rod,*" in *Reminiscences,* p. 232.

30. John Middleton Murry, *Son of Woman: The Story of D. H. Lawrence* (London: Cape, 1931), 186–87.

31. Murry, *Reminiscences,* p. 110.

32. Murry, *Son of Woman,* p. 308.

33. Murry, Journal, July 21, 1934, quoted by Lea, p. 119.

34. D. H. Lawrence, "The Border Line," in *The Woman Who Rode Away and Other Stories* (Harmondsworth, England: Penguin, 1950), p. 105.

35. Murry, *Son of Woman,* p. 310.

36. D. H. Lawrence, "On Coming Home," in *Phoenix II*, ed. Warren Roberts and Harry T. Moore (New York: Viking, 1970), pp. 250–56.

37. D. H. Lawrence to John Middleton Murry, Jan. 29, 1926, in *Letters of Lawrence*, vol. 2, p. 886.

38. Murry, review of *The Poems of D. H. Lawrence*, in *Reminiscences*, p. 260.

39. Ibid., p. 261.

40. Murry, "The Doctrine of D. H. Lawrence," in *Reminiscences*.

41. John Middleton Murry and James Carruthers Young, "Modern Marriage," *Forum* 81 (Jan. 1929), pp. 22–26.

42. John Middleton Murry, *God: An Introduction to the Science of Metabiology* (London: Cape, 1929), p. 269.

43. D. H. Lawrence to John Middleton Murry, May 20, 1929, in *Letters of Lawrence*, vol. 2, p. 1154.

44. Murry, *Reminiscences*, p. 14.

45. Harry T. Moore, *The Intelligent Heart: The Story of D. H. Lawrence* (New York: Farrar, Straus and Young, 1954), p. 437.

46. Murry, *Son of Woman*, p. 366.

47. Ibid., p. 319.

48. T. S. Eliot, "Books of the Quarter," *Criterion* 10 (July 1931), p. 769.

49. Murry, *Son of Woman*, p. 71.

50. F. R. Leavis, *D. H. Lawrence: Novelist* (London: Chatto and Windus, 1955), p. 627.

51. E. M. Forster, "The Cult of D. H. Lawrence," *Spectator* 47 (April 18, 1931), p. 627.

52. Murry, *Son of Woman*, pp. 153–54.

53. Murry to Freida Lawrence, Oct. 26, 1955, in *Frieda Lawrence: The Memoirs and Correspondence*, p. 362.

54. Green, p. 294.

55. Iris Barry, review of *Son of Woman*, *Bookman* 72 (Jan. 1931), p. 547; review of *Son of Woman*, *Forum* 86 (July 1931), p. 10; Aldous Huxley, Introduction to *Letters of Lawrence*, p. x.

56. Rees, *A Theory of My Time*, p. 59.

57. Percy Hutchinson, review of *Son of Woman*, *New York Times Book Review* (April 16, 1931), p. 2.

58. T. S. Eliot, review of *Son of Woman* in "Books of the Quarter," *Criterion* 10 (July 1931), pp. 768–74.

59. Review of *Reminiscences of D. H. Lawrence*, *Spectator* 150 (Feb. 10, 1933), p. 191.

60. John Middleton Murry, "On Marriage," *Wanderer* (Jan., Feb., March, 1934), pp. 17–24, 37–47, 50–59.

61. Ibid., pp. 23–24.

62. Murry, *Adam and Eve*, p. 87.

63. Ibid., p. 136.

64. John Middleton Murry, "The Living Dead—1: D. H. Lawrence," *London Magazine* 3 (May 1956), p. 57.

65. John Middleton Murry, *Love, Freedom and Society* (London: Cape, 1957).

66. John Middleton Murry, *The Challenge of Schweitzer* (London: Jason Press, 1948), p. 74.

67. Murry, *Love, Freedom and Society,* p. 38.

68. Murry to G. Wilson Knight, quoted in Knight's "J. Middleton Murry," in *Neglected Powers,* p. 365.

69. J. B. Beer, "John Middleton Murry," *Critical Quarterly* (spring 1961), pp. 59–66.

70. Ernest G. Griffin, "The Circular and the Linear: The Middleton Murry–D. H. Lawrence Affair," *D. H. Lawrence Review* 2 (spring 1969), pp. 76–92.

71. F. R. Leavis, "The Literary Mind," *Scrutiny* 1 (May 1932), p. 27.

72. Leavis, *D. H. Lawrence: Novelist,* p. 27.

73. F. R. Leavis, " 'Lawrence Scholarship' and Lawrence," in *Anna Karenina and Other Essays* (New York: Simon and Schuster, 1969), p. 172.

74. Rees, *A Theory of My Time,* p. 47.

75. T. S. Eliot to John Middleton Murry, Aug. 29, 1925, as quoted by John D. Margolis, *T. S. Eliot's Intellectual Development: 1922–1939* (Chicago: University of Chicago Press, 1972), p. 62.

76. T. S. Eliot, "The Poetic Drama," *Athenaeum* 1 (May 14, 1920), p. 635.

77. T. S. Eliot to John Middleton Murry, July 29, 1919, quoted by Margolis, p. 53.

78. Murry to Katherine Mansfield, March 30, 1920, quoted by Lea, p. 72.

79. Virginia Woolf, *The Diary of Virginia Woolf,* vol. 2, 1920–1924, ed. Anne Olivier Bell (New York: Harcourt Brace Jovanovich, 1978), pp. 124–25.

80. T. S. Eliot to John Middleton Murry, Oct. 13, 1922, quoted by Margolis, note 42.

81. Murry to T. S. Eliot, quoted by Lea, p. 117.

82. T. S. Eliot to Marianne Moore, Feb. 3, 1927, quoted by Margolis, p. 66.

83. Lea, p. 250; Murry's remark appears in *Proceedings of Archbishop of York's Malvern Conference* (London: Longmans, Green, 1941), p. 197, and is quoted by Lea, p. 278.

84. Murry, Journal, Nov. 16, 1956, quoted by Lea, p. 347; T. S. Eliot quoted by Margolis, p. 67.

85. Murry, Journal, April 29, 1954, quoted by Lea, p. 72.

86. John Middleton Murry, "The Classical Revival," parts 1 and 2, *Adelphi* 3 (Feb. and March 1926), pp. 585–95 and 648–53.

87. Ibid., p. 590.

88. Ibid., p. 589.

89. Ibid., p. 649.

90. Ibid., pp. 650–53.

91. John Middleton Murry, "Mr. Eliot at Lambeth," *Adelphi* 2 (April 1931), p. 70.

92. Murry, Journal, Aug. 3, 1956, quoted by Lea, p. 110.

93. John Middleton Murry, "On Romanticism," *Adelphi* 1 (Aug. 1923), p. 84.

94. T. S. Eliot, "The Function of Criticism," *Criterion* 2 (Oct. 1923), pp. 34–39.

95. John Middleton Murry, "More about Romanticism," *Adelphi* 1 (Dec. 1923), p. 559.

96. John Middleton Murry, "Romanticism and the Tradition," *Criterion* 2 (April 1924), p. 283.

97. F. M. [Vivien Eliot], "Letters of the Moment," *Criterion* 2 (April 1924), p. 362; "Books of the Quarter," *Criterion* 2 (July 1924), p. 484. Margolis discusses

the identity of F. M. and adduces that Murry did not know that the initials had been used by Vivien Eliot.

98. John Middleton Murry, "Towards a Synthesis," *Criterion* 5 (June 1927), p. 312.

99. M. C. D'Arcy, "The Thomistic Synthesis and Intelligence," *Criterion* 6 (Sept. 1927), pp. 227–28, and Charles Mauron, "Concerning 'Intuition,' " trans. T. S. Eliot. *Criterion* 6 (Sept. 1927), p. 233.

100. Ramon Fernandez, "A Note on Intelligence and Intuition," trans. T. S. Eliot, *Criterion* 6 (Oct. 1927), pp. 332–39; T. S. Eliot, "Mr. Middleton Murry's Synthesis," *Criterion* 6 (Oct. 1927), pp. 340–47; T. Sturge Moore, "Towards Simplicity," *Criterion* 6 (Nov. 1927), pp. 409–17.

101. John Middleton Murry, "Concerning Intelligence," *Criterion* 6 (Dec. 1927), pp. 524–33; Murry to T. S. Eliot, Sept. 22, 1927, quoted by Lea, p. 152.

102. T. S. Eliot, "Books of the Quarter," *Criterion* 20 (July 1931), pp. 768–74.

103. T. S. Eliot, "Books of the Quarter," *Criterion* 5 (May 1927).

104. T. S. Eliot, "Commentary," *Criterion* 12 (April 1933), pp. 472–73, and *Criterion* 14 (April 1935), pp. 432–33.

105. T. S. Eliot, "Books of the Quarter," *Criterion* 15 (July 1936), p. 708.

106. T. S. Eliot to John Middleton Murry, July 31, 1953, quoted by Margolis, p. 67.

107. T. S. Eliot, Foreward to *Katherine Mansfield and Other Literary Studies,* p. xxi.

108. John Middleton Murry, review of *The Craft of Letters in England,* ed. John Lehmann, *London Magazine* 3 (Dec. 1956), p. 72.

109. John Middleton Murry, "War, Poetry, and Europe," in *Looking Before and After* (London: Sheppard Press, 1948), pp. 151–68.

110. Murry, *Love, Freedom and Society,* p. 38.

111. John Middleton Murry, "A Note on 'The Family Reunion,' " *Essays in Criticism* 1 (Jan. 1951), p. 73.

112. John Middleton Murry, "The Plays of T. S. Eliot," in *Unprofessional Essays* (London: Cape, 1956), p. 191.

113. Murry, *Love, Freedom, and Society,* p. 38.

114. Leavis, *D. H. Lawrence: Novelist,* pp. 26–30.

115. Murry, Journal, May 29, 1954, quoted by Lea, p. 72.

116. Griffin, p. 51; Northrop Frye, *The Anatomy of Criticism,* (1957; reprint ed., New York: Atheneum, 1968), p. 19.

117. Murry, "Mr. Eliot at Lambeth," p. 70.

118. Murry to J. P. Hogan, March 8, 1955, quoted by Lea, p. 346.

119. Murry, "William Godwin," in *Countries of the Mind,* 2nd ser. pp. 181–87.

Chapter 5

1. Robert Langbaum, "Romanticism as a Modern Tradition," in *A Grammar of Literary Criticism,* ed. Lawrence Sargent Hall (New York: Macmillan, 1965), pp. 252–61.

2. Murry, "On Romanticism," p. 84.

3. Murry, "More About Romanticism," p. 559.

4. Murry, *Adam and Eve,* p. 32.

5. Murry, "The Poet's Poet," in *Countries of the Mind,* 2nd ser. pp. 63–77.

6. Murry, "George Chapman," in *Katherine Mansfield and Other Literary Portraits,* pp. 178–79.

7. Anne Finch, Countess of Winchelsea, *Poems,* sel. and intro. John Middleton Murry (London: Cape, 1928).

8. Murry, "The Poetry of John Clare," in *Countries of the Mind,* 1st ser., pp. 103–19; Murry, "The Case of John Clare," in *John Clare and Other Studies,* pp. 19–30; Murry, "Clare Revisited," in *Unprofessional Essays,* pp. 55–111

9. Murry, "Clare Revisited," pp. 77 and 89.

10. Griffin, p. 64.

11. Murry, "Keats and Shelley," in *Katherine Mansfield and Other Literary Portraits,* pp. 230–40. Page numbers in text refer to this edition.

12. Katherine Mansfield to Murry, Dec. 5, 1919, in *Letters to John Middleton Murry,* p. 431.

13. Murry, "Coleridge and Wordsworth," in *Katherine Mansfield and Other Literary Portraits,* pp. 63–64. Page numbers in text refer to this edition.

14. Murry, *Between Two Worlds,* pp. 326–27.

15. Rees, p. 62; Lea, p. 255; Beer, p. 64.

16. John Middleton Murry, *Heaven—and Earth* (London: Cape, 1938), p. 3.

17. Ibid., pp. 3–4.

18. Ibid., p. 106.

19. Ibid., pp. 165–66.

20. Ibid., p. 237.

21. Ibid., p. 367.

22. Ibid., pp. 327 and 333.

23. Ibid., p. 170.

24. Beer, p. 64.

25. Murry, Journal, Feb. 14, 1953, quoted by Lea, p. 332.

26. Murry to Henry Williamson, Sept. 7, 1953, quoted by Lea, p. 340.

27. Murry, Aug. 12, 1953, quoted by Lea, p. 340.

28. Murry to F. A. Lea, March 12, 1953; Murry to Richard Murry, March 21, 1954; both quoted by Lea, p. 340.

29. John Middleton Murry, *Jonathan Swift: A Critical Biography* (London: Cape, 1954), p. 13.

30. Ibid., pp. 81–82.

31. John M. Bullitt, "Labyrinthine Recesses of Satire," *Saturday Review of Literature* 39 (Jan. 7, 1956), p. 10; Herbert Davis also criticized Murry's mingling of criticism and biography in his review of *Jonathan Swift* in *Review of English Studies* 6 (1955), p. 320.

32. G. Wilson Knight, "The Challenge of Genius," in *Poets of Action* (London: Methuen, 1967), p. 178.

33. Murry, *Jonathan Swift,* pp. 351–55.

34. Ibid., pp. 354–55.

35. Ibid., p. 101.

36. John Middleton Murry, *Swift* (London: Longmans, Green, 1955), pp. 26–27.

37. Murry, *Jonathan Swift,* p. 37.

38. Ibid., pp. 225–26.

39. Ibid., p. 432.

40. Ibid., p. 60.

41. Philip Mahone Griffith, "Middleton Murry on Swift: 'The *Nec Plus Ultra* of Objectivity'?" *D. H. Lawrence Review* 2 (spring 1969), pp. 60–67.

42. Denis Donoghue, review of *Jonathan Swift, Studies* 44 (spring 1955), p. 121.

43. F. R. Leavis, "The Irony of Swift," in *The Common Pursuit* (London: Chatto and Windus, 1952), p. 86.

44. Donoghue, p. 121.

45, Knight, "The Challenge of Genius," p. 177; Geoffrey Moore, "A Man Terrible and Proud," review of *Jonathan Swift, New York Times Book Review* (Jan. 1, 1960), p. 10.

46. Murry, *Jonathan Swift,* p. 148.

47. Davis, pp. 319–21; Bullitt, pp. 9–10; see also Irvin Ehrenpreis, review of *Jonathan Swift, Philological Quarterly* 34 (July 1955) pp. 322–23.

48. V. S. Pritchett, "Books in General," *New Statesman and Nation* 47 (May 8, 1954), pp. 601–2.

49. Murry to Richard Murry, April 21, 1954, quoted by Lea, p. 341.

50. Murry, "George Gissing," in *Katherine Mansfield and Other Literary Studies,* pp. 1–68.

51. Gross, p. 252.

52. A phrase of Desmond McCarthy's appropriated by Gross to describe Murry, p. 245.

53. Mary Middleton Murry, *To Keep Faith* (London: Constable, 1959), p. 138.

54. F. R. Leavis, *The Great Tradition* (Garden City, N.Y.: Doubleday, 1954), p. 12.

55. Murry, "In Defense of Fielding," in *Unprofessional Essays,* pp. 9–52.

56. Murry to Katherine Mansfield, Nov. 23, 1919, quoted by Lea, p. 86.

57. Murry, "Poetry and Reality," in *Things to Come,* pp. 177–86.

58. Murry, "Analytical Criticism," review of William Empson's *Seven Types of Ambiguity in Poets, Critics, Mystics,* in *A Selection of Criticism Written between 1919 and 1955 by John Middleton Murry,* ed. Richard Rees (Carbondale: Southern Illinois University Press, 1970), pp. 78–82.

59. Murry, review of *The Lion and the Honeycomb* by R. P. Blackmur and *The Man of Letters in the Modern World* by Allen Tate, *London Magazine* 4 (May 1957), pp. 66–69.

60. Martin Green, *Children of the Sun* (New York: Basic Books, 1976).

61. Murry, "D. H. Lawrence," in *Collected Essays of Aldous Huxley* (New York: Harper, 1958), p. 128.

62. John Middleton Murry, *The Pledge of Peace* (London: Joseph, 1938), p. 183.

63. Huxley to Mary Murry, March 6, 1960, in *The Letters of Aldous Huxley,* ed. Grover Smith (London: Chatto and Windus, 1969), p. 888.

64. John Middleton Murry, "Mr. Yeats' Swan Song," in *Aspects of Literature,* pp. 39–45.

65. Murry, "The Break-up of the Novel," in *Discoveries,* pp. 129–52.

66. Murry, "Thomas Hardy," in *Katherine Mansfield and Other Literary Portraits,* pp. 215–29.

67. Murry, "Generosity in Literature," *Listener* 56 (Dec. 6, 1956). pp. 925–27.

68. Murry, "The Novels of Henry Williamson," in *Katherine Mansfield and Other Literary Studies*, p. 152.

69. Murry, "The End of an Egoist," *Wanderer* (1934), pp. 84–87.

70. Katherine Mansfield to Murry, Dec. 1920, in *Letters to John Middleton Murry*, p. 620.

71. Murry, "The End of an Egoist," p. 85.

72. Rees, *A Theory of My Time*, p. 87.

73. Maurice Cranston, review of *John Middleton Murry* by F. A. Lea, *Listener* 62 (Oct. 29, 1959), p. 743.

74. Kermode, p. 3.

75. Thayer, p. 47.

76. Rees, *A Theory of My Time*, p. 56.

77. Hilary Corke, "John Middleton Murry," *Encounter* 14 (Jan. 1960), p. 75.

78. John Jones, "Murry Revaluated," *New Statesman* 58 (Dec. 12, 1959), p. 848.

79. Heppenstall, *Four Absentees*, p. 203.

Bibliography

Primary Sources

Books by John Middleton Murry

Parenthetical dates refer to original publication when a later edition has been cited.

Fyodor Dostoevsky: A Critical Study. London: Secker, 1916.
Still Life (1916). New York: Dutton, 1922
Poems: 1917–1918. Hampstead, England: Heron Press, 1918.
The Critic in Judgement. Richmond: Hogarth Press, 1919.
Aspects of Literature (1920). 2nd ed. London: Cape, 1934.
Cinammon and Angelica. London: Cobden-Sanderson, 1920.
The Evolution of an Intellectual (1920). 2nd ed. London: Cape, 1927.
Poems: 1916–1920. London: Cobden-Sanderson, 1921.
Countries of the Mind. London: Collins, 1922.
The Problem of Style (1922) London: Oxford University Press Paperbacks, 1960.
The Things We Are (1922). New York: Dutton, 1930.
Pencillings (1923). New York: Seltzer, 1925.
Discoveries (1924). 2nd. ed. London: Cape, 1930.
To the Unknown God: Essays towards a Religion. London: Cape, 1924.
The Voyage. London: Constable, 1924.
Keats and Shakespeare. London: Oxford University Press, 1925.
Jesus, Man of Genius. New York: Harper, 1926. (Published in England as *The Life of Jesus.*)
Things to Come. London: Cape, 1928.
God: An Introduction to the Science of Metabiology. London: Cape, 1929.
Studies in Keats. London: Oxford University Press, 1930.
D. H. Lawrence: Two Essays. Cambridge: Minority Press, 1930.
Countries of the Mind. 2nd ser. London: Oxford University Press, 1931.
Son of Woman: The Story of D. H. Lawrence. New York: Cape and Smith, 1931.
The Fallacy of Economics. London: Faber and Faber, 1932.
The Necessity of Communism (1932). New York: Seltzer, 1933.
The Life of Katherine Mansfield. (With Ruth E. Mantz). London: Constable, 1933.
Reminiscences of D. H. Lawrence. London: Cape, 1933.
William Blake. London: Cape, 1933.
Wanderer. December 1933-November 1934. (Twelve issues.)
Between Two Worlds (1935). New York: Messner, 1936.
Shakespeare (1936). London: Cape Paperback, 1965.
The Necessity of Pacifism. London: Cape, 1937.
Heaven—and Earth. London: Cape, 1938. (Published in the United States as *Heroes of Thought.*)
The Pledge of Peace. London: Joseph, 1938.

The Defense of Democracy. London: Cape, 1939.
The Price of Leadership. New York: Harper, 1939.
Studies in Keats: New and Old. London: Oxford University Press, 1939.
The Betrayal of Christ by the Churches. London: Dakers, 1940.
Europe in Travail. New York: Macmillan, 1940.
Christocracy. London: Dakers, 1942.
Adam and Eve. London: Dakers, 1944.
The Free Society. London: Dakers, 1944.
The Challenge of Schweitzer. London: Jason Press, 1948.
Looking Before and After. London: Sheppard Press, 1948.
Katherine Mansfield and Other Literary Portraits. London: Nevill, 1949.
The Mystery of Keats. London: Nevill, 1949.
John Clare and Other Studies. London: Nevill, 1950.
The Conquest of Death. New York: Nevill, 1951.
Community Farm. London: Nevill, 1952.
Jonathan Swift: A Critical Biography. London: Cape, 1954.
Swift. London: Longmans, Green, 1955.
Keats. 4th ed. rev. and enlarged (1955). New York: Minerva, 1968.
Unprofessional Essays. London: Cape, 1956.
Love, Freedom and Society. London: Cape, 1957.
Katherine Mansfield and Other Literary Studies. London: Constable, 1959.
Not as the Scribes. Ed. and intro. Alec Vidler. London: S. C. M. Press, 1959.
Selected Criticism. Sel. and intro. Richard Rees. London: Oxford University Press,
    1960.
*Poets, Critics, Mystics: A Selection of Criticism Written between 1919 and 1955 by John
    Middleton Murry.* Sel. and intro. Richard Rees. Carbondale: Southern Illinois
    University Press, 1970.

Selected Essays of John Middleton Murry

For a full listing of Murry's uncollected essays see George P. Lilley, *A Bibliography
of John Middleton Murry.*

"Art and Philosophy." *Rhythm* 1 (summer 1911), pp. 9–12.
Review of *La Chute. Blue Review* 1 (May 1913), pp. 8–9.
"Simichidas in the Mountains." *Nation-Athenaeum* 21 (Dec. 3, 1921), p. 381.
"Katherine Mansfield." *Literary Review* 3 (Feb. 17, 1923), pp. 461–62.
"Romanticism and the Tradition." *Criterion* 2 (April 1924), pp. 272–95.
"The Classical Revival." Parts 1 and 2. *Adelphi* 3 (Feb. and March 1926), pp.
    585–95 and 648–53.
"Towards a Synthesis." *Criterion* 5 (June 1927), pp. 294–313.
"Concerning Intelligence." *Criterion* 6 (Dec. 1927), pp. 524–33.
Introduction. *Poems by Anne, Countess of Winchelsea, 1661–1720,* ed. John Mid-
    dleton Murry. London: Cape, 1928.
"Modern Marriage." (With James Carruthers Young.) *Forum* 81 (January 1929),
    pp. 22–26.
"Western Mysticism." *Aryan Path* 1 (February 1930), pp. 83–88.

"The Purgation of Suffering." *Aryan Path* 1 (October 1930), pp. 648–51.

Review of *Wheel of Fire* by G. Wilson Knight. *Adelphi* 1 (January 1931), p. 347.

"Mr. Eliot at Lambeth." *Adelphi* 2 (April 1931), pp. 70–73.

"The Doctrine of Will in Shakespeare." *Aryan Path* 4 (July 1933), pp. 479–83.

"Professors and Poets." *Aryan Path* 6 (July 1935), pp. 446–50.

"The Value of Poetry in the Social Order." *Aryan Path* 11 (September 1940), pp. 439–42.

"A Note on 'The Family Reunion.' " *Essays in Criticism* 1 (January 1951), pp.67–73.

Review of *The Fire and the Fountain: An Essay on Poetry* by John Press, *London Magazine* 2 (November 1955), pp. 79–82.

"The Living Dead—1: D. H. Lawrence." *London Magazine* 3 (May 1956), pp. 57–63.

"Coming to London—8." *London Magazine* 3 (July 1956), pp. 30–37.

"Generosity in Literature." *Listener* 56 (Dec. 6, 1956), pp. 925–27.

Review of *The Craft of Letters in England*, ed. John Lehmann. *London Magazine* 3 (Dec. 1956), pp. 69–75.

Review of *Form and Meaning in Drama* by H. D. F. Kitto and *The Harvest of Tragedy* by T. R. Henn. *London Magazine* 4 (May 1957), pp. 66–69.

Review of *The Lion and the Honeycomb* by R. P. Blackmur and *The Man of Letters in the Modern World* by Allen Tate. *London Magazine* 4 (May 1957), pp. 66–69.

Secondary Sources

Books

Aldington, Richard. *Portrait of a Genius But . . .* London: Heinemann, 1950.

Alpers, Anthony. *Katherine Mansfield: A Biography.* New York: Knopf, 1954.

Armstrong, Edward A. *Shakespeare's Imagination.* Omaha: University of Nebraska Press, 1963.

Benet, Mary Katherine. *Writers in Love.* New York: Macmillan, 1977.

Bentley, G. E., and Martin K. Murni. *A Blake Bibliography.* Minneapolis: University of Minnesota Press, 1964.

Bowra, C. M. *The Romantic Imagination.* New York: Oxford University Press, 1961.

Brewster, Dorothy. *East-West Passage.* London: Allen and Unwin, 1954.

Carrington, Dora. *Carrington: Letters and Extracts from Her Diaries*, ed. David Garnett. New York: Holt, Rinehart and Winston, 1970.

Carswell, Catherine. *The Savage Pilgrimage.* Rev. ed. London: Secker, 1932.

Collis, J. S. *Farewell to Argument.* London: Cassell, 1935.

Eliot, T. S. Foreword to *Katherine Mansfield and Other Literary Studies*, by John Middleton Murry, pp. i–xii. London: Constable, 1959.

———. *The Sacred Wood.* London: University Paperbacks, 1969.

Foster, Malcolm. *Joyce Cary: A Biography.* Boston: Houghton Mifflin, 1968.

Fruman, Norman. *Coleridge, The Damaged Archangel* New York: George Braziller, 1971.

Frye, Northrop. Introduction to *Blake: A Collection of Critical Essays*, ed. Northrop Frye, pp. 1–7. Englewood Cliffs, N.J.: Prentice-Hall, 1966.

Glenavy, Lady Beatrice. *Today We Will Only Gossip*. London: Constable, 1964.

Green, Martin. *Children of the Sun*. New York: Basic Books, 1976.

_____. *The Von Richthofen Sisters: The Triumphant and the Tragic Modes of Love*. New York: Basic Books, 1974.

Griffin, Ernest G. *John Middleton Murry*. New York: Twayne, 1969.

Gross, John. *The Rise and Fall of the Man of Letters*. New York: Macmillan, 1970.

Heppenstall, Rayner. *Four Absentees*. London: Barrier and Rockliff, 1960.

_____. *John Middleton Murry: A Study in Excellent Normality*. London: Cape, 1934.

Holroyd, Michael. *Lytton Strachey: A Critical Biography*. 2 vols. London: Heinemann, 1967.

Hough, Graham. *The Dark Sun: A Study of D. H. Lawrence*. Harmondsworth, England: Penguin, 1961.

Huxley, Aldous, "D. H. Lawrence." In *Collected Essays of Aldous Huxley*. New York: Harper, 1958, pp. 115–28.

_____. Introduction to *The Letters of D. H. Lawrence*, pp. ix–xxxiv. New York: Viking, 1932.

_____. *The Letters of Aldous Huxley*, ed. Grover Smith. London: Chatto and Windus, 1969.

Keats, John. *The Letters of John Keats*, ed. Maurice Buxton Forman. 2nd ed. London: Oxford University Press, 1935.

Knight, G. Wilson. "The Challenge of Genius." In *Poets of Action*, pp. 176–78. London: Methuen, 1967.

_____. *The Imperial Theme*. London: Methuen, 1931.

_____. "J. Middleton Murry." In *Neglected Powers: Essays on Nineteenth and Twentieth Century Literature*, pp. 358–66. London: Routledge and Kegan Paul, 1971.

Langbaum, Robert. "Romanticism as a Modern Tradition." In *A Grammar of Literary Criticism*, ed. Lawrence Sargent Hall, pp. 252–61. New York: Macmillan, 1965.

Lawrence, D. H. *Fantasia of the Unconscious*. New York: Viking Paperbacks, 1960.

_____. *The Letters of D. H. Lawrence*, ed. Harry T. Moore. New York: Viking, 1962.

_____. *Phoenix II*, ed. Warren Roberts and Harry T. Moore. New York: Viking, 1970.

Lawrence, Frieda. *Frieda Lawrence: The Memoirs and Correspondence*, ed. E. W. Tedlock. London: Heinemann, 1961.

Lea, Frank A. *John Middleton Murry*. New York: Oxford University Press, 1960.

_____. *Voices in the Wilderness: From Poetry to Prophecy in Britain*. London: Bentham Press, 1975.

Leavis, F. R. *D. H. Lawrence: Novelist*. London: Chatto and Windus, 1955.

_____. *The Great Tradition*. New York: Doubleday, 1954.

_____. "The Irony of Swift." In *The Common Pursuit*, pp. 73–87. London: Chatto and Windus, 1952.

_____. " 'Lawrence Scholarship' and Lawrence." In *Anna Karenina and Other Essays*, pp. 167–78. New York: Simon and Schuster, 1969.

Lilley, George P. *A Bibliography of John Middleton Murry*. Toronto: University of Toronto Press, 1975.

Lodge, David. *The Language of Fiction*. New York: Columbia University Press, 1966.

Mairet, Philip. *John Middleton Murry*. London: Longmans, Green, 1958.

Mais, S. P. B. *Some Modern Authors*. London: Richards, 1923.

Mansfield, Katherine. *Journal of Katherine Mansfield*, ed. John Middleton Murry. London: Constable, 1954. (Definitive edition.)

_____. *Katherine Mansfield's Letters to John Middleton Murry, 1913–1922*, ed. John Middleton Murry. London: Constable, 1951.

_____. *The Letters of Katherine Mansfield*, ed. John Middleton Murry. 2 vols. London: Constable, 1928.

_____. *Passionate Pilgrimage: A Love Affair in Letters: Katherine Mansfield's Letters to John Middleton Murry from the South of France, 1915–1920*, ed. Helen McNeish. London: Joseph, 1977.

_____. *The Scrapbook of Katherine Mansfield*, ed. John Middleton Murry. London: Constable, 1939.

Margolis, John D. *T. S. Eliot's Intellectual Development: 1922–1939*. Chicago: University of Chicago Press, 1972.

Marsh, Edward. *A Number of People*. London: Heinemann, 1939.

Meyers, Jeffrey. *Katherine Mansfield: A Biography*. New York: New Directions, 1978.

Moore, Harry T. *The Intelligent Heart: The Story of D. H. Lawrence*. New York: Farrar, Straus and Young, 1954.

Morrell, Ottoline. *Ottoline at Garsington: Memoirs of Lady Ottoline Morrell, 1915–1918*, ed. Robert Gathorne-Hardy. London: Faber and Faber, 1974.

Muir, Kenneth. Introduction to *Shakespeare: The Comedies: A Collection of Critical Essays*, ed. Kenneth Muir. Englewood Cliffs, N.J.: Prentice-Hall, 1965.

Murry, Colin Middleton. *I at the Keyhole*. New York: Stein and Day, 1975. (Also published under the title *One Hand Clapping* [London: Gollancz, 1975].)

_____. *Shadows on the Grass*. London: Gollancz, 1977.

Murry, Mary Middleton. *To Keep Faith*. London: Constable, 1959.

Plowman, Max. *Bridge into the Future: The Letters of Max Plowman*, ed. D. L. P. London: Dakers, 1944.

Pondrom, Cyrene M. *The Road from Paris: French Influence on English Poetry. 1900–1920*. Cambridge: Cambridge University Press, 1974.

Rees, Richard. *A Theory of My Time: An Essay in Didactic Remembrance*. London: Seckert and Warburg, 1963.

Rowse, A. L. *William Shakespeare: A Biography*. New York: Harper and Row, 1964.

Seaver, George. *Albert Schweitzer: A Vindication—Being A Reply to "The Challenge of Schweitzer" by John Middleton Murry*. London: Clarke, 1950.

Sullivan, J. W. N. *But for the Grace of God*. New York: Knopf, 1932.

Tillyard, E. M. W. *The Miltonic Setting: Past and Present*. New York: Barnes and Noble, 1966.

_____. *Shakespeare's History Plays*. 1944. Reprint. Harmondsworth, England: Penguin, 1956.

Wimsatt, W. K., Jr., and Monroe Beardsley. "The Intentional Fallacy." In *The Verbal Icon*, pp. 3–18. Lexington: University of Kentucky Press, 1954.

Woolf, Leonard. "Look Up There, with Me!" In *Essays on Literature, History, Politics, Etc.*, pp. 240–44. Freeport, N.Y.: Books for Libraries Press, 1927.

Woolf, Virginia. *The Diary of Virginia Woolf*, ed. Anne Olivier Bell. New York and London: Harcourt Brace Jovanovich, 1978.

Periodicals

Barnes, R. R. Review of *William Blake. Scrutiny* 2 (March 1934), pp. 424–26.
Barry, Iris. Review of *Son of Woman. Bookman* 72 (Jan. 1931).
Beer, J. B. "John Middleton Murry." *Critical Quarterly* 3 (spring 1961), pp. 59–66.
Bennett, J. R. "The Problem of Style." *D. H. Lawrence Review* 2 (spring 1969), pp. 32–46.
Blunt, Wilfred. "Blake and the Scholars." *New York Review of Books* (Oct. 28, 1965), p. 280.
Bullitt, John M. "Labyrinthine Recesses of Satire." *Saturday Review of Literature* 39 (Jan. 7, 1956), 9–10.
Corke, Hilary. "John Middleton Murry." *Encounter* 14 (Jan. 1960), p. 75.
Cranston, Maurice. Review of *John Middleton Murry* by F. A. Lea, *Listener* 62 (Oct. 29, 1959), p. 743.
Crépin, Andre. "John Middleton Murry et le sens allégorique de la vie." *Etudes anglaises* 14 (Oct.–Dec. 1961), pp. 321–30.
D'Arcy, Father M. C. "The Thomistic Synthesis and Intelligence." *Criterion* 6 (Sept. 1927), pp. 227–28.
Davis, Herbert. Review of *Jonathan Swift. Review of English Studies* 6 (1955), pp. 319–21.
Donoghue, Denis. Review of *Jonathan Swift. Studies* 44 (spring 1955), pp. 119–21.
Ehrenpreis, Irvin. Review of *Jonathan Swift. Philological Quarterly* 34 (July 1955), pp. 322–23.
Eliot, T. S. "Books of the Quarter." *Criterion* 10 (1931), pp. 768–74.
_____. "Books of the Quarter." *Criterion* 15 (1936), pp. 708–10.
_____. "Commentaries." *Criterion* 12 (April 1933), pp. 472–73.
_____. "Commentaries." *Criterion* 14 (April 1935), pp. 432–33.
_____. "The Function of Criticism." *Criterion* 2 (Oct. 1923), pp. 31–42.
_____. "Mr. Middleton Murry's Synthesis." *Criterion* 6 (Oct. 1927), pp. 340–47.
_____. "The Poetic Drama. *Athenaeum* 1 (May 14, 1920), pp. 635–36.
Fernandez, Ramon. "A Note on Intelligence and Intuition," trans T. S. Eliot. *Criterion* 6 (Oct. 1927), pp. 332–39.
F. M. [Vivien Eliot] "Books of the Quarter." *Criterion* 2 (July 1924), p. 484.
_____. "Letters of the Moment." *Criterion* 2 (April 1924), p. 362.
Fogle, Richard Harter. "Beauty and Truth: John Middleton Murry on Keats." *D. H. Lawrence Review* 2 (spring 1969), pp. 68–75.
Forster, E. M. "The Cult of D. H. Lawrence." *Spectator* 147 (April 18, 1931), p. 627.
Girard, Denis. "John Middleton Murry, D. H. Lawrence, et Albert Schweitzer." *Etudes anglaises* 12 (July–Sept. 1959), pp. 212–21.
Griffin, Ernest G. "The Circular and the Linear: The Middleton Murry–D. H. Lawrence Affair." *D. H. Lawrence Review* 2 (spring 1969), pp. 76–92.
Griffith, Philip Mahone. "Middleton Murry on Swift: The *Nec Plus Ultra* of Objectivity?" *D. H. Lawrence Review* 2 (spring 1969), pp. 60–67.
Heath, William R. "The Literary Criticism of John Middleton Murry." *PMLA* 70 (March 1955), pp. 45–47.
Hutchinson, Percy. Review of *Son of Woman. New York Times Book Review.* (April 16, 1931), p.2.

Jones, John. "Murry Revaluated." *New Statesman* 58 (Dec. 12, 1959), p. 848.

Kaufmann, R. J. "On Using an Obsessed Critic: John Middleton Murry." *Graduate Student of English* 3 (winter 1960), pp. 4–8.

Kermode, Frank. "On the Frontiers of Criticism." *Manchester Guardian* (June 10, 1960), p. 8.

Lea, F. A. "Murry and Marriage." *D. H. Lawrence Review* 2 (spring 1969), pp. 1–21.

Leavis, F. R. "Keats." *Scrutiny* 4 (March 1936), pp. 376–400.

_____. "The Literary Mind." *Scrutiny* 1 (May 1932), p. 27.

Mauron, Charles. "Concerning 'Intuition,'" trans. T. S. Eliot. *Criterion* 6 (Sept. 1927), pp. 229–35.

Meyers, Jeffrey. "Murry's Cult of Mansfield." *Journal of Modern Literature* 7 (1979), pp. 15–38.

Moore, Geoffrey. "A Man Terrible and Proud." *New York Times Book Review* (Jan. 1, 1960), p. 10.

Moore, T. Sturge. "Towards Simplicity." *Criterion* 6 (Nov. 1927), pp. 409–17.

Paris, Rosemary. Review of *Katherine Mansfield's Letters to John Middleton Murry. Furioso* 7 (winter 1952), pp. 66–69.

Plowman, Max. "The Key to Blake." *Aryan Path* 5 (July 1934), pp. 462–66.

Pritchett, V. S. "Books in General." *New Statesman and Nation* 47 (May 8, 1954), pp. 601–2.

Rees, Richard. "The Politics of a Mystic." *D. H. Lawrence Review* 2 (spring 1969), pp. 24–31.

Selincourt, Basil de. "The Problem of Blake—Self and Its Annihilation." *Observer* (Oct. 1, 1933), p. 4.

Stanford, Derek. "Middleton Murry as Literary Critic." *Essays in Criticism* 8 (January 1958), pp. 60–67.

Thayer, C. G. "Murry's *Shakespeare*." *D. H. Lawrence Review* 2 (spring 1969), pp. 47–59.

Tims, Margaret. "A Biography of John Middleton Murry." *Aryan Path* 31 (January 1960), pp. 34–35.

Unsigned Review of *Dostoevsky*. *Bookman* 44 (November 1916), pp. 299–300.

Unsigned Review of *Dostoevsky*. *Nation* 104 (Jan. 4, 1917), p. 23.

Unsigned Review of *Reminiscences of D. H. Lawrence*. *Spectator* 150 (Feb. 10, 1933), p. 191.

Unsigned Review of *Son of Woman*. *Forum* 6 (July 1931), p. 10.

Unsigned Review of *William Blake*. *Times Literary Supplement* (Oct. 26, 1933), p. 727.

Van Doren, Mark. "Criticism by Exclamation." *Nation* 142 (April 22, 1936), pp. 520–22.

Waldron, Philip. "Katherine Mansfield's Journal." *Twentieth Century Literature* 20 (Jan. 1974), pp. 11–18.

Watson, J. H. "A Good Workingman and His Friends: Recollections of John Middleton Murry." *London Magazine* 6 (May 1959), pp. 51–55.

West, Rebecca. Review of *The Things We Are*. *New Statesman* 19 (June 24, 1922), p. 326.

Index

Adelphi, 2, 25–29, 63, 71, 84, 89–92, 95, 105
Andreev, Leondin, 27
Aristotle, 44
Arnold, Matthew, 6, 44–45, 50, 59, 129
Athenaeum, 1, 2, 19–23, 25, 35, 42, 43, 52, 85, 88, 102–3, 132
Auden, W. H., 131, 133
Austen, Jane, 130

Baker, Ida, 84
Bell, Clive, 20
Bergson, Henri, 9–11, 13
Blackmur, Richard, 131
Blake, William, 54, 63–69, 82, 85–86, 94, 100, 121, 122; *Jerusalem,* 67
Bloomsbury group, 2, 23, 43, 103, 131
Blue Review, 1, 14
Bowden, George, 12, 16
Bradley, A. C., 70
Brawne, Fanny, 60, 62
Brett, Dorothy, 82, 90

Campbell, Beatrice (Lady Glenavy), 84
Campbell, Gordon (Lord Glenavy), 15, 17, 84
Carco, Francis, 10, 16
Carlyle, Thomas, 129
Carrington, Dora, 2
Carswell, Catherine, 3, 95
Cary, Joyce, 8
Chapman, George, 75, 114
Chatterton, Thomas, 80
Chaucer, Geoffrey, 66, 113
Chekhov, Anton, 23, 34, 40–42, 48, 83, 85
Clare, John, 114
Cockbayne, Betty (Mrs. Elizabeth Murry), 5, 29–30, 63–64, 67, 69, 92, 97, 128
Coleridge, Samuel Taylor, 44, 65, 70, 83, 114–19; relation with Wordsworth, 114–19; "Dejection: An Ode," 116; "Frost at Midnight," 117
Criterion, 102, 105–7
Cromwell, Oliver, 120–21

Danby, John, 78
Dante, 104
Davies, W. H., 14

De La Mare, Walter, 14
Derain, E., 13
Derème, Tristan, 10
Dickens, Charles, 128
Dostoevsky, Fyodor, 1, 15, 17–18, 24, 39–42, 83; Murry's treatment of novels, 39
Drinkwater, John, 14
Dryden, John, 44

Egoist, 13, 43
Eliot, George, 23, 95
Eliot, T. S., 3, 20, 23, 32, 35, 43–45, 47–51, 54, 98, 100–13, 127, 131–34; *Sacred Wood,* 43, 102; objective correlative, 47; romanticism-classicism debate with Murry, 48, 51, 105–7; "Wasteland," 54, 103–4; *Cocktail Party,* 98; "Hollow Men," 103; *The Idea of a Christian Society,* 108
Eliot, Vivien, 102

Fergusson, J. D., 9, 10
Fielding, Joseph, 130
Finch, Anne (Countess of Winchelsea), 114
Flecker, James, 14
Forster, E. M., 46
Freud, Sigmund, 7, 88

Gamble, Mary. *See* Murry, Mrs. Mary Middleton
Garnett, Constance, 39
Gaudier-Brzeska, Henri, 33
Gazinin, Edouard, 10
Georgian poets, 20
Gertler, Mark, 16
Gibson, Wilfred, 14
Gissing, George, 128–29; novels, 129; marriage to Ellen Underwood, 129
Gittling, Robert, 62
Godwin, William, 111, 121
Goethe, Johann, 121, 133
Gorky, Maxim, 27
Gurdjieff, G., 24

Hardy, Thomas, 45, 76, 133
Harris, Frank, 13

Hogarth Press, 35
Homer, 66
Hulme, T. E., 11
Hunt, Leigh, 114
Hutchinson, Sara, 117
Huxley, Aldous, 3, 20, 97, 127, 131–32; parody of Murry, 3

Imagists, 11, 13
Imlay, Fanny, 122
Independent Labor Party, 64, 68

James, Henry, 38
Jesus, 27, 53, 57–58, 62, 67, 85, 92–93, 97, 100, 108
Johnson, Samuel, 78
Jonson, Ben, 73
Joyce, James, 23, 54, 89, 133; *Ulysses*, 23, 54
Judas theme, 27, 93

Kean, Edmund, 76
Keats, John, 2–3, 23–24, 54–62, 65–66, 68–70, 80, 82–83, 85–87, 94, 98, 100, 114–15; "Ode on a Grecian Urn," 58, 82; "Hyperion," 60; "Endymion," 62; Letters, 56–66 passim
Knight, G. Wilson, 70
Koteliansky, Samuel, 27, 85

Lamb, Charles, 83
Larrouy, Maurice, 9
Lawrence, D. H., 1–3, 7, 14–19, 20–68 passim, 87–134 passim; "The Crown," 15, 18; *The Rainbow*, 15, 18, 21, 87–88; *Sons and Lovers*, 15, 87; "Study of Thomas Hardy," 15; *Women in Love*, 15, 19, 88, 99; *Aaron's Rod*, 17, 89; "The Whistling of the Birds," 21; *Fantasia of the Unconscious*, 25, 88–97 passim; Café Royal dinner, 26–27, 90; *The Lost Girl*, 88; short story parodies of Murry, 90; "On Coming Home," 90; *The Plumed Serpent*, 91; *Lady Chatterley's Lover*, 91; "The Man Who Died," 93; "The Escaped Cock," 93; *St. Mawr*, 98; *David*, 99
Lawrence, Frieda, 14–18, 27, 29, 89–96 passim; affair with Murry, 27, 29, 92
Leavis, F. R., 2, 87, 99–100, 110, 127, 129–30, 133

le Maistre, Violet (Mrs. Violet Middleton Murry), 5, 28–29, 52, 63–64, 85, 91, 97, 126
Lessing, Gotthold, 121
Lewes, George Henry, 23
London Mercury, 43
Lucy, Sir Thomas, 76

McCarthy, Desmond, 43
Mansfield, Katherine (Mrs. Katherine Middleton Murry), 1–63 passim, 83–137 passim; "Man Without a Temperament," 24; short stories, Murry's treatment of, 86
Marguéritte, 10
Marsh, Edward, 14
Marx, Karl, 120–21
Marxism, 3, 63–64, 108
Melville, Herman, 112
Milton, John, 61, 65–66, 101, 104, 120–21
Moore, Marianne, 102
Morrell, Lady Ottoline, 2, 68
Morrell, Philip, 68
Morris, William, 120
Murry, Colin Middleton ("Col"), 28–29, 64
Murry, David Middleton, 29
Murry, Mrs. Elizabeth Middleton. *See* Cockbayne, Betty
Murry, John, Jr. (Murry's father), 6–8
Murry, John Middleton: *Dostoevsky*, 1, 18, 33, 38–52 passim; *Love, Freedom and Society*, 1–2, 68, 87, 97–98; *Problem of Style*, 2–3, 20, 43, 45–53, 71, 77, 103; *Jonathan Swift*, 3, 31, 122–28; *Son of Woman*, 3, 29, 63, 89–99 passim, 108; *Between Two Worlds*, 6, 24, 39, 84–85, 92, 118; *Still Life*, 10, 33–34, 36; *God*, 24, 64, 92; *Reminiscences of D. H. Lawrence*, 27, 29, 95; *Keats and Shakespeare*, 28, 40, 50, 52, 55–63, 71, 73–74, 127, 134; *Adam and Eve*, 30, 96–97; *Heaven—and Earth (Heroes of Thought)*, 30, 119–22; *Shakespeare*, 30, 51, 69–81, 108, 119, 136; *Poems*, 34–35; *Cinammon and Angelica*, 35–36; *Critic in Judgement*, 35; *Things We Are*, 36–37; *Voyage*, 37–38, 106; "Critical Credo," 43, 45–46; "Function of Criticism," 44–45; *Aspects of Literature*, 50, 134; *Countries of the Mind*, 50; "Nature of Poetry," 53–54;

Discoveries, 54; *Jesus: Man of Genius*, 58, 64; *Keats*, 62; *William Blake*, 63–69, 136; *Necessity of Communism*, 64; *Katherine Mansfield and Other Studies*, 86, 128; "On Marriage," 96; *Wanderer*, 96; *Challenge of Schweitzer*, 98; *Free Society*, 101, 109; *Price of Leadership*, 108; *Katherine Mansfield and Other Literary Portraits*, 114–15
Murry, Miss Katherine Middleton ("Weg"), 28, 64
Murry, Mrs. Katherine Middleton. *See* Mansfield, Katherine
Murry, Miss Mary Middleton, 29, 30
Murry, Mrs. Mary Middleton (Mary Gamble), 5, 30–31, 96, 132
Murry, Mrs. Violet Middleton. *See* le Maistre, Violet

Nation, 20
New Age, 13
New Criticism, 3, 43, 50, 130
New Statesman, 43

Ouspensky, P. D., 24
Owen, Wilfred, 133

Pacifism, 3, 5, 68–69, 122
Peace Pledge Union, 69, 132
Peachey family, 8–9
Picasso, Pablo, 10–13
Plato, 10–11, 35, 44
Plowman, Max, 25, 65
Pound, Ezra, 11, 131, 133
Priestley, J. B., 130
Proust, Marcel, 133

Ravagli, Angelo, 29, 92
Read, Herbert, 20
Rees, Sir Richard, 4, 25
Rhythm, 1, 11–14. *See also Blue Review*
Richards, I. A., 130
Romanticism-Classicism debate, 48, 105–7
Rousseau, Jean, 97, 108, 120–21
Rozanov, Vasilii, 39
Russell, Bertrand, 20

Sadlier, Michael, 10
Salinger, J. D., 133
Schweitzer, Albert, 90, 98
Shakespeare, William, 3, 23, 41, 53–58, 61, 65–66, 69–81, 82–83, 86–87, 94, 100–1, 113–14, 121–22, 131; works, 71–81
Shaw, George Bernard, 127
Shelley, Percy Bysshe, 65, 83, 111, 114–15
Signature, 1, 18
Southampton, Earl of, 75
Spanish Civil War, 69
Spenser, Edmund, 113–14
Squire, J. C., 20, 43
Stendhal, 47
Stevens, Wallace, 131, 133
Strachey, Lytton, 20, 84
Swift, Jonathan, 122–29; works, 123–25

Tate, Alan, 131
Times Literary Supplement, 20
Tolstoy, Leo, 40–41, 83
Toynbee, Arnold, 8

University Wits, 73

Valéry, Paul, 20
Virgil, 66

Walpole, Hugh, 13
Wells, H. G., 20
Westminster Gazette, 12
Whitman, Walt, 112
Williamson, Henry, 133
Winchelsea, Countess of (Ann Finch), 114
Woolf, Leonard, 23, 25
Woolf, Virginia, 20, 23, 83, 86, 102–4; *Jacob's Room*, 103
Wordsworth, Dorothy, 117
Wordsworth, William, 57, 65, 113, 114–19, 121

Yale Review, 84
Yeats, William Butler, 131–33